Team Building

Proven Strategies for Improving Team Performance

Fifth Edition

W. Gibb Dyer Jr.

Jeffrey H. Dyer

William G. Dyer

JOSSEY-BASS
A Wiley Imprint
www.josseybass.com

Published by Jossey-Bass
A Wiley Imprint
One Montgomery Street, Suite 1200, San Francisco, CA 94104-4594—www.josseybass.com

Jossey-Bass books and products are available through most bookstores. To contact Jossey-Bass directly call our Customer Care Department within the U.S. at 800-956-7739, outside the U.S. at 317-572-3986, or fax 317-572-4002.

Wiley publishes in a variety of print and electronic formats and by print-on-demand. Some material included with standard print versions of this book may not be included in e-books or in print-on-demand. If this book refers to media such as a CD or DVD that is not included in the version you purchased, you may download this material at http://booksupport.wiley.com. For more information about Wiley products, visit www.wiley.com.

Library of Congress Cataloging-in-Publication Data

Dyer, W. Gibb, 1954–
  Team building : proven strategies for improving team performance / W. Gibb Dyer Jr., Jeffrey H. Dyer, William G. Dyer. — 5th ed.
      p. cm. – (The Jossey-Bass business & management series)
  William G. Dyer appeared as the first named author on the earlier ed.
  Includes bibliographical references and index.
  ISBN 978-1-118-10513-9 (pbk.)
  ISBN 978-1-118-41878-9 (ebk.)
  ISBN 978-1-118-41614-3 (ebk.)
  ISBN 978-1-118-43366-9 (ebk.)
1. Teams in the workplace.   2. Organizational change.   I. Dyer, Jeffrey H.
II. Dyer, William G. III. Title.
  HD66.D94 2013
  658.4'022—dc23

                              2012038248

Printed in the United States of America
FIFTH EDITION
PB Printing   10 9 8 7 6 5 4 3 2 1

Contents

About the Online Assessments   v

Introduction   1

Part One: The Four Cs of Team Development   9

1   The Search for the High-Performing Team   11

2   Context: Laying the Foundation for Team Success   21

3   Composition: Getting the Right People on the Bus   37

4   Competencies: Developing Team Skills for High Performance   57

5   Change: Devising More Effective Ways of Working Together   85

6   Bringing the Four Cs Together: Designing a Team-Building Program   103

Part Two: Solving Specific Problems Through Team Building   127

7   Managing Conflict in the Team   129

8   Overcoming Unhealthy Agreement   155

9   Reducing Conflict Between Teams   169

10   Leading Innovative Teams   183

Part Three: Team Building in Different Types of Teams   205

11   Managing the Temporary Team   207

12   Creating Effective Cross-Cultural Teams   219

13   High-Performing Virtual Teams   235

14   Managing Interorganizational Alliance Teams   247

Part Four: The Challenge of Team Building for the Future   267

15   Challenges for Building Effective Teams   269

Notes   278

The Authors   287

Index   289

About the Online Assessments

In order for teams to improve their performance through team building, it is critical for them to have accurate information on how they are performing—in particular, their areas of weakness. The Dyer Team Assessment draws on the concepts in this book to evaluate a team's performance in terms of context (Does the team have the appropriate organizational and environmental support for success?), composition (Do people on the team have the right set of skills and capabilities?), competencies (Does the team display process competencies in eleven areas that predict effective team functioning?), and change capabilities (Does the team know how to make changes regularly as necessary to improve performance?).

The Dyer Team Assessment culminates in a report that gives teams insight into their specific areas of strength and weakness. Thus, it is an extremely useful tool for them to use as they build their change capabilities.

Want to assess your student or corporate team performance?

Visit www.josseybass.com/go/dyerteamassessments to get more information about the online assessments based on the Dyer 4 Cs model. The Dyer Student Team Assessment is designed to assess student teams within the classroom. The Dyer Team Assessment is designed for use in corporate team settings. To register and pay for either assessment, please visit www.josseybass.com/go/dyerteamassessments.

To our parents, Bonnie and Bill, and to our wives,
Theresa and Ronalee, who have taught us the importance
of our most important team: the family

Team Building

The Jossey-Bass Business & Management Series

INTRODUCTION

This book is for everyone concerned about effective team performance. Four previous editions of *Team Building* have been well received by managers, team leaders, and team consultants. In fact, over 100,000 copies have been sold in several languages over the almost three decades since our father, William G. "Bill" Dyer, wrote the first edition, making it one of the most widely read books on the subject. Bill was the consummate social scientist, trained in sociology at the University of Wisconsin after World War II. He had grown up in a family of seven children (one was his half-brother Jack Gibb, another prominent social scientist) in a rather poor section of Portland, Oregon. Bill's father ran a small grocery store attached to their home, and it was there that Bill learned the importance of hard work and teamwork as he worked in the family store. From these experiences, he also recognized that education was the key to his future.

After finishing his doctorate at the University of Wisconsin, Bill and his wife, Bonnie, moved on to Iowa State University and shortly after that to Brigham Young University. His early research studies in the 1950s were on family dynamics and role conflict within families. In the late 1950s, he was introduced by his brother Jack Gibb into the world of T-groups (the T stood for "training"), which at the time were largely sponsored by National Training Laboratories. The assumption underlying the T-group was that individuals—and particularly organizational leaders—were impaired by the authoritarian assumptions they

1

held about those they worked with and needed to change their assumptions about people and ways of doing work.

Organizations were largely seen as being oppressive—creating "organization men"—and stifling creativity and innovation. Stanley Milgram's studies during this period pointed out that anyone could become a victim of authoritarianism, and Douglas McGregor in *The Human Side of Enterprise* noted that most managers in organizations operated using theory X assumptions (people are basically untrustworthy and lazy) but should have been basing their actions on theory Y assumptions (people essentially are good and want responsibility).[1] Other writers such as Chris Argyris and Abraham Maslow argued that organizations as human systems needed to allow people to achieve their potential and become self-actualized. It was in this context that the group dynamics and humanistic psychology movement began to flourish in the 1960s.

T-groups were composed of strangers led by a T-group trainer, whose job was to allow group members to explore what it meant to be part of a group that would provide them with feedback about their own behavior, require them to respond in an "open and honest" manner, and encourage group members to accept responsibility for their behavior, as well as be willing to engage in relationships based on equality rather than hierarchy or status. It was in this environment that Bill, as a T-group trainer, initially learned about the dynamics of groups and the individuals who were part of them.

For several years, Bill consulted with many organizations that wanted to use the T-group to improve the performance of their employees and their teams. Those within the movement believed that the T-group could be the vehicle to change the values of organization leaders and, that by so doing, these new values would filter down throughout the organization. Organizations in this way could be transformed into more humane and creative systems. Bill also was influenced at this time not only by Jack Gibb but others, such as Dick Beckhard and Ed Schein, who later became the founders of a new field of practice, organization development. Moreover, famous psychologist Abe Maslow had a significant influence on Bill, since Maslow attended a T-group sponsored by National Training Laboratories in Bethel, Maine, and Bill was chosen to be Maslow's T-group trainer.

As children growing up in the Dyer home, we often heard our father tell stories about Maslow and his wit and wisdom. These stories invariably had to do with the importance of being honest and being a "congruent" person—sharing openly what we think and feel—and acting in a way consistent with our values. One story that our father shared was about Maslow and his wife when they invited a friend, Harry, to stay with them. The first morning at breakfast, Abe's wife, Bertha, burned the toast and profusely offered an apology to Harry. To which, Harry replied, "Don't worry. I kind of like burned toast." So every morning after that, Bertha remembered to burn the toast for Harry. Finally, one morning Harry had had enough and blurted out at the breakfast table, "What's with the burned toast? Why are you giving me burned toast every morning?" To this, the Maslows replied, "But we thought you liked burned toast—that's what you told us." Harry then came clean: "I don't like burned toast. I only said that to be nice." After that incident, when either Abe or Bertha felt they weren't being completely honest with one another, one of them would often say, "Remember Harry's toast." In Bill's office hung a sign that read "The cruelest lies are often told in silence." Bill often talked about the importance of being a congruent person and wanted his children to apply the ideas of personal congruence that Maslow taught him.

Growing up in the home of a social scientist like Bill also created some interesting opportunities for learning. For example, on one occasion, he had a long conversation with a friend about the different dynamics in their two families. The two of them decided that it would be a useful exercise for each of their families to gain some deeper insights into how families functioned (e.g., rules about chores, homework, bedtime, and so on). To gain this insight, they decided to swap a child for a week and then have each child report back on what it was like to be a member of the "new" family. Then the two families would get together to discuss the differences between the families. Apparently Bill and Bonnie felt that Mike, the second oldest, was expendable, so Mike spent the week with the McLean family, and we received Herb McLean in return. It proved to be an insightful and memorable experience for us, and we remember it even forty or so years later.

Bill had a unique ability to share his philosophies regarding management in a way that others—even his children—could understand. On one occasion, his son Jeff commented that Bill wasn't catching very many fish on a family fishing trip. The four Dyer boys were outcatching him—and Bill was supposed to be the expert fisherman. Bill proceeded to describe his role as "manager" of a group of Dyer children (four boys and a girl) on a fishing trip. He explained that in order for the trip to be a success, all of the members of the Dyer fishing group needed to experience success in catching fish. That meant that Bill needed to spend much of his fishing time showing each of his children how to tie on hooks and cast and basically coaching us in the art of fishing. As a result, his personal production decreased, but the team production increased. Collectively we caught more fish because the manager, Bill, was less concerned with his individual achievement than with team achievement. This analogy offered a poignant lesson on the art of management and what it takes to be an effective team manager.

Many of the ideas in this book come from Bill's belief that groups can be used to help people learn, can bring out the best in people, and can create much of what is good in the world. Through his T-group experience, he also learned the importance of team skills such as problem solving, communication, and conflict management and how to develop those competencies in a team. His thoughts on these topics are central to what is presented in this edition of *Team Building*.

The early 1960s were an exciting time for those involved with T-groups. Many felt that the T-group would be the vehicle that would help change the nature of authoritarian organizations and help unleash the human potential that had been suppressed. However, a study conducted by Campbell and Dunnette in 1968 was to change most of that thinking.[2] Campbell and Dunnette reviewed the major studies that had looked at the impact of T-group training on individuals and on organizations. Not surprisingly, they found that the T-group did in fact help individuals become more comfortable with themselves and their ability to manage interpersonal relationships. However, the study also showed that T-group training had virtually no impact (and sometimes a negative effect) on organizational or team performance. The T-group experience often helped people become more open and honest, but this sometimes led to dysfunctional confrontations in the team and didn't necessarily translate into solving the team's specific performance problems.

Given these findings, Bill had to make a decision regarding his work as a T-group trainer. It was at this point that he decided to create a new paradigm for working with groups—the team-building paradigm. He wrote about this change from T-groups to team building as follows:

> As practitioners developed more experience in applying the T-group methods to work units, the T-group mode shifted to take into account the differences of the new setting. It became clear that the need was not just to let people get feed-back, but to help the work unit develop into a more effective, collaborative, problem-solving unit with work to get out and goals to achieve. Slowly the methodology shifted from the unstructured T-group to a more focused, defined process of training a group of interdependent people in collaborative work and problem-solving procedures.[3]

Bill's experience in working with T-groups proved helpful as he worked as a consultant to many teams facing problems, and in 1977, he published the first book on team building that captured the essence of his consulting experience and his model for helping teams become more effective. The book was an instant success because the theories, methods, and exercises he described in the book worked. They proved invaluable to managers, team leaders, and consultants. Over the years, in subsequent editions, Bill added new material to keep up with the changing times and the evolution of the field.

Bill passed away in 1997. In many ways, we have continued in the tradition of our father. Gibb went to MIT to obtain his PhD degree in management and worked closely with Ed Schein and Dick Beckhard. Jeff worked as a strategy consultant for several years at Bain & Company before completing his PhD work at UCLA, where he collaborated with Bill Ouchi, who popularized theory Z management. He then spent a number of years as a professor at the Wharton School. We both have had our own experiences in consulting with various teams that have found themselves in trouble. And Bill's models of team building have helped us immensely as we have worked with those teams. In fact, on many occasions we turned to this book for help and advice in working with clients or have given it to others to help them with their teams.

A few years ago, a graduate student came to us for help. He was going to Mozambique on an internship to work for a nonprofit agency that was apparently in disarray due to a lack of clear goals and strategy and poor teamwork. After we oriented the student to team building and armed him with the team-building book, he went off to his assignment. During his stay in Mozambique, he communicated with us by e-mail about his progress. He reported that the team-building activities that he used from the book had made a significant difference in the organization's performance. Moreover, because the agency liked his work so much, he was hired permanently as director of operations in southern Africa. Like this student, we, too, have found Bill's ideas to have had a significant impact on our clients.

We decided to revise the Fourth Edition as a result of some recent changes in the world and in organizations. We have added a chapter on cross-cultural teams to highlight the challenges many organizations face today as they bring together people in teams that have different cultures and backgrounds. Jeff's work on innovation in organizations, which is found in his recent book with Hal Gregersen and Clayton Christensen, *The Innovator's DNA*, encouraged us to write a chapter on leading innovative teams in today's competitive environment.[4] Moreover, we've updated this edition with some new case examples and have strengthened the Four Cs framework that we developed for the Fourth Edition.

We believe that this Fifth Edition of *Team Building* will provide the next generation of team leaders, team members, and team consultants with the knowledge and skills they need to create effective teams in the future. We believe Bill is pleased that the work he started over a half-century ago is continuing today.

Part One

THE FOUR Cs OF
TEAM DEVELOPMENT

THE SEARCH FOR THE HIGH-PERFORMING TEAM

"Fired?" John Smith, president of DigiCorp, couldn't believe it (all names have been disguised): he had just come from a meeting with Peter Davis, chairman of the board, who had asked for John's resignation.

A few days earlier, several members of John's executive management team had met privately with Davis to air their grievances about John and demand that he be fired. The executives reported that he was unable to create an "effective team atmosphere" for them to work in. Team meetings were unproductive, they said, and led to confusion rather than clarity for team members, in part because consensus about decisions was rarely reached. John imposed top-down decisions when many members of the executive team felt capable of sharing the decision-making responsibility. The team was afflicted with interpersonal conflict, not only between a small subgroup of team members but also between John and a couple of key team members. He had taken no action to address or resolve those conflicts. Moreover, they called John "untrustworthy" because he often said one thing and did another, and thus he had slowly lost the support of his team. Team morale, motivation, and productivity had been dropping for several weeks. In the end, the team had had enough: either John would have to leave or they would.

A panicked John phoned us, since he knew we were team consultants, and explained his situation. "What should I do?" he inquired. "Can I save my job? What did I do wrong? What should

I do now?" After we asked John several questions, it became clear to us that at the heart of John's problem was his lack of knowledge regarding how to create and lead a high-performing team. Moreover, he lacked the fundamentals in diagnosing team problems as well as developing team-building skills that could have been used to solve the team's problems before they spiraled out of control.

John Smith's case illustrates some of the more serious problems that we have seen in teams that we have worked with over the years, but his situation is, unfortunately, not all that unusual. Many, maybe most, teams function far below their potential. The reasons for poor team performance are many: the team may not have clear goals or performance metrics; the team may be composed of the wrong people with the wrong set of skills for the task at hand; the team's dynamics may not foster creativity and good decision making; or the team may not know how to solve its own problems and improve performance. Our experience is that poor team performance is largely due to a team's inability to systematically engage in team-building activities—team processes for evaluating team performance and engaging in problem-solving activities that lead to improved team performance.

Poor team performance is a major concern because most of the work performed today is done in a team environment—research teams, product development teams, production teams, sales and marketing teams, cross-functional problem-solving teams, and top management teams. One reason that work is done more by teams now is that products and services have become increasingly complex, requiring a wide range of skills and technologies. No single person is capable of developing, manufacturing, and selling increasingly complex products, which means that teams of individuals with complementary knowledge must coordinate effectively in order to be successful. This requires teamwork. A second reason is that in a global economy, individuals must collaborate across cultural, organizational, and geographical boundaries to accomplish their goals. Hence, the need for cross-cultural, virtual, and alliance teams (teams collaborating across organizational boundaries) has increased in recent years. Thus, to be a high-performing company in today's competitive landscape essentially requires high-performing work teams. The two unavoidably go hand in hand.

High-performing teams are those with members whose skills, attitudes, and competencies enable them to achieve team goals. These team members set goals, make decisions, communicate, manage conflict, and solve problems in a supportive, trusting atmosphere in order to accomplish their objectives. Moreover, they are aware of their own strengths and weaknesses and have the ability to make changes when they need to improve their performance.

The purpose of this book is to give managers, team leaders, team members, and team consultants specific guidance on how to improve team performance. Although the team-building activities we propose may be particularly well suited for poorly performing or dysfunctional teams, they also can transform average or even good teams into great teams.

Determinants of High-Performing Teams: The Four Cs

Over the past several decades, as we have consulted with teams and conducted research on team performance, we have come to the conclusion that four factors—the Four Cs—must be understood and managed for teams to achieve superior performance (figure 1.1):

1. The context for the team
2. The composition of the team
3. The competencies of the team
4. The change management skills of the team

Figure 1.1 The Four Cs of Team Performance

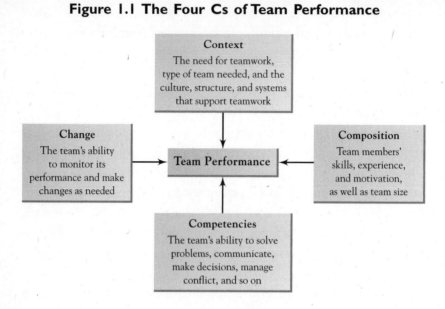

We describe each of these factors briefly here and discuss them in more depth in the following chapters in Part One.

Context for the Team

Team context refers to the organizational environment in which the team must work. Understanding context and how it influences team performance requires an understanding of the answers to two questions:

1. Is effective teamwork critical to accomplishing organizational goals? If so, are there measurable team performance goals around which we can organize a team?

2. Do my organization's senior managers, reward systems, information systems, human resource practices, structure, and culture support teamwork?

Experience has shown that the teamwork required to achieve high performance is much more important when the team must complete a complex task characterized by a high degree of inter-dependence. In addition, we have found that some organizations deploy formal organization structures or reward systems that become barriers to effective teamwork. For example, reward systems that provide strong individual incentives often create strong disincentives to engage in cooperative behavior within a team. Unfortunately, many organizations, while paying lip-service to the importance of teamwork, do little to encourage and support those who work on teams. Thus, they do not foster a culture in which teams can succeed.

High-performing teams manage context effectively by (1) establishing measurable team performance goals that are clear and compelling, (2) ensuring that team members understand that effective teamwork is critical to meeting those goals, (3) establishing reward systems that reward team performance (more than individual performance), (4) eliminating roadblocks to teamwork that formal organization structures might create, (5) establishing an organizational culture that supports teamwork-oriented processes and behaviors (e.g., everyone in the orga-nization understands that success is predicated on effective collaboration; consequently, informal norms and processes support team-oriented behavior), (6) creating information sys-tems to provide the team with needed information to make decisions, and (7) establishing human resource systems to pro-vide training, team member selection, methods, and so on to support teamwork.

Composition of the Team

The composition of the team concerns the skills and attitudes of team members. You have to have the "right people on the bus" to make things happen as a team and achieve top performance.[1] To effectively manage the composition of the team, team leaders must understand that team leadership and processes differ depending on the answers to the following questions:

- Do individual team members have the technical skills required to complete the task?
- Do they have the interpersonal and communication skills required to coordinate their work with others?
- Are individual team members committed to the team and motivated to complete the task?
- Is the team the right size to complete the task successfully?

Teams saddled with members who are not motivated to accomplish the task or lack the skills to achieve team goals are doomed to failure from the outset. Of course, team composition also refers to assembling a group of individuals with complementary skills. High-performing teams use the diverse skills and abilities of each team member in a synergistic way to achieve high performance. The members of high-performing teams clearly understand their roles and assignments and carry them out with commitment.

Team size also plays a significant role in team effectiveness. A team that is too large may be unwieldy and cause team members to lose interest due to a lack of individual involvement. Having too few team members may place unnecessary burdens on individual team members, and the team may not have the resources needed to accomplish its goals.

High-performing teams effectively manage team composition by (1) establishing processes to select individuals for the team who are both skilled and motivated, (2) establishing processes that develop the technical and interpersonal skills of team members as well as their commitment to achieving team goals, (3) cutting loose individuals who lack skills or motivation, (4) managing the team according to the skills and motivation of team members, and (5) ensuring that the team is the right size, that is, neither too large nor too small to accomplish the task.

Competencies of the Team

We have found that successful teams have certain competencies that exist independent of any single member of the team but are embedded in the team's formal and informal processes—its way of functioning. High-performing teams have developed processes that allow the team to:

- Clearly articulate their goals and the metrics for achieving those goals
- Clearly articulate the means required to achieve the goals, ensuring that individuals understand their assignments and how their work contributes to team goals
- Make effective decisions
- Effectively communicate, including giving and receiving feedback
- Build trust and commitment to the team and its goals
- Resolve disputes or disagreements
- Encourage risk taking and innovation

Thus, while the context and composition of the team set the stage, these competencies propel it to high performance. If the team hopes to be extraordinary, it must develop competencies for goal setting, decision making, communicating, trust building, and dispute resolution. In chapter 4, we discuss these and other key competencies in greater detail.

Change Management Skills of the Team

High-performing teams must change and adapt to new conditions to be effective over time. Factors related to team context, composition, and competencies may need to change for the team to succeed in reaching a new goal. A team that is able to monitor its performance and understand its strengths and weaknesses can generate insights needed to develop a plan of action to continuously improve. Toyota, a company that we've researched extensively, uses the *kaizen,* or continuous-improvement, philosophy to help its teams identify the bottlenecks they are facing and then develop strategies to eliminate the bottlenecks.[2] Toyota's managers are never fully satisfied with their team's performance because once they've fixed one problem, they know that continuous improvement requires that they find and fix the next one. We have found that teams in most companies, unlike Toyota, are oblivious to their weaknesses. And even when they do recognize them, they do not have the ability to manage change effectively to overcome those weaknesses. It is possible to view change management skills as just another team competency, but this meta-competency—what we call team-building skills—is so important that it deserves special attention.

High-performing teams have developed the ability to change by (1) establishing team-building processes that result in the regular evaluation of team context, team composition, and team competencies with the explicit objective of initiating needed changes in order to better achieve the desired team goals and (2) establishing a philosophy among team members that regular change is necessary in order to meet the demands of a constantly changing world.

What Happened to John Smith?

You might be wondering what happened to John Smith, the CEO in trouble at DigiCorp. After John called us, we were engaged to conduct several team-building sessions with his team. The board of directors agreed to suspend John's firing until the team's problems, and John's role in those problems, could be more fully explored. Initially we conducted interviews and gathered data from team members and members of the board of directors to diagnose the team's problems. John's team then met with us in a team-building session designed to clear the air and develop a plan of action to improve team performance.

The problems were serious: trust had been lost, and the team had significant philosophical differences with John regarding how team decisions should be made and what the priorities of the company should be. However, the company was facing its busiest time of the year, and to avoid a total collapse, the team members needed to figure out a way to work together effectively to serve the company's clients—at least for the next three months, until the busy season passed.

In the team-building sessions, team members agreed to set aside their differences and work cooperatively so they could function effectively in the short run. Moreover, the board of directors agreed to give John the opportunity to turn things around. After the initial data-gathering and team-building sessions, our role as consultants was to meet periodically with the team to monitor its performance. The results: the team did work together successfully during the busy season and served the company's clients well. But at the end of the busy season, most of the team members decided to leave the organization: the damage had been done and couldn't be fully repaired. They lacked confidence in John's ability to develop important team competencies such as how to establish consensual decision-making processes, resolve interpersonal conflicts, and make changes in team composition and team processes when necessary. The resignation of most of John's team gave him the opportunity to create a new, more effective team. He apparently learned from his previous team failure by hiring the right people with the right skills and motivation. Moreover, he created the appropriate context to strengthen his team and developed greater competencies in the team. Today John remains the CEO of a highly successful organization.

In Summary

To avoid the problems that John encountered with his team, team leaders must create the appropriate context to support teamwork. Team members should also have the requisite knowledge, skills, and motivation to do their individual jobs, while working in a team environment. Team competencies in areas such as decision making, meeting management, and conflict management need to be developed by the team. And effective teams should be able to monitor their performance and take corrective action when needed. By paying attention to the Four Cs, teams can truly become high performing.

2

CONTEXT

Laying the Foundation for Team Success

We have discovered that successful teams are found in organizations in which senior executives know how and when to emphasize and support teamwork and have well-thought-out strategies for assigning people to work in teams. Unfortunately, most organizations pay only lip-service to developing high-performing teams and do little to create an atmosphere that fosters successful teams.

In this chapter, we discuss the first C of our Four Cs model: context. By creating a context for developing effective teams, managers are more likely to achieve the successful team dynamics and team results they desire.

The Context Problem: Why Teamwork Often Doesn't Work

Over the years we have surveyed dozens of personnel and human resource managers in both large and small companies and gathered data from hundreds of managers about their organizations' efforts to improve team performance. Although most report that their companies believe teamwork is important, only about one-third were engaged in a serious effort to initiate team-building practices that would improve team performance. When the managers of the other two-thirds were asked why they didn't spend much time and effort to improve their teams, they reported the following problems, listed in order of the frequency of response:

1. I don't know how to build a more effective team.

2. I'm concerned that the possible negative effects will outweigh the benefits.

3. I don't feel that developing an effective team is rewarded in our company.

4. My subordinates feel they don't need it, and it takes too much time.

5. I don't have the support of my boss to spend time in team development.

Let's look at each of these:

1. *I don't know how to build a more effective team.* With the business world's emphasis on teamwork, it is interesting that the primary obstacle to team building is that managers feel they do not know how to build an effective team. Virtually every recent publication on organizations and management has emphasized the importance of effective teams in achieving high levels of performance. However, rarely do these writings describe exactly how to develop effective teams. There is almost a sense that because everyone agrees that teams are important and almost everyone has participated on some type of team, everyone must therefore understand how to put an effective team together.

Very few academic programs deal with understanding team processes and dynamics. Students—whether in undergraduate courses or in MBA programs—are assigned to work in teams, and often the team product is graded. However, few professors know enough or take the time to help these teams deal with the problems and group issues that often occur. Frequently in these class teams, a few students do the work while others coast along and get undeserved credit; in other cases, conflicts and problems arise, and because the team does not know how to handle them, the students wind up with strong negative feelings about team projects that they carry into the business world.

To overcome this lack of skill and knowledge in developing teams, some organizations have a speaker come in and talk about team building or circulate a book or other information. However, most people find it difficult to engage in complex activities just by reading or hearing information. They need some direct experience and some clear examples of what to do. It's one thing to read about how to hit a fastball of a major league pitcher; it's quite another thing to actually do it yourself. This lack of practical know-how is a major obstacle. And even when people know how to develop teams, they still may not succeed if some of the other obstacles are present.

2. *I'm concerned that the possible negative effects will outweigh the benefits.* Most managers are pragmatic in their approach to taking action: they weigh the possible gains against the costs and risks and usually follow a course of action designed to maximize benefits and minimize negative consequences. Many managers we have interviewed have talked about some of the negative effects of team-building programs they have heard about. Some have heard of (but very few have ever directly experienced) team-building efforts that resulted in a "bloodbath." They heard that the entire session was devoted to unmercifully giving people harsh, negative feedback. The result was a lot of hard feelings and a drop in team morale and performance.

Other horror stories include reported incidents of people quitting or getting fired, suffering a mental breakdown, invading other people's private lives, or spending long sessions talking about their "feelings" but accomplishing little. Moreover, many managers realize that team building might improve morale but not necessarily improve team performance. It appears to them that the time devoted to team building might be better spent working on team tasks directly related to output. With these possible negative effects, coupled with managers' not really understanding how to do team building or clearly seeing the benefits, it is easy to see why many managers do not engage in ongoing team development.

3. *I don't feel that developing an effective team is rewarded in our company.* Another key obstacle is the lack of apparent connections between team building and formal rewards in the organization. For many years, a major oil company had a program of management development for middle managers that included clear instruction about doing effective team building. However, few of these managers implemented their team development plans on the job. When asked the reason, they overwhelmingly replied that their performance reviews by their bosses did not include anything about their team-building efforts. The team building that was emphasized in the management program was not included in either performance reviews or subsequent raises or promotions, and therefore managers could see no personal payoff from spending time building teams. Moreover, the organization did not provide the resources or the time to engage in a serious team-building effort during work hours.

4. *My subordinates feel they don't need it, and it takes too much time.* Our surveys revealed that because many people have never experienced working on an effective work team, they have no standard against which to compare their current team. Many describe their current team functioning as "Okay," "We're doing all right," or "We are as good as most." In a similar vein, many managers believe that team building is a kind of "touchy-feely" activity, not associated with getting work done. As one manager said, "What I need is help in getting a lot of work done with reduced manpower. I don't need to waste time while people talk about their feelings." When the attitude that teams are unimportant is coupled with the assumption that the team building will waste valuable working time, many managers understandably decide that they don't really need team building.

5. *I don't have the support of my boss to spend time in team development.* Some managers in the organizations we studied indicated that although they would like to engage in team building and thought they knew what to do, they did not get any

support for these activities from their bosses. These managers said that their bosses gave the following reasons for not supporting team development:

"It will take too much time from our heavy workload."

"It isn't supported by upper management."

"Team development is not part of the company goals or the performance review system."

"We have heard that it is a waste of time."

"We understand that it requires an outside consultant, which we can't afford."

When your boss doesn't support an initiative, it is virtually impossible to feel it is important.

The Importance of Context

What we have learned from our own experience in consulting with teams over the years is that context matters. Without a team-supportive organization context, team development is difficult, even impossible. To create an organizational context that will support teamwork, managers should ask themselves the following questions:

1. How important is effective teamwork to accomplishing this particular task?
2. What type of team is needed?
3. Does the organization's context of culture, structure, and systems support teamwork?

How Important Is Effective Teamwork to Accomplishing This Particular Task?

Although all teams represent a collection of people who must collaborate to some degree to achieve common goals, some tasks

Figure 2.1 Continuum of Teamwork

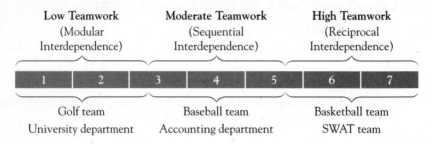

Low Teamwork (Modular Interdependence)		Moderate Teamwork (Sequential Interdependence)			High Teamwork (Reciprocal Interdependence)	
1	2	3	4	5	6	7

Golf team	Baseball team	Basketball team
University department	Accounting department	SWAT team

require more team collaboration than others. Figure 2.1 represents a continuum of the teamwork or collaboration needed for a team to function. The continuum is based on the notion that the importance of teamwork will vary according to the task environment, notably the degree of interdependence required to complete the team's tasks.[1]

Modular Interdependence   Sometimes the nature of the task doesn't require the team to work closely together all the time because the team tasks are modular in nature. In these tasks, individuals on the team are connected through *modular or pooled interdependence*, performing tasks independently and pooling only the results to create a team output. For example, a golf team may do some general planning and share information about the golf course and competition, but in the final analysis, play is by the individual performer. Team performance is based on individual performances that are pooled together.

Similarly, an academic department requires relatively little teamwork. Each professor can do most of the required work— teach, research, write—alone. Of course, faculty members share ideas on how to be effective in teaching and research. But the performance of the department, as measured by student teaching evaluations or the number of faculty publications in top journals, is based largely on individual performance that is pooled together.

When important decisions need to be made or departmental goals set that require the efforts of all department members, then those members must function as a decision team. However, these situations occur relatively infrequently.

Sequential Interdependence Individuals on teams are sequentially interdependent when one person cannot perform his or her task until another has completed his or her task and passed on the results. Under these circumstances, team members must meet more regularly and consistently to coordinate their work.

A baseball team is an example of a team that requires a moderate amount of teamwork. All nine players must be on the field at once, but for much of the game, the effort is individual in nature. However, whether a batter bunts or tries to hit to the opposite field depends on what the previous hitters have done. Relay throws from outfield to home base and double plays require sequential coordination. Moreover, the catcher and pitcher interact constantly in a coordinated fashion as they try to prevent batters from reaching base.

An accounting or financial department requires sequential coordination. Everyone in such a department must work within a common accounting framework, and the work of one part of the accounting process depends on the work of other parts. The accuracy of the tax people depends in part on how well internal auditors have done their work. Although each accountant may be doing individual work, each sometimes may be unable to proceed without input from others.

Most company executive committees require a moderate amount of teamwork. Historically, for much of their work, the heads of marketing, finance, personnel, and manufacturing have done their work autonomously in their own areas. At key times, they have come together to build a common strategy, set common goals, and coordinate work activities, such as getting marketing and manufacturing to agree on the type and amount of product that should be produced for the marketplace. However, effective companies realize that success in coordinating product development and manufacturing, or manufacturing and sales and marketing activities, requires reciprocal rather than sequential interdependence.

Reciprocal Interdependence In some groups, the nature of the task requires a high degree of teamwork because tasks are reciprocally interdependent. Team outputs are achieved through work done in a simultaneous and iterative process in which each individual must work in close coordination with other team members because he or she can complete tasks only through a process of iterative knowledge sharing. Thus, team members must communicate their own requirements frequently and be responsive to the needs of the other team members.

Similarly, members of a basketball team are on the court together and must coordinate constantly as they run offense plays and play team defense. Every member interacts with every other member. Thus, one would predict that a basketball team would suffer more from the lack of teamwork than would a golf team or even a baseball team. Indeed, this seems to be the case, as evidenced by the fact that major league baseball teams that acquire a few free-agent stars occasionally come from a low ranking the prior year (even last place) to win the World Series. This rarely happens with NBA basketball teams, which must learn how to coordinate and work together to be successful.

Experience has shown that even having the best individual basketball talent on one team is no guarantee of team success. Consider the events that led to the historic failure of the U.S. basketball team in the 2004 Olympics, which included players like Tim Duncan and Allen Iverson, as well as in the 2006 International Basketball Federation (FIBA) World Championship, when players like Dwyane Wade and Carmelo Anthony were part of the team. The need for better teamwork prompted the United States to require a three-year commitment from NBA players so that they could learn to work together as a team. Since then, the U.S. basketball team has won the 2008 Olympic gold medal, the 2010 FIBA World Championship, and the gold medal in the 2012 Olympic Games.

Product development teams for complex products such as automobiles, aircraft, robotics, and consumer electronics work together in a reciprocally interdependent fashion. For example, when a commercial aircraft is being designed, decisions regarding the weight and thrust of a jet engine and the aerodynamic design of the fuselage and wings must be made taking each other into account.[2] Team members must share information back and forth as they iteratively solve problems. Similar arguments could be made for a police SWAT team or the surgical team in a hospital operating room. All of the tasks are highly connected, and members cannot do their respective work without others doing theirs in a coordinated fashion.

Understanding the level of teamwork and the nature of interdependence required by the task is important for three reasons. First, they dictate the amount of attention that managers need to pay to teamwork and team processes: the greater the team interdependence, the more important it is to make sure the team is working together effectively and everyone understands the nature of the interdependence. Second, by understanding the nature of interdependencies in the team, managers will have greater insight into why certain common problems arise and will know how to fix them. For example, team members of modularly interdependent tasks frequently feel frustrated when team processes are designed for frequent meetings and interaction. They rightly want to be left alone to get their work done rather than be bothered by group processes. Similarly, highly interdependent teams often run into trouble when they are organized as virtual teams and have no opportunities for frequent, rich interactions.

Third, understanding the different levels of teamwork and the nature of interdependence will allow managers to adapt business and team structures to the nature of the task and thereby prevent some problems from occurring in the first place.

What Type of Team Is Needed?

Once the nature of the teamwork needed for a particular task has been determined, decisions can be made about the type of team needed to accomplish that task. Although there are many typologies of teams that have been developed, we describe three generic team types that are simple yet sufficient to cover the important distinctions: (1) decision teams, (2) task teams, and (3) self-directed teams. The first two types of teams are manager led but differ from each other in the roles that they play in the organization. The third type, the self-directed team, is based on different authority and autonomy from the traditional manager-led team that is merely a tool of the manager to get work done.

Decision Teams All teams have a basic activity and a goal. Many teams in organizations have as their basic activity making decisions. People on these decision teams meet to make decisions about a whole range of matters: defining goals, developing strategy to achieve those goals, giving assignments, allocating resources, cutting or expanding resources for various functions, preparing budgets, setting schedules and deadlines, and so on. It is important for a decision team to understand that the quality and acceptance of their decisions can have an immense impact on many other people. For example, if a top management team is making decisions about downsizing or restructuring and if that group is not open to all information—both hard data, such as the profit picture, and soft data, such as morale—its decisions may be resisted and resented and cause serious problems throughout the entire organization.

Task Teams By contrast, members of a task team must together perform a set of interlocking tasks in order to accomplish an end result—a certain product, service, or activity. Examples are a production unit that is making the total product (such as a Volvo automobile), a SWAT team, a surgical team in a hospital, and a utility company service crew. Obviously task teams also must make decisions, and the quality of those decisions will have an impact, positive or negative, on the team's work. The ability to make effective decisions is thus a key element of all teams. But the task team has the additional function of physically coordinating efforts to achieve a given goal.

Self-Directed Teams Much of organization restructuring in recent years has been based on the desirability of allowing work teams to have more authority to deal with the issues that they face. Such self-directed work teams are also called autonomous or semiautonomous work teams.

An autonomous team does not have a formally designated leader. It can select its own leader, rotate leadership among members, or operate without a leader—a kind of "leadership by committee" process during which leadership functions are assigned to different members of the team.

A semiautonomous team, by contrast, does have a designated leader with a formal title and position, but the leader's role is defined in such a way that the team makes its own decisions and takes actions independent of the leader. This has led to one of the dilemmas of the semiautonomous team: determining the role of the leader if the team has the right to function without the direct influence and control of that formal leader.

Organizations that have successfully adopted semiautonomous teams have begun to redefine the role of the formal leader in some combination of the following:

- The leader functions primarily as a training resource or facilitator to help the team examine how it is working and

give the team the needed training, coaching, or
facilitation.

- The leader spends most of his or her time dealing with
  issues with other units or with upper management. Or the
  leader may increase the interaction and relationships with
  customers.

- The leader acts as a consultant to the team and can be
  asked to help deal with team problems, conflicts, problem
  members, or other concerns.

- The leader may attend all team meetings or attend only
  when invited. The leader may formally open the meeting
  but then turn over the activities of the meeting to team
  members.

It is apparent that some teams are autonomous or semiautonomous in name only; that is, the formal leader is not willing
to relinquish power and continues to function in the traditional
leader role of having all activities flow from and through the
leader. It should also be apparent that the team can find itself
beset with a multitude of problems if team members have never
had training or experience in how to work together as a team.
Sometimes teams are asked not only to plan, schedule, and
coordinate work but also to make decisions about hiring, termi-
nations, allocation of pay raises or bonuses, vacation schedules,
training needs, or awarding time off to attend meetings or other
activities. These issues, which are central to a number of personal
concerns of team members, have proved difficult even for experienced teams, and an untrained autonomous or semiautonomous
work team can get buried under a load of activities it is not prepared to handle.

We know of one organization using semiautonomous teams
that even made budget cutting and layoff decisions as a team,
decisions typically reserved for senior management. When the
business experienced a serious downturn, the organization's

senior management gave the work teams data on the kinds of budget cuts that were needed to help the business survive, and the teams were then given the autonomy to decide how they would reduce costs, the bulk of which were in payroll. The teams came up with some creative solutions: some team members decided to take unpaid vacations, others decided to job-share or work part time, and still others who wanted to leave the company and had other opportunities were let go, with relatively few bad feelings. By allowing the team to use its autonomy and creativity in the face of a difficult situation, the company was able to weather the crisis and emerge even stronger.

Identifying the Team Needed These descriptions of decision, task, and self-directed teams suggest that managers must think through the type of team they need to accomplish their goals. Should the team be focused on making quality decisions to improve performance, or should its role be to carry out certain tasks of the organization? Furthermore, does the team need clear direction and leadership from a strong manager, or does it need autonomy to be flexible to adjust to various contingencies that may arise? By answering these questions, the manager can help the team understand what role it is to play in the organization and understand what degree of autonomy it has to do its work.

Does the Organization's Context of Culture, Structure, and Systems Support Teamwork?

Three of the most powerful factors in shaping the context for team development are the organization's culture, structure, and systems.

Culture is probably the most significant factor in team development. While powerful, culture is often difficult to detect and change. An organization's culture represents the basic shared values and assumptions held by most people in the organization. It defines what things are viewed as right or wrong, what is valued, how one gets into trouble, and how people are expected to see the whole corporate world. It is critical to the collaborative team organization that the shared culture emphasize that teamwork is essential and that people at all levels get into trouble if they do not collaborate with others and respond readily as members of the total team. If the culture is either openly or passively resistant to the importance of teamwork, any attempts to foster collaboration, participation, or involvement will be seen as a temporary action or a management manipulation.

In one organization we studied, the culture was permeated by one key assumption or basic rule: no one does anything without checking with Fred, the CEO, first. The rule was clearly demonstrated each time an employee walked past the thermostat in the hall and read the sign: "DO NOT ADJUST THIS THERMOSTAT WITHOUT FRED'S PERMISSION!!!" In an atmosphere in which one must wait for the boss before taking any action, it is difficult to encourage teamwork and collaboration.

Structure refers to the basic design of the organization as represented in an organization chart. It reflects authority, communication patterns, and the responsibility for certain functions in the organization. Organization structure largely determines who works with whom and whether teams are designated formally to carry out organization tasks. Although all organizations have informal groups that form for a variety of reasons, the formal organization structure can encourage and support teamwork, or it can make it much more difficult for teams to form and function effectively.

We have found that organizations that rely on an organization structure that fails to account for the teamwork that must occur across the various functions (engineering, marketing, manufacturing, and so on) tend to foster conflict, miscommunication, and poor coordination. To illustrate, Chrysler experienced teamwork problems in developing new cars up through the early 1990s when it was organized around functional silos in engineering, manufacturing, finance, marketing, and purchasing. New cars were developed in temporary project teams that pulled individuals from each of the functional areas. However, using this organizational structure, Chrysler took six years to develop a new car, while its Japanese competitors, Toyota and Honda, were consistently developing new cars in four years. The teamwork required to quickly develop new car models simply wasn't there.

To address the teamwork problem, Chrysler reorganized around car platform teams: large car, small car, truck, and minivan. In this way, individuals from the different functional areas worked together consistently within the same team over long periods of time. This structure even brought supplier partners onto the team—giving the supplier "guest engineers" desks and work space within the platform team. This reorganization improved teamwork and coordination within the product development teams at Chrysler. Within three years, they were developing new car models on a four-year basis, just like their Japanese competitors. Chrysler's experience shows that organizations that are designed based on a team concept can use organization structure to bring people together in formal, and sometimes informal, teams to accomplish the organization's goals.

Systems are the agreed-on methods for doing work in the organization. These integrated agreements, or systems, regulate almost all aspects of organization life. Pay systems, evaluation and promotion systems, decision-making systems, and management information systems are all examples of this component. It is critical that the systemic aspects of the organization support team development. People encounter major problems in a company that is attempting to build teamwork into the organization when the pay system is based entirely on individual performance, or if information is given only to individual senior managers rather than all team members.

In one cell phone assembly plant, the work was done almost entirely using an assembly line with no emphasis on teamwork among employees on the line. Costs were high and quality was low, and top management gave the plant an ultimatum: fix the problems, or we will shut down the plant.

The plant manager brought in a consultant who redesigned the assembly-line system, putting employees into semiautonomous work teams. Just as important, the teams were given information, heretofore kept secret, on costs and quality and given the authority to make changes as needed. As a result, the teams came up with over a thousand suggestions for improvement in the first year after the changes were made. Not surprisingly, quality improved significantly, and the plant recognized cost savings of more than $7 million over a one-year period. Jobs were saved and employees rewarded for improving performance. In this case, changes in the culture, structure, and systems led to improved teamwork, which resulted in significant productivity gains.

In Summary

To create the right context to support high-performing teams, it is important to:

- Identify the type of teamwork needed for success
- Determine the type of team needed to accomplish team goals
- Ensure that the organization's culture, structure, and systems support teamwork

Without the proper context to support teamwork, it is difficult, if not impossible, to develop effective teams. We have found that our efforts to do team building are often undermined by an unfriendly team context. Improving team performance without the proper contextual support is like paddling a canoe upstream through rapids: you might eventually get to your destination but not without expending a lot more effort than necessary.

3

COMPOSITION

Getting the Right People on the Bus

If the organizational context is supportive of teamwork, the next task is to determine the appropriate size of the team, who should be on it, and how they should be managed depending on their skill set and motivation.

In this chapter, we discuss the importance of getting the right people on a team, as well as the optimal team size. To illustrate the importance of both team composition and context, we examine the practices of Bain & Company, a management consulting firm that has achieved superior results through the effective management of team context and composition. We also provide an assessment instrument for evaluating team composition and context.

WEB www.josseybass.com/
go/dyerteamassessments

Team Composition and Performance

For a team to succeed, its members need two things: the skills and experience to accomplish the task and "fire in the belly," that is, the motivation to succeed. Team leaders play a critical role in identifying and attracting people with those attributes to the team. Beyond that, we have found that effective team leaders have the following characteristics:[1]

- Clear vision of the team's goals and the metrics that will accurately measure team performance
- Ability to set clear direction for the team with regard to how to achieve team goals

- Ability to motivate and inspire team members as they pursue team goals
- Ability to teach and coach team members in developing the skills necessary to complete team tasks
- Ability to make each team member feel that she or he is valued and an important contributor to the team
- Ability to hold team members accountable for their contributions to team performance
- Ability to include and listen to team members when making decisions that affect the team
- Ability to manage conflict and solve team problems effectively
- Ability to gain support and resources for the team from key executives and other constituencies

We often find that team leaders do not receive adequate training and as a result are ill equipped to lead the team.

In addition to effective leaders, successful teams need members who have the following characteristics:

- Strong technical skills, knowledge, or experience related to accomplishing the team's tasks
- High motivation to be an effective contributor to the team effort
- Effective interpersonal and communication skills
- A willingness to help and support other team members in their efforts to achieve team goals
- Good conflict management skills (i.e., they are capable of working through disagreements)
- Ability to adapt to new situations
- Dependability and ability to take initiative to help the team achieve its goals

Figure 3.1 Team Composition: Evaluating and Managing Team Members Based on Skills and Motivation

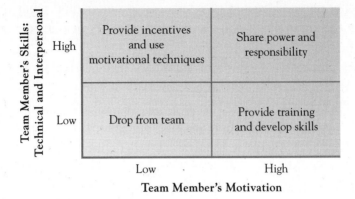

Effective team leaders understand that the way they manage the team and individual team members is strongly influenced by the degree to which team members are skilled and motivated (see figure 3.1). In some instances, team members may not have the necessary skills or may not be properly motivated to work on the team. When team members are neither skilled nor motivated, team leaders may be wise to drop them from the team because the challenge of building their skills and motivating them is simply too daunting. When team members are skilled but not motivated, the team leader's role is largely a motivational one. We have found that empowering skilled team members with greater responsibility for team tasks and performance can be an effective way to increase a team member's commitment to the team and its goals. Naturally, it is preferable if team members are intrinsically rather than extrinsically motivated. In fact, when selecting someone for the team, try to determine to what extent the person has a passion and love for this kind of work and to what extent she or he is committed to the team goals.

Finding people who are passionate about the work and internally committed to the organization's goals can save team leaders headaches down the road. However, in some cases, it may be necessary and desirable to motivate through increased pay, rank, or other perks. The key, of course, is to understand what motivates the particular team member to give his or her best effort for the team.

In contrast, when team members are motivated but not skilled, the leader's task is largely one of coaching and skill building. This requires that the leader play the roles of educator and coach. It also means that assessments of skill deficiencies are necessary so that an individual development and training program can be established to ensure that the person develops the technical skills necessary to be effective in completing the team's tasks.

Finally, when team members are both skilled and motivated, the wise team leader will share power and responsibility with the members, since they are capable of assisting the leader in developing team competencies and motivated to achieve the team's goals.

As teams are formed, team leaders should meet with potential team members before selection to ascertain their ability to contribute to the accomplishment of the team's goals as well as their motivation to be part of the team. Offering a meaningful team goal or significant performance challenge generally can rally individuals to a team and motivate them. When team members believe they are being asked to contribute to something important—something that counts, that has vision—they are more likely to give their best effort than will people who are asked to serve on another team or committee that seems to serve little purpose.

Amazon.com, the Internet discount retailer, is known for attracting and retaining some of the best and brightest technical talent around. It does this in part by maintaining one constant in its selection process: "Does this candidate have a strong desire to change the world?" Leaders are looking for people who want to achieve something important. In addition, job applicants are interviewed by teams of Amazon employees—in many cases, by the entire team that they will join. The team interviews help ensure that new employees bring diversity to the team (which is critical for innovation and is an explicit goal of the team interviews) and tests whether the recruits have the collaboration skills necessary to succeed in Amazon's team environment.

Team Size

There is no clear answer as to the size of an optimal team because size is determined in part by the nature of the task. Some managers like large teams because they believe that these teams generate more ideas and call attention to the importance of a project or functional area. Moreover, some managers think that putting people on a team is a good experience, and they don't want to leave anyone out. However, in general, small teams are preferable to large teams, and there are rules of thumb and certain pitfalls to avoid in determining team size.[2]

We find that large teams (typically over ten people) have lower productivity than smaller teams. Research reported by Katzenbach and Smith in their book *The Wisdom of Teams* suggests that "serious deterioration in the quality and productivity of team interactions sets in when there are more than 12 to 14 members of the team."[3] The greater the number of team members, the more difficult it is to achieve a common understanding and agreement about team goals and team processes. Large teams lead to less involvement on the part of team members and hence lower commitment and participation, which leads to lower levels of trust.

Although team size clearly should be determined by the nature of the task, much of the research suggests that the most productive teams have four to ten members. In summarizing research on team size, researcher Glenn Parker notes, "Although optimal size depends on the specific team mission, in general, the optimal team size is four to six members, with ten being the maximum for effectiveness. It is important to remember that many team tools in decision making, problem solving, and communicating were created to take advantage of small-group dynamics. Consensus, for example, just does not work as a decision-making method in a team of twenty members."[4]

Amazon.com has experienced an explosion of growth throughout its short life and employs more than ten thousand people. However, it typically deploys its workforce into "two pizza" teams (the number of people who can be adequately fed by two pizzas) to promote team identity and foster commitment, accountability, and innovation within the team. Because two large pizzas typically feed eight to ten people, you rarely find larger teams within Amazon. Thus, the rule of thumb is to choose the smallest number of people possible that will still allow the team to effectively accomplish its mission.

Effective Team Context and Composition: The Case of Bain & Company

Bain & Company, a top-tier global consulting firm, has made team development a high priority. Although the company and its teams certainly have their problems, most organizations can learn some valuable lessons from Bain's team development efforts. (Jeff Dyer experienced the impact of Bain's team culture personally as a Bain consultant for several years.)

Bain's ability to develop productive teams hinges largely on a program that includes the following key elements:

- A strong team culture that features:
  - A team orientation explicitly stated in the company's mission statement
  - Promotion and rewards for those who demonstrate team leadership skills

- Team processes that emphasize interdependency as exemplified by the mantra: "A Bainie never lets another Bainie fail"
- Attention to team dynamics and structure, including:
  - Lean and flat semiautonomous teams with high responsibility
  - Attention to complementary team skills and team chemistry
  - High priority on personal and leadership skill development
- Systems that measure team satisfaction and performance on a monthly basis

Getting the right people on the team is a critical first step, and Bain focuses its recruiting efforts at top universities around the globe that it has determined do an effective job of finding (and sometimes preparing) individuals for management consulting. Bain also invests heavily in two rounds of interviews with recruits as it looks for three skill sets: analytical and problem-solving skills, client and communication management skills, and team collaboration skills.

In the first round of interviews, recruits are largely tested on their analytical and problem-solving skills as they are asked to solve business cases during the interviews. The second round focuses more on whether recruits have the client and communication skills necessary and whether they will be effective team players. As part of the client and communication skill evaluation, interviewers assess whether the person has the appropriate degree of confidence and optimism without showing arrogance. (Arrogance is the kiss of death.) They also assess whether a recruit can comfortably communicate with all sorts of people, from shop foreman to CEO. Finally, recruits must pass the airplane test: "Is this someone I would want to hang out with for six hours on an airplane?" "Is this someone I want to work on *my* team?"

Another key way that Bain gets the right people on the bus is to watch them perform on a Bain team before they are hired as a full-time consultant. To do this, Bain invests heavily in a summer intern program, bringing in a large percentage of MBA students to work over the summer between the first and second years of their program to see whether they have the "right stuff" (i.e., analytical skills, communication skills, and team collaboration skills). Thus, Bain puts potential team members on a simulated "bus ride" before putting them on the bus for good.

According to Mark Howorth, senior director of global recruiting for Bain, roughly two-thirds of new consultants hired have either worked at Bain as summer interns or as analysts (associate consultants) after graduating from college. This dramatically reduces the risk of getting the wrong people on the bus. Once Bain has determined that a person has the ability to be successful, it brings that person into an organizational environment that supports effective teamwork in the following ways.

Cultural Characteristics: A Team Orientation

Bain understands what it means to foster a culture that supports teamwork. Most organizations just talk about it, but at Bain it is not just talk. The importance of the team is highlighted in the company's mission statement as one of three keys to success. The statement reads (italics added for emphasis):

> Bain & Company's mission is to help our clients create such high levels of economic value that together we set new standards of excellence in our respective industries. This vision demands:
>
> - The Bain vision of the most productive client relationship and single-minded dedication to achieving it with each client.
> - *The Bain community of extraordinary teams.*
> - The Bain approach to creating value, based on a sharp competitive and customer focus, the most effective analytical techniques, and our process for collaboration with the client.[5]

Extraordinary teams is a term often heard within Bain & Company. Historically, one of the senior directors in the firm had responsibility for researching and understanding what made an extraordinary team. He then gave his report at the annual company meeting on the company's progress in this area. An extraordinary team was selected and featured in the biannual company newsletter with a description of how and why the team was extraordinary. These teams were also recognized at company meetings and celebrated with a team event. All teams within the company are encouraged—and given the resources—to celebrate successful projects or particularly effective teamwork. Celebrating can range from a team dinner to a weekend of skiing together. The company wants to let the team know that it appreciates a job well done.

Promoting Team Leadership Skills

No one is promoted to manager at Bain without clearly demonstrating the skill mix necessary to be an effective team leader. The company has adopted a promotion process that essentially results in the flip side of the Peter principle. Rather than promoting people to their level of incompetence, Bain requires that prospective managers demonstrate the full complement of managerial skills, and particularly intellectual leadership, in a case team leader role before they are promoted to manager.

Just like any other manager or partner, they receive a monthly evaluation from the team regarding their leadership performance (more on this in a moment). Over time the company has studied what makes for an effective team leader. In the early days in the firm, they found that extraordinary teams (as measured by quantifiable results for the client) were led by team leaders who exhibited great "intellectual leadership." Intellectual leadership might best be defined as the ability to create and communicate a clear vision for the team, as well as to brainstorm and generate value-added ideas. Although this is still important, more recent studies of employee satisfaction have found that the most effective team leaders are those who "motivate, inspire, and value" their team members. In other words, just being smart isn't enough to inspire a team of individuals who are mostly from the Gen X or millennial generation. These practices have resulted in a core of managers who are generally highly effective at building productive teams.

Team Process Emphasizing Interdependency and Productivity

Bain's approach to emphasizing interdependency and productivity is unique. At the beginning of each project, a "blank slide" presentation is created that is essentially a structured problem-solving method that clearly outlines the data and analysis required to solve the problem facing the team. This represents the manager's hypothesis (with input from the partner, or senior manager, and team members) on the key aspects of the problem being addressed and is the manager's vision of the logic and structure behind the final presentation (product). Consequently the team understands the working hypothesis and knows precisely what the overall team objective is from the very beginning.

The team goal is to do the analysis that proves or disproves the hypothesis and leads to a set of recommendations. Each person is responsible for a piece of the puzzle and understands how this piece is vital to the success of the combined team effort. This is a strong motivating factor for team members because they know that their work is critical to the team's final product and that they will be held accountable.

The presentation is divided among team members, and the manager develops a work plan with each member to ensure that he or she understands what is expected. Because of the interdependent nature of the work, Bain tries to ensure that a "Bainie" never fails. This philosophy is shared at every recruiting event that the firm holds and is frequently mentioned within training and other company events. This saying boldly reinforces the idea that "we are a team" and "we need each other."

Team Dynamics and Structure: Lean, Flat Teams with High Responsibility

Bain's internal study of extraordinary teams found that lower-performing teams were generally larger and had multiple reporting relationships. Consequently, efforts are made to keep teams small and structures flat. The logic is that people work harder and are happier when they are given heavy responsibility and are not burdened by layers of management. Moreover, on a small team, individuals have more direction from supervisors and are less likely to get lost in the shuffle and end up frustrated and unproductive. Therefore, teams are generally organized to consist of only four to six members. These individuals report to a manager, who then reports to a partner, the end of the line of authority. All are closely involved in the work and are held accountable for team performance.

Attention to Team Chemistry

Bain devotes significant time to determining the right mix of people given the demands of the team project and the professional development needs of potential team members. The team assignment process begins with a discussion among the office staffing officer, partners or managers, and potential members. The staffing officer typically discusses the skills required to be successful on a particular client project with the partner or manager. Three issues are generally reviewed when a person is considered for a team:

- Does this person have the skills and experience necessary to help the client be successful in this particular assignment?

- Does this project fit with this person's skill plan and professional development needs?
- Will this person work well with the client, manager, and other team members?

The staffing officer in charge of case team assignments speaks with managers and potential team members before an assignment is made to make sure the fit is good. In most cases potential team members can refuse an assignment if they make a strong argument that they cannot answer these questions with a "yes."

By taking time in advance to consider these issues, Bain ensures that team members are considerably more committed to the team and are less likely to become frustrated and unproductive. As a result, management saves time by avoiding team problems down the road.

High Priority on Personal Development

This may seem paradoxical but although creating extraordinary teams is the overall goal, Bain doesn't lose sight of the fact that extraordinary teams are composed of successful and productive individuals. To ensure that individual needs are considered, professional development is a company priority. Managers and team members jointly develop skill plans to outline the skills that the team member needs to develop in order to advance in the organization.

Skill plans are prepared every six months, with the manager providing coaching and feedback. Most managers also conduct a monthly or bimonthly lunch with each member to discuss professional development needs. The system is supported by a professional development department whose primary responsibility is to help employees with their personal growth and development. Team "buddies," or colleagues, are assigned when a new member joins the company to ensure that he or she is properly integrated into the team. Remembering the individual is

Bain's way of keeping its turnover among the lowest in the consulting industry.

Monthly Measurement of Team Satisfaction and Performance

Overall team satisfaction and team leadership effectiveness are evaluated every month through a formal review process. Members fill out a survey and rate their satisfaction on such issues as these:

- Value addition and impact of work
- Ability of team leaders to motivate and inspire team members
- Clear and prompt downward communication
- Reasonable time demands
- Upfront planning and organization
- Fun, motivation, and a sense of teamwork
- Interest level of work
- Clear performance expectations
- Level of responsibility
- Opportunities for professional growth and development
- General level of respect for each person

The data are compiled and given to both the team members and the team's leaders (manager and partner). The team then meets alone, without the leader, to discuss the results and develop recommendations regarding what could be done to improve team satisfaction and performance. Team leaders also meet to develop their own recommendations. Then the members and leaders meet together to discuss each other's recommendations and determine what should be done to improve team satisfaction and performance over the next month. If the team satisfaction scores are particularly low, a facilitator meets with the entire team in a team-building discussion.

Team satisfaction and performance scores are posted publicly each month for all to see, so there are strong incentives for team leaders to ensure that they are taking actions that improve team satisfaction if their scores have been low. When asked whether monthly reviews were too frequent, Krista Ridgeway, director of HR for the consulting and business operations, said: "We used to do reviews every two months in the Chicago office and thought that was enough. But the other offices started doing it every month and we eventually decided we would give it a try. We discovered that we were able to discover and respond to team problems much more quickly when we did it monthly. Problems were less likely to escalate. And it really only takes people about five minutes to do the evaluation, so we've found that it is definitely worth the effort."

Bain has found that productive teams can pay big dividends for both itself and its clients. It has grown rapidly from a small Boston Consulting Group spin-off to one of the largest and most prestigious strategy consulting firms in the world with nine years straight as *Consulting* magazine's "Best Firm to Work for" and fourth place on a list of MBAs' Top 50 Dream Companies.[6] Moreover, Bain consulting teams have helped clients achieve stock price appreciation four times greater than that of the S&P 500, an indication that Bain's team approach helps get results for clients.[7]

Assessing Context and Composition

Bain & Company's experience demonstrates what teams can achieve when an organization takes both team context and composition seriously. Because context and composition are indeed the foundation for team success, we believe that organizations should periodically do an assessment to see if their context and methods for assigning team members support team development. Figure 3.2 provides an assessment for determining whether that foundation is in place.

WEB www.josseybass.com/ go/dyerteamassessments

Creating the Context and Composition
for Team Performance

Almost all organizations and teams will likely be deficient in some way related to providing the right context and composition to create a high-performing team. In summarizing this chapter, we suggest the following ideas and actions that we have found useful for managers in creating the appropriate context and composition for teamwork.

Provide Clear Top Management Support for Team Development

In any organization, people at lower levels respond to cues from upper management about what is truly important to the organization. A key role for leaders is to create a vision for others of what is possible for the organization to achieve. A company with a clear team-related mission statement will assign a top corporate officer or group to monitor how well teams are functioning. This sends a clear signal that teams are fundamentally important and that to succeed, everyone must learn to contribute to the team effort. Too many organizations give some emphasis to team building in a middle management seminar or training program, but there is little evidence that upper management takes any of this seriously. Bain & Company is a good example of an organization that clearly states in its mission and goals the need for teamwork.

Create Organizational Rewards to Support Teamwork

Managers must be able to see that if they develop a successful team, their efforts will be rewarded. This means having some criteria of team effectiveness and having those criteria emphasized in the performance review system. Managers at all levels

Figure 3.2 Team Context and Composition Scale

Instructions: Using your observations of your organization and work unit or team, circle the number that applies to each question (on a scale of 1 to 5).

1. Is teamwork needed for your team to accomplish its goals (that is, is reciprocal interdependence important for the team to succeed)?

1	2	3	4	5
No, not really.		It is somewhat important.		Teamwork is critical to success.

2. Is the team's role in the organization clear (that is, is it clear whether the team is a decision team or task team or plays some other role)?

1	2	3	4	5
No, the role is unclear.		The role is somewhat clear.		Yes, the role is very clear.

3. Does the team have the authority needed to accomplish its goals?

1	2	3	4	5
No, the team has little authority.		It has some authority, but not all that is needed.		Yes, the team has the authority it needs.

4. Does the team have the resources it needs to accomplish its goals?

1	2	3	4	5
No, more resources are needed.		Some resources are available.		Yes, the resources needed are available.

5. Does the organization's culture (its rules and values) encourage teamwork?

1	2	3	4	5
No, teamwork is not encouraged.		Teamwork is somewhat encouraged.		Teamwork is encouraged as part of the organization's culture.

6. Does the organization's structure (organization chart, roles, job descriptions, and so on) support teamwork?

1	2	3	4	5
No, the structure hinders teamwork.		The structure somewhat supports teamwork.		Yes, the structure supports teamwork.

7. Do the organization's systems (compensation, appraisal, information, and so on) support teamwork?

1	2	3	4	5
No, the systems undermine teamwork.		The systems somewhat support teamwork.		Yes, the systems support teamwork.

8. Does your organization have a well-thought-out method for assigning people to be on a team?

1	2	3	4	5
No, team assignments are rather haphazard.		Some thought goes into team assignments.		Yes, careful thought is taken before making team assignments.

9. How effective is the leadership in the team?

1	2	3	4	5
The leadership is not effective.		The leadership is somewhat effective.		The leadership is very effective.

10. Does the team have the necessary technical skills, knowledge, and experience to achieve its goals?

1	2	3	4	5
No, it needs more skills, knowledge, and experience.		It has some of the skills, knowledge, and experience it needs.		Yes, it has all the skills, knowledge, and experience it needs.

11. Do team members have the interpersonal skills needed to work effectively as a team?

1	2	3	4	5
No, they don't have the interpersonal skills needed.		They have some of the interpersonal skills needed.		Yes, they have the interpersonal skills needed to work well as a team.

12. Is the team the appropriate size to accomplish its goals?

1	2	3	4	5
No, it is either too large or too small.		The team might need to add or subtract a member or two.		Yes, the team is the right size for the task.

13. Are team members motivated to help the team achieve its goals?

1	2	3	4	5
No, there is little motivation.		There is some motivation on the part of team members.		Yes, team members are highly motivated to achieve team goals.

Scoring: Add up your score and divide by 13.

A score of 3.75 or higher indicates that the organization's context and team composition generally support team performance. Scores between 2.50 and 3.75 indicate moderate support for team performance. Scores between 1.00 and 2.50 indicate some serious problems related to context and composition that are hindering team performance.

If responses to even one or two items are very low (1 or 2), this suggests that action may need to be taken soon to improve the context or team composition. However, if the response to item 1 (the need for teamwork) is low (either a 1 or 2), which typically means that the interdependence of team members is largely modular or sequential, then the mean score may not need to be as high as on a team in which teamwork is essential to achieve its goals (in other words, when there is a need for reciprocal interdependence).

should monitor and be monitored on what is being done to build effective teams, and organizational resources need to be made available to support such action. Teams should not only be allowed but also required to take time out regularly to critique their own team effectiveness and make plans for improvement. Effective teams should be singled out for praise in company meetings and in official publications, and organizations should recognize effective teams with some clear, special rewards.

It is not necessary to always connect pay to team performance, although this is possible, and such rewards are being used with increasing frequency. Regardless of the nature of the reward, it is important for managers to see that they are being rewarded for engaging in team development activities that result in effective work.

We often find organizations today using multiple criteria— individual, team, and organizational—to determine pay raises and bonuses. For example, an organization might base its bonuses using the following percentages: 40 percent on individual achievement, 40 percent on team achievement, and 20 percent on the achievement of organizational goals. Thus, someone would receive 100 percent of his or her bonus if the goals were achieved in all three areas. The bonus would decrease by the corresponding percentage if performance was unsatisfactory in one or more of the areas. In this way, organizations can focus an employee's attention not only on individual achievement but on achieving the goals of the team and organization.

Make Time Available for Team Development

Managers must feel that team development is a high-priority activity and that the organization supports time spent in team-building activities. If managers believe that upper-level management views team development as a frill that prevents people from getting work done, few will be inclined to spend time in this area. There is some advantage to taking the team away from the work setting for development activities. This is not a requirement, however, and time can be saved if team building is done at the workplace.

One of our clients, a large credit union, was having difficulty in coordinating the activities in its branches to serve its customers. When we asked employees why they didn't spend time in team meetings to solve their problems, they replied, "We don't have time—we just can't close the branch office to solve those problems. We have to wait on customers." When asked why they didn't come to work earlier or stay later after hours to discuss and solve their problems, they replied, "The president would never pay us to spend time as a team working on these issues."

To test this assumption, we met with the president and informed him of his employees' desires to spend time in branch problem-solving meetings. His response was, "If it will improve performance, let's do it." The president made the decision to give all employees one paid hour per week to meet as a branch team to discuss problems in the branch and make plans to take corrective action. Most branch teams decided to meet one hour before their branch opened on Friday. The results were almost instantaneous: problems were solved, customer service was improved, and employee morale was strengthened.

Regularly Assess Whether the Organization's Culture, Structure, and Systems Support Teamwork

One reason for poor team performance is the lack of congruence between an organization's culture, structure, and systems and team development. To avoid this problem, an organization should periodically assess how these three factors are affecting teamwork in the organization. The assessment in figure 3.2 could be used for this purpose. The organization needs to be designed to support teams, conduct compensation and performance reviews that encourage teamwork, and demonstrate that it values the work of those who participate in teams. After such an assessment, management can take corrective action to ensure that these three factors support teamwork.

Develop a Systematic Process for Making Team Assignments

Without the right players (those who are motivated and have the right skills), a team is unlikely to succeed. Thus, organizations need to develop clear methods and criteria for making team assignments. In this process, the organization should identify (1) the goals for the team; (2) the knowledge, skills, and experience that the team leader and team members need for the team to achieve its goals; and (3) the optimal number of members needed for the team to achieve its goal. Moreover, after identifying those who should be on the team, team members should be "signed" up by the team leader (possibly with the assistance of others in senior management), and the team assignment should be explained along with the importance of this assignment. In this way, the team members will more likely be motivated to be part of the team and recognize how they can contribute to team success.

In Summary

Context and composition are the initial building blocks of effective team performance. When culture, structure, systems, and processes support teamwork along with strong support from top management, an environment is created for teams to flourish. Moreover, when organizational leaders take the composition of teams seriously, they identify the skills, abilities, experience, and motivation that are needed for a team to succeed and create clear processes for "signing up" team members and evaluating their performance. As illustrated by Bain & Company, organizations that carefully craft the context and composition of their teams and regularly evaluate how the organization is performing along these dimensions are well on their way to developing high-performing teams.

4

COMPETENCIES

Developing Team Skills for High Performance

Once team context and team composition support team effectiveness, the next step is to develop team competencies. Such competencies are not solely the attributes of individual team members but are competencies that are developed and shared by members of the team.

In this chapter, we discuss the competencies of high-performing teams and provide an assessment tool in figure 4.2 to determine to what extent a team has those competencies. Before doing so, however, we discuss how managers can develop important competencies in their teams over time. We have found that most managers, while believing that they and their subordinates function as a team, are really more interested in having their subordinates carry out orders and operate independently under their direct supervision. To move from this type of "staff" relationship to that of a "team" requires a series of developmental steps, and they are largely the focus of this chapter. We conclude the chapter with the team competencies assessment instrument in figure 4.2 and a case study of the Wilson Corporation, which illustrates how one organization created a highly effective team that has made a significant impact on its performance.

Developing the Competencies of High-Performing Teams

Most managers and supervisors have worked with their subordinates primarily in boss–staff (subordinate) relationships. Such relationships typically are based on the assumption that the boss should set the direction and lead, and the subordinates' role is to carry out the directives of the supervisor. However, we have found that to develop effective teams, managers need to think of their subordinates as being members of a team rather than merely seeing them as members of their staff. A staff differs from a team in a number of significant ways. Managers and team leaders who are making the transition from staff to a team must first understand these differences (see table 4.1).

The Shift from Management to Team Leadership

It is clear that a critical difference between a staff and a team resides in the power and role of the "boss." With a staff, the superior is in charge and staff members are workers who carry out the assignments or actions decreed by the superior. There is little, if any, synergy among team members or empowerment of team members. Effective teams are successful because they take advantage of the complementary knowledge and skills of team members: everyone on the team contributes something different to team performance. The team still has a recognized leader, but that person's use of power and definition of the role are very different. The team's leader tends to give more responsibility to the team, opens up lines of communication, encourages collaboration and mutual helping among members, and allows—even encourages— differences of opinion and helps the team work through those differences. The leader spends time building the team so that team members feel responsible for working together to accomplish common goals.

Table 4.1 Differences Between a Staff and a Team

Characteristics	A Staff	A Team
Goals and decisions	Made by the boss	Made jointly by team and boss
Assignments	Made by the boss	Made jointly by the boss and subordinates
Communications	Are primarily between the boss and a subordinate	Are open among all team members
Role of subordinate	Primarily to carry out assignments determined by the boss	Team members initiate action, make suggestions, and help plan work assignments
Primary virtues	Loyalty and being a "good soldier"	Trust, helping, creativity, and giving constructive feedback
Sharing of data	Data shared on the basis of what people feel the boss wants	All relevant data shared in the team
Critical feedback	Rare and anxiety provoking	Regarded as important to improvement
Differences and conflicts	Avoided or smoothed over	Regarded as enriching; worked through by the team
Work	Each staff person is responsible for own, individual work	Team members feel responsible for one another
Goal	Boss's primary goal is to get the job done	Team leader works to get results and develop the team

To achieve this shift from a staff to a team, managers or team leaders need to move more power and responsibility to team members and redefine their leadership role. Figure 4.1 shows how power and roles need to shift to change a staff, or any immature team, into an effective team.

In the beginning of this change from a staff to a team, the superior is usually in a traditional leadership role. Ultimate

Figure 4.1 Team Development Model

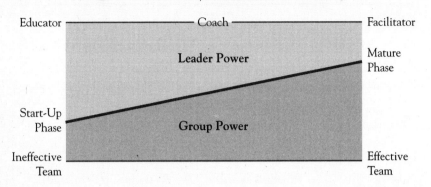

authority resides with "the boss," and a minimal amount of real power or authority is delegated to subordinates. The boss must be helped (trained, oriented, educated) to see the leadership role in an effective team in a radically new way. The boss who is to become a leader must experience a true paradigm shift in order for the development of the team to take place.

Team Leader as Educator

Assuming that the leader is committed to leading a high-performing team, the first task for the leader in the team development model in figure 4.1 is to understand the competencies needed for this type of team and educate the team regarding those competencies. This model describes how the role of the team leader and team dynamics change as a team matures and develops new competencies. In future chapters, we describe specific team-building activities for helping a team move through various developmental stages to gain new competencies and become high performing.

Although there are several theories about which competencies high-performing teams (see, for example, McGregor) possess,[1] we have found the following five task-related competencies and five relationship- or process-related competencies to be the most important.

Task-Related Competencies

1. The team sets clear, measurable goals and generates the commitment of all members to team goals by all team members.

2. The team knows how to make assignments clear and shows team members how their work contributes to the goals of the entire team.

3. The team has clear processes for making decisions, and team members influence decisions through appropriate participation (typically through a process of consensus).

4. The team knows how to establish high performance standards and hold members mutually accountable for results.

5. The team knows how to run effective meetings so that time spent together is productive.

Relationship- or Process-Related Competencies

1. The team knows how to build trust and support among team members so that they are committed to each other and to the team.

2. The team develops open lines of communication, and members are willing to share information, express feelings, and provide feedback to the others.

3. The team has a process for managing conflicts. Conflicts are recognized and managed, not brushed aside or ignored.

4. Team members show mutual respect and collaborate with one another to accomplish their work.

5. Team members are willing to take risks to bring innovative ideas that will improve the team.

In addition to these ten task and relationship competencies, effective teams have developed an eleventh competency: "team building" (what we refer to as a "meta-competency"). Team building is critical because it is the competency to systematically evaluate how the team is performing and then identify how to develop or adjust the other ten competencies to solve problems and improve team performance. For example, if the team has a weakness in setting goals (task competency 1) or managing conflict (relationship competency 3), team-building processes help the team to (1) identify the problems they have with setting goals or managing conflict, (2) identify a set of possible solutions to those problems, and (3) implement a solution that helps the team improve its competency at setting goals or managing conflict.

Ideally, the team leader should educate the team members about the key competencies and the important roles of team members and the leader. If the leader feels inadequate to conduct these education sessions, an outside facilitator or consultant might help in the education of the team, though not in running the team meetings—because that's still the role of the team leader.

In this education phase, the leader:

- Demonstrates a willingness to share power and responsibility with team members
- Encourages team members to become more active in sharing leadership responsibilities
- Develops with team members the basic competencies of an effective team and their acceptance as goals for the team
- Develops team performance metrics and guidelines on how the team will function in the future to achieve those performance goals
- Presents and practices the key competencies that the team needs: being trusting and trustworthy, fostering open communications (sharing all relevant data), giving and receiving feedback, making decisions that have the

commitment of all, and observing and critiquing group processes

We briefly discuss the first four of these in turn and then examine the fifth in more detail.

Sharing Power

The team leader shows commitment to the new paradigm or philosophy of management by sharing power with team members. This can be done in a variety of ways: asking a team member to build a team meeting agenda by contacting all of the other members for agenda items; allowing a member to chair a team meeting; asking members for their ideas, suggestions, or criticisms of proposals on the table; setting goals and making decisions that require full participation; or delegating significant work to team members without continually checking up on them.

Sharing power is the basis of true participative management. Team members must feel that they are partners with the team leader in the work to be done, that their ideas are listened to and respected, and that they can disagree with the team leader without fear of reprisal.

Sharing Leadership

The concept to be taught and practiced is that leadership is not something deposited in a position but is instead a process that can be shared with others. A person who shares in the leadership process sees an action that is needed to move the team ahead and then has the initiative to take the action. Leadership is truly shared when every team member tries as much as possible to initiate an action whenever he or she sees the team struggling or getting bogged down. Team members do not wait and say, "If the leader doesn't do something soon, we are going to waste a lot of time and make some very poor decisions." Thus all team members, not just the leader, feel responsible for improving the functioning of the team.

Developing the Competencies of an Effective Team

Although the eleven characteristics of high-performing teams can provide guidance, each team should identify its own set of competencies that it will need to achieve success, since certain competencies are more important than others given a team's unique mission and task. Using our list of eleven competencies as a guide, team members should meet and generate a list of the competencies they believe are most important to success. The team leader should ask, "If we are to become a truly effective team, what would we look like? Let's spend some time now identifying what we think are the most important competencies of an effective team." With the team leader participating but not dominating, the members develop their list. The leader could also ask, "For which of these competencies do we have some strength, and which ones do we need to work on?"

This is an important first discussion leading to building an effective team. The discussion should lead to some kind of action that both team members and the leader need to be more effective in the areas identified.

Developing Team Guidelines and Metrics

What guidelines does the team need to become effective according to its own criteria and to avoid pitfalls? Again with the leader participating but not dominating, the team develops its own set of guidelines. The leader might say, "We need guidelines that will promote open discussion on how we will make decisions and how we will deal with disagreements among team members. We need guidelines on how to ensure that people follow through on assignments. We need clear metrics to know if we are meeting our goals."

These guidelines and metrics should be agreed on by all team members and can be written up and posted for display at all team meetings. Periodically the team should stop and consider whether it is following its own guidelines and whether any guidelines need to be added or changed.

Developing Team Competencies

In this educative phase of team development, team members should discuss and practice competencies that seem to be imperative if the team is to improve. In this section, we briefly discuss some of the important issues surrounding the development of each of the eleven competencies.

Setting Clear, Measurable Goals High-performing teams develop the competency to set clear and measurable goals to which all team members are highly committed. Clear goals are those that are realistic, prioritized, and measurable. As the team discusses its goals, it should always try to make sure that the goals are realistic (even though they may be "stretch" goals) and measurable (otherwise the team has no way of knowing whether it is achieving its goals). The team must be careful not to have too many goals. If it has multiple goals, it should make sure the goals are prioritized so that everyone knows which goals are the most important ones.

A problem that many teams experience is a lack of commitment to the team goals because they are made by the team leader and just handed to the team. When team members participate in setting the team goals, as well as in how they will be measured, their commitment to those goals increases substantially.

Making Assignments Clear and Ensuring Competence Once clear goals are set, the team then must have a process for making individual assignments so that everyone knows exactly what they are supposed to do and how it contributes to the team goals. This means clearly documenting who is to do what and by when. It also means identifying the skills and resources each team member needs to fulfill his or her assignment.

There is nothing more frustrating than to be given an assignment that you don't have the skills or resources to complete successfully. Sometimes this may require that certain team members get additional training or that someone from another part of the company (or even from outside the company) is brought in to help complete the assignments. But effective teams have developed a process for making clear assignments and then making sure that the team has the skills and resources to complete those tasks.

Using Effective Decision-Making Processes Making effective decisions that have the commitment of all of the team members is another key competency. Teams must make a wide range of decisions—about goals, programs, use of resources, assignments, schedules, and so forth. It should be made clear that in an effective team, not all decisions are made by consensus; moreover, all team members should agree that the decision made is one they understand and can implement, even if it is not necessarily their first choice. As research on decision making shows, sometimes team leaders should make decisions by themselves, sometimes they should consult with team members before making a decision, and sometimes they should let the team make the decision by consensus. The mode of decision making used depends on how critical the decision is, whether the leader has all the data, and whether the team's commitment will be affected if the leader makes the decision alone.

These various decision methods need to be discussed, the key decisions identified, and agreement reached on the decision-making process to be used. A team exercise on decision making is useful for practicing decision-making skills in this phase of team development.

Establishing Accountability for High Performance High-performance teams encourage high-performance standards, and team members hold each other accountable for performance. Once individual assignments are made, the team needs a process for periodically checking up on team members and holding them accountable for fulfilling their assignments in a way that is acceptable to the team.

Most of us know how frustrating it is to work on a team where people are lazy or shirk their duties. When team members are not held accountable for their work, it demoralizes the entire team. *After all,* they may think, *why should I work hard to achieve team goals when my efforts are rendered useless due to the poor performance of my teammates?* On effective teams, team members hold each other mutually accountable for team performance— it's not just the team leader's job. This is something we see on successful sports teams: players hold each other mutually accountable for performance and do not expect that to be solely the job of the coach.

Running Effective Meetings The team also needs to be competent in meetings. The general approach to effective meeting management has the following steps:

1. Set out a clear purpose and goal for each meeting.
2. Develop an agenda before the meeting, and send it to team members. Team members can then come to the meeting prepared.
3. Structure the items on the agenda to follow a logical sequence. Given time constraints that are usually present, the team may need to put time limits on certain items to make sure all the important issues are discussed.

4. Identify when the discussion is moving off the subject and into areas unrelated to the goals of the meeting. The team can then bring the discussion back to focus on the important issues.

5. Summarize and record the actions, decisions, and assignments made at the meeting and disseminate them to team members after the meeting, usually by e-mail. The team then can follow up to ensure that the meeting's objectives are achieved and assignments are carried out.

6. Make it clear that all team members have the responsibility (and obligation) to call for a meeting if the meeting will help improve the team's performance. The team leader is not solely responsible for initiating team meetings.

By following these simple steps of effective meeting management, a team is more likely to be productive. To train teams in effective meeting management, we have often shown the training video *Meetings, Bloody Meetings*, produced by the Monty Python comedy group, which illustrates the differences between effective and ineffective meetings.[2] One might also videotape a team meeting so the team can critique it and see what might be done to improve their meetings.

Building Trust One of the most important team competencies is trust behavior—trusting and being trustworthy. This is sometimes referred to as creating "psychological safety" within the team so that team members are willing to express opinions, acknowledge mistakes, and have confidence that they can engage in risky, learning-related behaviors without punishment. The fundamental emotional condition in a team is not "liking" but "trusting."

People do not need to like one another as friends to be able to work together, but they do need to trust one another. Thus, each team member must be both trustworthy and trusting of others, assuming that the others are also trustworthy. Being trustworthy means keeping confidences; carrying out assignments and following through on promises and commitments; supporting others when they need support; giving both honest, positive feedback and helpful constructive feedback; being present at team meetings; and being available to help other team members.

If trust among team members has been low, this issue needs to be aired in the team meeting. Trust on the team will increase if specific trustworthy and untrustworthy behaviors are identified and all team members verbally commit themselves to being trustworthy and trusting others. Some teams have developed a guideline for amnesty; team members will grant amnesty for all past behaviors and will respond only to current and future behaviors of others they may have previously distrusted. The amnesty guideline indicates that a team member who feels that another has behaved in an untrustworthy way will go to that person and say, "I could be wrong, but I have felt that you were not as trustworthy as I thought was appropriate. Could we talk about this?" These encounters are sensitive and delicate, and the hope is that the matter can be discussed without either party becoming defensive or belligerent. Sometimes a third party can help to mediate this discussion.

The key to developing trust in a team is to make agreements and then follow through on those agreements. Actions speak louder than words. We often find teams that build trust relatively quickly by making commitments to short-term objectives and following through to meet those commitments. However, we have also found that trust can be lost quickly when the leader or team member fails to meet a commitment. Trust typically takes a long time to build and can be lost quickly. Thus, it is important for the team to ask and discuss the following questions:

- What is the current level of trust in the team?
- What specific actions and commitments need to be made to increase trust?
- How will the team hold its members accountable for their commitments?
- What should we do when someone on the team fails to keep a commitment and trust is undermined?
- What should be our process for regaining trust in the team and the members?

Establishing Open Communication Channels Another needed competency is open communications. This involves some risk if the norm has been to keep quiet and say only what you think the boss wants to hear. It is helpful if the team leader, consistent with the new team philosophy, can say, "I honestly want every person to speak up and share his or her thinking, regardless of whether it is in agreement." As part of the educative phase, the leader can initiate a team-oriented exercise so that the team has a chance to practice being open, making decisions, testing the trust level, and observing the leader's behavior.[3] The team then has an opportunity to critique its performance after the conclusion of the exercise. In the training, team leaders should be introduced to various exercises to give them some experience in how to administer and use them.

A natural extension of open communications is giving and receiving feedback. Some guidelines of effective feedback should be discussed. For example, feedback is best given if it is asked for rather than unsolicited. Feedback is more easily accepted if given in the form of a suggestion, for example, "I think you would be more effective if you asked a number of people for their ideas rather than just one or two." This is easier feedback to hear than evaluative feedback, such as, "I think you play favorites and listen only to people you like." Feedback should also be positive:

people need to hear what they do well just as much as what they need to improve.

Sometimes feedback needs to be shared in the team setting if, for example, a person's behavior is blocking the group. Sometimes, however, it is best if the feedback is solicited and given in a one-on-one situation. If a person giving feedback feels uncertain, it can be useful to express that uncertainty: "John, I have a dilemma. I have some feedback I think would be useful to you, but I am reluctant to share it with you for fear it might disrupt our relationship. I value our relationship, and it is more important than giving the feedback. How do you think I should deal with this dilemma?" Given this context, the person usually will ask for the feedback to be shared.

Managing Conflict Effective teams learn how to give and receive constructive feedback (as opposed to "critical" feedback) without becoming defensive or combative. This is an important competency because continuous improvement requires that team members frequently give and receive constructive feedback so that change is possible. However, when team members give feedback to each other, conflict often results.

Every team has conflicts, and unresolved conflict can destroy a team's ability to function. For this reason, managing conflict effectively is a critical competency. In ineffective teams, conflicts are not discussed openly or resolved. As a result, much team effort is expended in having offline conversations about the unresolved conflict, and people don't focus on their tasks. Most conflict is the result of unmet expectations on the part of team members. An exercise in which the team clearly outlines the expectations that each team member has of each other (e.g., the role clarification exercise described in chapter 7) can be a useful tool for managing conflict.

Creating Mutual Respect and Collaboration Another competency of effective teams is that they know how to collaborate in a spirit of cooperation and mutual respect. This requires that team members understand the need to collaborate and understand that they are each better off if they all help each other. High-performing teams develop a norm of reciprocity that involves quickly helping each other when asked. This works only when team members develop a healthy mutual respect for each other's skills, learn to care about each other as individuals, and realize that they are truly better off if they collaborate.

Encouraging Risk Taking and Innovation We have found that team members in high-performing teams are willing to take risks and encourage innovation to help make their teams better. Unfortunately, most teams tend to put down or punish team members who come up with new ways of working together or new solutions to old problems. "We have always done it that way. Why change?" is heard too often in those teams that we've worked with.

To encourage risk taking, the team leader needs to describe to the team the kinds of behaviors that should be rewarded—for example, sharing with the team new approaches to making decisions, providing the team with information about how to run effective meetings, or identifying for the team roadblocks to the team's performance. Then the team leader, while encouraging such behaviors, also needs to clearly and explicitly praise and reward team members when they engage in such behaviors to improve the team. Of course, the team leader should help team members recognize when risk taking is appropriate—after careful thought, planning, and collaboration—versus "risks" based on sloppy thinking and poor planning. Team members also should be praised for "thoughtful failures," since taking risks inevitably leads to some failures. If the team leader rewards only successful risks, little risk taking will take place. (We discuss how to create innovative teams in more detail in chapter 10.)

Engaging in Team Building Most organizational team members are not going to become skilled group observers or facilitators of team-building sessions. But they can become skilled at observing and critiquing group processes. They can build a set of processes that will allow them to deal with most problems that occur as the team works together. These processes should include setting a time for the team to stop and critique how it has been functioning. It is not that difficult to save some time at the end of a team meeting and ask, "What did we do in this meeting that allowed us to be productive? What did we do in this meeting that bogged us down or decreased our effectiveness? What do we need to do to improve our effectiveness in team meetings?"

To be successful at team building, it is useful if the team can understand that all groups function and develop competencies at two levels: (1) a task level, at which people are trying to set goals, make assignments and decisions, and get work done; and (2) a relationship level, at which people are dealing with one another's feelings and ongoing relationships. At the task level, teams need people to proffer ideas and suggestions, evaluate ideas, make decisions and assignments, and allocate resources. At the relationship level, team members need to support and encourage one another, invite more hesitant members to contribute, ease tension and provide some humor (without disrupting the task), and generally provide group maintenance, just as one would engage in the maintenance of a piece of machinery.

Successful teams show a concern for getting the task done but also a concern for managing relationships and always need to balance these concerns. Sometimes it is easy to become so worried about completing the tasks and getting the work done that relationships are trampled on, and other times it is necessary to get down to work and spend less time being concerned about relationships. Team members should be aware of actions and behaviors that block the team at either of these two levels and at least be able to say, "I think we are getting bogged down on nonwork activities and need to move ahead on our work," or, "I think we have lost the participation of two members, and I would like to stop and see how they are feeling about what we are doing." Such actions could occur during the team meeting or might be shared during the critiquing session at the end.

Helping teams develop these important competencies and creating the opportunity to practice them should be part of team development programs. The goal is to prepare team leaders to conduct the education phase of team development or support a resource person who may be asked to handle this phase in collaboration with the team leader. Team-building competencies are discussed in greater detail in the following chapters.

Team Leader as Coach

As the team matures and the leader shifts more power and responsibility for team functioning from his or her shoulders to the team, the leader's role begins to change from educator to coach. This should not occur until team members understand the team orientation and have developed some competence in the new skills. Team members also should have experienced the willingness of the team leader to share responsibility and authority with them.

Coaching, not a new concept in the field of management, means stopping work at some point as necessary to identify for the team some mistake or disturbance in the way it is functioning. It is also a way to reinforce and encourage positive behaviors that the team exhibits. Coaches must observe and have regular contact with members of their team. Hence, they must be "out with the troops" watching how they perform, critiquing their performance, and providing specific, helpful feedback.

Effective coaches tend to ask questions more than give answers. Certainly coaches may have their own views about what the team should be doing, but they encourage team members to develop their own insights regarding what to do and how to do it. This Socratic method of asking questions helps team members discover what they need to do to help the team succeed and gain insights about how to improve themselves personally. This coaching process helps team members develop a deeper understanding of the competencies necessary to achieve team excellence. Most important, team members must recognize that the coach's role is to help them succeed—not merely to be a critic or a purveyor of advice. People generally are willing to listen, take advice, and make needed changes if they see the source of such advice as being both authoritative and caring. Thus the team leader needs to be seen as a "knowledgeable helper" in order to function effectively.

One of the mistakes a leader can make is to move too quickly and start to coach when the team has not been adequately educated. If the leader starts to make decisions by consensus and the team members do not understand what consensus is, they could be confused by and suspicious of the leader's behavior. But if they understand what is happening in the team, coaching becomes a natural activity for the leader.

Sometimes coaching is best done for the whole team, reviewing again the guidelines for consensus or for critiquing group processes. But sometimes coaching is most appropriate for a particular team member in a private session. In chapter 5, we discuss the use of the personal management interview as a follow-up to team meetings, and in this private interview coaching can also be done productively.

Team Leader as Facilitator

In this final phase in making the transition to a high-performing team, the leader may function as a facilitator. Here his or her primary role is to intervene in the group's actions only when attention needs to be focused on a matter the team has not dealt with. Like coaches, facilitators often get more mileage out of asking questions than giving answers. Thus, the leader as facilitator might say, "It seems to me that a vote is being taken before everyone has been able to speak. Do you see the same things I do?" Or the leader might intervene by saying, "If we move ahead in this direction, will this really get us to the overall mission or goals we have set? Have we reached a real or a false consensus? Does everyone feel satisfied with the way we have been functioning at this meeting?"

At this stage in the team's maturity, the intervention of the leader at certain points is enough to get the team back on track, for members are now used to handling team actions themselves. However, the movement up the power line is never fixed and one-way. It is quite possible that when new ideas, concepts, or skills are identified, the leader may need to shift back to the educator role or perhaps to the coaching role if some reminding or skill rehearsal is needed.

Measurement of Team Competencies

In addition to following a process for turning an immature group or staff into a competent, mature team, an ongoing team can use an assessment tool (see figure 4.2) to examine its processes to see what level of competence it has achieved. Members of the team should fill out the scale, compute an average for the total team, and identify which areas they believe need improvement. One should think of this scale in connection with the model in figure 4.1. Think of the power line in the middle of the model in this figure as representing a scale from 1 (less competent or immature team) to 5 (a mature, competent team), with 3 being the midpoint.

Creating a High-Performing Team at the Wilson Corporation

One company that we have worked with is what we will call the Wilson Corporation (all names disguised). We were asked

Figure 4.2 Team Competencies Scale for Assessment

Instructions: Using your observations of your work unit, evaluate the maturity of your team by answering the following questions on a scale of 1 (a less competent or immature team) to 5 (a mature, competent team).

Team Competency 1: Setting Clear, Measurable Goals

1. Does the team know how to set clear, measurable goals?

1	2	3	4	5
Team goals are unclear, and team performance is not measured.		Team goals are somewhat clear and occasionally measured.		The team effectively sets clear goals and tracks performance.

2. Does the team develop commitment within team members to achieve team goals?

1	2	3	4	5
People demonstrate surface-level commitment to the goals.		People only work at achieving the goals with which they agree.		Everyone is deeply committed to all of the goals.

Team Competency 2: Making Assignments Clear and Ensuring Competence

3. Does the team make assignments that are clearly understood by all team members?

1	2	3	4	5
People are often confused about their assignments and how they relate to others' work.		Team members are occasionally confused about their assignments and how they contribute to team performance.		Each team member clearly understands his or her assignment and how it contributes to team performance.

4. Does the team know how to develop the skills in team members to accomplish their assignments?

1	2	3	4	5
Team members lack skills, and there is no plan to help them develop the skills necessary to complete their assignments.		There is some effort to develop team members' skills.		The team regularly assesses individual skills and develops plans to improve the skills of individual team members.

(Continued)

Figure 4.2 (Continued)

Team Competency 3: Using Effective Decision-Making Processes

5. Does the team know how to effectively make decisions effectively?

1	2	3	4	5
The team has no processes for making decisions. The boss tells us what the decisions are.		The team has some processes for decision making, but there is often confusion as to how decisions are made.		The team has clear processes for making decisions, and the team knows how and when to use consensus decision making.

6. To what extent do people appropriately participate in, accept, and implement decisions with commitment?

1	2	3	4	5
There is often a failure to involve people in decision making. There is little personal commitment to decisions.		At times, there is some involvement and commitment to decisions; at other times, there is not.		There is appropriate participation and full commitment by everyone to all decisions.

Team Competency 4: Establishing Accountability for High Performance

7. Does the team encourage high-performance standards and hold team members accountable?

1	2	3	4	5
There is little encouragement of high performance. Team members are not held accountable.		There is some accountability and encouragement of high performance.		Team members set high performance standards and hold each other accountable.

Team Competency 5: Running Effective Meetings

8. Does the team run effective meetings?

1	2	3	4	5
Meetings are ineffective; there is little preparation, no clear agenda, and little follow-through on decisions made.		Meetings are somewhat effective.		Meetings are very effective. There is significant preparation; agendas are well organized, and the team follows through on decisions made at the meeting.

Figure 4.2 (Continued)

Team Competency 6: Building Trust

9. Does the team know how to build trust among team members?

1	2	3	4	5
There is almost no trust. Team members don't follow through on promises and commitments.		Some trust exists, but it is not widespread.		There is high trust among all team members. Everyone follows through on promises and commitments.

Team Competency 7: Establishing Open Communication Channels

10. How would you describe the team leader's management style?

1	2	3	4	5
She or he is authoritarian and runs things her or his way without listening to others.		She or he is somewhat consultative; consults with us but has final decision.		She or he is participative; is part of the team and willing to listen and be influenced.

11. Does the team know how to foster open and free communications?

1	2	3	4	5
Communication is very closed, guarded, and careful; information is not shared.		Communication is somewhat open; people will talk only about matters that are safe.		Communication is very open and information is shared; everyone feels free to say what he or she wants.

Team Competency 8: Managing Conflict

12. Does the team know how to manage conflict effectively?

1	2	3	4	5
Conflicts are ignored, or people are told not to worry about them.		Conflicts are sometimes looked at but are usually left hanging.		Conflicts are discussed openly and resolved.

(Continued)

Figure 4.2 (Continued)

13. Does the team know how to give and receive feedback without becoming defensive or combative?

1	2	3	4	5

1
No, information and feedback are not shared. If given, the feedback is not constructive or makes people defensive.

3
Yes, some information is shared, and constructive feedback is given without people becoming too defensive.

5
Yes, information is shared, and feedback is clear, timely, and helpful. Team members welcome feedback without becoming defensive.

Team Competency 9: Creating Mutual Respect and Collaboration

14. How well do team members collaborate with others?

1
Each person works independently of others without recognizing the need to collaborate.

3
There is some collaboration when people are pushed to it.

5
People quickly offer to help each other on assignments; they easily work with others as needed.

15. How supportive and helpful are the team leaders and members toward one another?

1
There is little cooperation and support; team members don't help each other.

3
There is some cooperation and support; team members help each other some of the time.

5
There is a high degree of cooperation and support; team members always help each other.

Team Competency 10: Engaging in Risk Taking and Innovation

16. Are people willing to take a risk and try out new actions to make the team better?

1
No one is willing to take risks or bring new ideas to the team. Risk takers are often punished.

3
There is some willingness to take risks and bring new ideas to the team.

5
There is a high willingness to take risks and bring new ideas to the team.

Figure 4.2 (Continued)

Team Competency 11: Engaging in Team Building

17. Do your team members ever stop and critique how well they are working together?

1	2	3	4	5
We never stop to critique how well we are doing or discuss ways to improve team competencies.		We occasionally take time to critique how well we are doing.		We regularly take time to critique team performance and discuss how to improve team competencies.

18. Does your team have the necessary team-building skills to identify its problems and take corrective action?

1	2	3	4	5
No, the team lacks the ability to identify its problems and take corrective action.		The team has some skills at identifying problems and taking corrective action.		Yes, the team is skilled at identifying its problems and selecting and implementing those team-building activities that can improve its performance.

Scoring: Each person should add up his or her score for the eighteen items and divide that total by 18. This will give the competency score of the team as perceived by that member. If you add up all of the individual scores and divide by the number of members of the team, you will find the team's rating of its competence. If the ratings are 3.75 or higher, there is evidence that there is an appropriate level of competence. If the scores are between 2.50 and 3.75, competency is at a midlevel, with still work to be done by the team and team leader. If the score is between 1.00 and 2.50, the team is at an immature or low competency level, and a great deal of team building is needed.

An item analysis, that is, looking at the individual and team scores for each item, will help the team see the areas that need the most work to move the team to a higher level of competence.

initially to serve as consultants to the company's president, Rod Wilson, his son, Jim, and his daughter, Lisa. Rod had founded Wilson Corporation and had developed it to be a rather successful business. However, Jim and Lisa felt that the company could do better and needed to employ more effective methods of marketing and production.

As a result of the consulting engagement, they decided to create a new team: an "outside" board of directors that would help the company develop a growth strategy and improve its operations. Although Rod was somewhat hesitant to create a board with outside members (the previous board was just himself, his wife, and Jim), he was willing to experiment with this new team to see if it would make a difference.

Once the decision was made to create a board, the question became: Who should serve on the board? After discussing this issue for quite some time, they decided that Rod, Jim, and Lisa would sit on the board along with three company outsiders—Tim and Rick, who were CEOs of family businesses in a related industry, and a consultant, Gibb Dyer. The two CEOs would bring strategic and operational expertise to the business, and Gibb would provide expertise regarding how to run an effective family business (he is the coauthor of *Consulting to Family Businesses* with Jane Hilburt-Davis).[4] Although the outside board members knew that we served at the pleasure of the family—they could fire us at any time—we also knew that the family members were paying us to be there and that acceptance of our advice would be important to the success of the business.

Rod was somewhat reluctant to participate actively in the initial board meetings, but over time (the board met quarterly) he became more willing to engage in the discussions. Moreover, the board members insisted on having all the financial information about the company each quarter, and this led to useful discussions about the company's strengths and weaknesses. Other members of the management team and consultants as well were asked to come periodically to the board meetings to share their insights and expertise. Thus, the board was not insulated from differing views.

As the team set goals, it became clear that the company was not organized properly to encourage growth. Jim, who was appointed president of the company soon after the board was created, was invited by the CEOs to visit their companies and see how they had dealt with growth (their companies were about twice the size of the Wilson Corporation). In particular, Jim was interested in implementing a "lean" manufacturing system in the company. Tim and Rick were able to show him how they had implemented lean in their organizations. As a result of these visits and discussions with the board, the Wilson Corporation developed a new strategic focus and reorganized its operations to foster growth. Over three years, the company almost doubled in size.

As we examined the functioning of the board of directors at Wilson Corporation, a number of things become clear:

- The context supported an effective team inasmuch as regular meetings were scheduled, company reports—such as income statements and balance sheets—were circulated before the meeting, and participation on the team was linked with financial rewards.

- The team included individuals who had the expertise and motivation to help the organization increase revenues and improve overall performance. When more information and expertise were needed, individuals not on the board were invited to share their ideas at a board meeting.

- The team had the competencies it needed to succeed: there were clear goals; assignments were made and accountability established during the board meeting; meetings were well organized, with an agenda describing the issues and minutes outlining what was decided at the previous meeting; and the team encouraged open communication and risk taking and created a collaborative problem-solving style. Since the Wilson family had already established relationships with the two CEOs and had developed a relationship with Gibb in his consulting role, a climate of trust and mutual respect was part of the team dynamics.

The board of directors of the Wilson Corporation is another example of a team that was successful because it paid attention to context and composition and, more important, developed the competencies it needed to make important strategic and operational decisions to foster growth.

In Summary

To develop the competencies of a high-performing team generally requires the team to go through a developmental process in which the team leader's role changes from one that is highly directive to one that facilitates effective team processes. To become a high-performing team, the team must be competent at goal setting, making assignments and ensuring that team members have the skills to complete them, consensus decision making, setting high standards and holding people accountable, and running effective meetings. Simultaneously, the team must be adept at managing team relationships through high trust, clear communications and feedback, effective conflict management, mutual respect and collaboration among team members, and a willingness to take risks and innovate to improve the team. And as we have seen in the case of the Wilson Corporation and many other teams that we have consulted with over the years, the key to developing such competencies is the commitment of the team to develop the competencies needed for success and then managing the developmental processes that we have outlined in this chapter. The "Team Competencies Scale" in figure 4.2 is one assessment tool that team leaders can use to help their teams understand where they are and where they need to go to improve their performance.

5

CHANGE

Devising More Effective Ways
of Working Together

The last "C" refers to change, the key meta-competency in our model. High-performing teams not only understand what is impeding their performance but are able to take corrective action to achieve their goals. Team building refers to the activities a team can engage in to change its context, composition, or team competencies to improve performance.

In this chapter, we discuss the common problems found in teams and how to diagnose them, how to determine whether the team itself can solve its problems or whether a consultant is needed, and the basic elements of a team-building program.

Common Problems Found in Teams

Usually a team-building program is undertaken when a concern, problem, issue, or set of symptoms leads the manager or other members of the team to believe that the effectiveness of the team is not up to par. The following symptoms or conditions usually provoke serious thought or remedial action:

- Loss of production or team output
- A continued unexplained increase in costs
- Increases in grievances or complaints from the team
- Complaints from users or customers about quality of service
- Evidence of conflict or hostility among team members

- Confusion about assignments, missed signals, and unclear relationships
- Misunderstood decisions or decisions not carried out properly
- Apathy and general lack of interest or involvement of team members
- Lack of initiative, imagination, or innovation
- Ineffective meetings, low participation, or poor decision making
- High dependence on or negative reactions to the team leader

Most of these symptoms are consequence symptoms; that is, they result from or are caused by other factors that are the root causes of the problems. Loss of production, for example, might be caused by such factors as conflicts between team members or problems with the team leader. Indeed, after years of studying and working with teams, we have found that the underlying causes of poor team performance can typically be attributed to differences between team members and the team leader and differences among team members.

Differences Between Team Members and the Team Leader

Usually this cause of team ineffectiveness is obvious to the subordinates on the team and an outside observer. Unfortunately, it often is not so apparent to the team leader. The problem is not that the leader and team members have differences of opinion with regard to how the team should function but rather how they deal with the differences. One common consequence of these differences is a condition of conformity. Team members may feel that the best way to get along with the team leader is just to go along with what they are told to do. They find that the easiest way to manage the relationship with the leader is to fall in line, which is less stressful than the alternative of ongoing conflict.

At times conformity may represent true acceptance of the leader's position. But at other times, it may simply represent avoidance of conflict. A leader who is surrounded by people who are dependent on him or her eliminates any possible conflict but also eliminates the richness of diverse opinion; or team members may have learned over time that conformity is the best strategy and automatically go along with whatever the leader suggests instead of making their own suggestions. At other times, conformity may represent passive resistance. People may agree with the leader publicly but privately resent and resist. Resistance may take subtle forms, such as avoiding the leader or ignoring or never fully implementing the leader's decisions.

Another type of consequence is overt resistance—openly fighting or resisting what the leader wants. In this situation, ordinary problem-solving procedures have been abandoned, and a struggle ensues whenever the leader gets together with team members. Or the struggle may go underground, and although on the surface the interaction seems compatible, heavy infighting is going on behind the scenes.

Some superiors try to manage subordinates and the possibility of resistance by assuming a strong authoritarian stance. The authoritarian leader demands obedience and uses a variety of control methods, formal and informal, to influence behavior. People who are threatened by authority or are used to high controls tend to become conforming. Those who do not accept authoritarian processes become resistant, either openly or under cover.

Other difficulties arise from a lack of trust. Team members may not trust the leader to give them honest information, represent them honestly, keep confidences, or carry through on promises. When trust is low, team members try to protect themselves. They are guarded in what they say and are suspicious of decisions and promises of action. Lack of trust between the leader and team members was a core problem in John Smith's team described in chapter 1. In fact, the trust level was so low between John and his team that team members refused to meet with him one-on-one. Because they believed John was lying to them, they wanted witnesses to all their conversations with him.

Differences Among Team Members

Differences among team members are one of the most widely observed symptoms of a team in trouble. These difficulties are described in different ways: people fight all of the time; they don't trust one another; there are personality conflicts; people have different philosophies, goals, or values. Usually the signals of team member problems are strong statements of disagreement, with no attempt to reach agreement; complaints to the leader, indicating an unwillingness or inability to work out differences; avoidance of one another except when interaction is absolutely required; missed meetings or deadlines; poor-quality work; building of cliques or subgroups to protect against the other side; and minimal or guarded communication.

Not surprisingly, most team leaders initiate team building when they discover serious problems among team members and the team members don't seem to be willing or able to work through their differences. Usually it is the manager who identifies one or more of the consequences or causal factors, although any unit member may share personal observations and diagnosis.

WEB www.josseybass.com/go/dyerteamassessments

Figure 5.1 is a checklist for identifying whether a team-building program is needed and whether an outside facilitator or consultant should be hired for such a program. Teams should develop metrics such as those listed in the figure that they regu-

Figure 5.1 Team-Building Checklist

Problem identification: To what extent is there evidence of the following problems in your team? Circle the number that best represents your opinion.

	Low Evidence		Some Evidence		High Evidence
1. Loss of production or output	1	2	3	4	5
2. Grievances or complaints within the team	1	2	3	4	5
3. Conflict or hostility among team members	1	2	3	4	5
4. Confusion about assignments or unclear relationships among people on the team	1	2	3	4	5
5. Lack of clear goals or low commitment to goals	1	2	3	4	5
6. Apathy or general lack of interest or involvement of team members	1	2	3	4	5
7. Lack of innovation, risk taking, imagination, or initiative	1	2	3	4	5
8. Ineffective meetings	1	2	3	4	5
9. Problems in working with the boss	1	2	3	4	5
10. Poor communications: people afraid to speak up, not listening to one another, or not talking together	1	2	3	4	5
11. Lack of trust between leader and members or among team members	1	2	3	4	5
12. People not understanding or agreeing with decisions	1	2	3	4	5
13. People feeling that good work is not recognized or rewarded	1	2	3	4	5
14. People not encouraged to work together in better team effort	1	2	3	4	5

Scoring: Add up the score for the fourteen items. If your score is between 14 and 28, there is little evidence that your unit needs team building. If your score is between 29 and 42, there is some evidence but no immediate pressure unless two or three items are very high. If your score is between 43 and 56, you should seriously think about planning a team-building program. If your score is over 56, team building should be a top priority for your work unit.

Figure 5.2 Checklist for Determining the Need for Outside Help

Directions: Answer the following questions by responding either "yes," "no," or "don't know." Circle the appropriate response.

1. Does the manager/team leader feel comfortable in trying out something new and different with the team?	Yes	No	Don't know
2. Does the team have prior positive experiences working through difficult issues when team members have different perspectives?	Yes	No	Don't know
3. Will group members speak up and give honest information ?	Yes	No	Don't know
4. Does your group generally work together without a lot of conflict or apathy?	Yes	No	Don't know
5. Are you reasonably sure that the manager/ team leader is not a major source of difficulty?	Yes	No	Don't know
6. Is there high commitment by the manager and team members to achieve more effective team functioning?	Yes	No	Don't know
7. Is the personal style of the manager and his or her management philosophy consistent with a team approach?	Yes	No	Don't know
8. Do you feel you know enough about team building to begin a program without help?	Yes	No	Don't know
9. Would your staff feel confident enough to begin a team-building program without outside help?	Yes	No	Don't know

Scoring: If you have circled six or more "yes" responses, you probably do not need an outside consultant. If you have four or more "no" responses, you probably do need a consultant. If you have a mixture of "yes," "no," and "don't know" responses, you should probably invite a consultant to talk over the situation and make a joint decision.

larly monitor so that the team can determine quickly if it is not performing up to its standards and needs to take corrective action, which generally requires team-building activities.

The checklist in figure 5.2 provides some guidance concerning whether an outside facilitator or consultant might be needed to help the team improve its performance. The checklist should be filled out by all team members and aggregated to determine the need for outside help.

Team Building as a Process

Team building should be thought of as an ongoing process, not as a single event. Indeed, as described in chapter 3, Bain & Company does team building on a monthly basis to ensure that team problems are quickly identified and resolved. People who want to get away for a couple of days and "do team building" but then return to doing business as usual have an incorrect notion of the purpose of team building.

Team building is a meta-competency that great teams develop that allows them to systematically evaluate and change the way the team functions. This means changing team processes, values, team-member skill sets, reward systems, or even the resources available to get teamwork done. These changes are initiated at a kickoff meeting and continue through the next several months or years while the group learns to function effectively as a team. The philosophy one should have about team building is the same as the philosophy behind *kaizen*, or continuous improvement: the job is never done because there are always new bottlenecks to improved team performance.

The team development process often starts with a block of time devoted to helping the group look at its current level of functioning and devise more effective ways of working together. This initial sequence of data sharing, diagnosis, and action planning takes time and should not be crammed into a couple of hours. Ideally the members of the work group should plan to meet for at least one full day, and preferably two days, for the initial program. A common format is to meet for dinner, have an evening session, and then meet all the next day or for whatever length of time has been set aside.

Most team-building facilitators prefer to have a longer block of time (up to three days) to begin a team development program.

This may not be practical in some situations, and modifications must be made. Since we are thinking of team development as an ongoing process, it is possible to start with shorter amounts of time regularly scheduled over a period of several weeks. Some teams have successfully conducted a program that opened with an evening meeting followed by a two- to four-hour meeting each week for the next several weeks. Commitment to the process, regular attendance, high involvement, and good use of time are all more important than length of time.

It is customary to hold the initial team development program away from the work site. The argument for this is that if people meet at the work location, they will find it difficult to ignore their day-to-day concerns in order to concentrate fully on the goals of the program. This argument is compelling, though there is little research evidence about the effect of the location on learning and change. Most practitioners do prefer to have development programs at a location where they can have people's full time and attention.

Use of an Outside Facilitator or Consultant

Managers commonly ask, "Should I conduct the team development effort on my own, or should I get an outside person to help us?" As we noted previously, "outside person" can mean a consultant from outside the organization or an internal consultant who is employed by the organization, often in human resources or organization development and with a background in team development.

Ultimately the manager should be responsible for team development. The consultant's job is to get the process started. The use of a consultant is generally advisable if a manager is aware of problems, feels that he or she may be one of those problems, and is not sure exactly what to do or how to do it but feels strongly enough that some positive action is necessary to pull the work group together to improve performance.

The Roles of Manager and Consultant

Ultimately the manager or team leader is responsible to develop a productive team and develop processes that will allow the team to regularly stop and critique itself and plan for its improvement. It is the manager's responsibility to keep a finger on the pulse of his or her team and plan appropriate actions if the team shows signs of stress, ineffectiveness, or operating difficulty.

Unfortunately, many managers have not yet been trained to do the data gathering, diagnosis, and planning and take the actions required to maintain and improve their teams. The role of the consultant is to work with the manager until the manager is capable of incorporating team development activities as a regular part of his or her managerial responsibilities. The manager and the consultant (whether external or internal) should form their own two-person team in working through the initial team-building program. In all cases, the manager will be responsible for all team-building activities, although he or she may use the consultant as a resource. The goal of the consultant's work is to leave the manager capable of continuing team development without the assistance of the consultant or with minimal help.

The Team-Building Cycle

Problem Identification

Ordinarily a team-building program follows a cycle similar to that depicted in figure 5.3. The program begins because someone recognizes one or more problems. Either before or during the team-building effort, data are gathered to determine the root causes of the problem. The data are then analyzed, and a diagnosis is made of what is wrong and what is causing the problem. After the diagnosis, the team engages in appropriate planning and problem solving. Actions are planned and assignments

Figure 5.3 Team-Building Cycle

made. The plans are put into action and the results honestly evaluated.

Sometimes there is no clear, obvious problem. The concern is then to identify or find the problems that are present but hidden and their underlying causes. One still gathers and analyzes the data, identifies the problems and the causes, and then moves to action planning. The manager and the consultant work together in carrying out the program from the time the problem has been identified through some form of evaluation.

Data Gathering

Because team building encourages a team to do its own problem solving and given that a critical condition for effective problem solving is accurate data, a major concern is to gather clear data on the causes behind the symptoms or problems originally identified. A consultant initially may assist in the data gathering, but eventually a team should develop the ability to collect its own data as a basis for working on its own problems. The following are some common data-gathering methods.

Surveys One of the most common approaches to gathering data is to conduct a survey of all team members. Surveys are helpful when there are relatively large numbers of team members or members would be more open in responding to an anonymous survey. It also can be helpful to use a survey if you want to compare the issues and problems facing different teams in an organization.

There are two general types of surveys: open- and closed-ended surveys. An open-ended survey asks questions such as: What do you like about your team? What problems does your team need to address? and What suggestions do you have to improve the team? Team members can give their responses in writing. The team leader or consultant summarizes these responses and presents them to the team in a team-building session. It may be somewhat messy to summarize such raw data, but it often helps to read the actual views of the team members to better understand the issues and how the members are feeling.

Closed-ended surveys force the person responding to choose a specific response. Most of the surveys in this book are closed-ended. Closed-ended surveys make tabulating the results easy and statistical comparisons possible. However, they may miss some of the important dynamics and problems of a team. Closed-ended surveys are a useful starting point, however, to create awareness of the problems facing a team and begin a discussion of how to solve those problems. We have found that the team-building checklist in this chapter and the Team Competencies Scale (figure 4.2) are helpful surveys to gather data about a team (the complete team assessment survey and report can be accessed online).

WEB www.josseybass.com/
go/dyerteamassessments

Interviews At times a consultant can perform a useful service by interviewing the members of the team. The manager or team leader could conduct such interviews, but in most cases, team members will be more open in sharing data with someone from outside the team. The consultant tries to determine the causes behind the problem in order to pinpoint those conditions that may need to be changed or improved. In these interviews the consultant often asks the following questions:

1. Why is this team having the kinds of problems it has?
2. What keeps you personally from being as effective as you would like to be?
3. What things do you like best about the team?
4. What changes would make the team more effective?
5. How could this team begin to work more effectively together?

Following the interviews, the consultant frequently does a content analysis of the interviews, identifies the major themes or suggestions that emerge, and prepares a summary presentation. At the team-building meeting, the consultant presents the summary, and the team, under the manager's direction, analyzes the data and plans actions to deal with the major concerns.

Some consultants prefer not to conduct interviews prior to the team-building meeting and do not want to present a data summary. They have found that information shared in a private interview with a consultant is not as readily discussed in the open, with all other team members present, especially if some of those members have been the object of some of the interview information. Consultants have painfully discovered that people often deny what they said in the interview, fight the data, and refuse to use what they said as a basis for discussion and planning. At times it may be appropriate for the consultant to interview people privately to understand some of the deeply rooted issues but still have people present their own definitions of the problems in an open session.

One question often arises about interviewing: Should the interviews be kept anonymous so that no one will be identified? We have found that if data are gathered from a team and those data are then presented to that team, team members often can figure out who said what. Keeping sources anonymous is often difficult, if not impossible. Thus, we typically say to a team member before starting an interview: "You will not be personally identified in the summary we present back to the team, but you must be aware that people might recognize you as the source of certain data. Thus, you should respond to the questions with information that you'd be willing to discuss in the team and might possibly be identified with. However, if you have some information that is important for us to know but you don't want it to be reported back, you can give such information off the record. This won't be reported, but it might prove useful to us to better understand the team's problems." We have found this approach helpful in getting team members to open up and share information with us about the team. It also encourages team members to own their own feelings and be willing to discuss them in the team.

Team Data Gathering An alternative to surveys and interviewing is open data sharing in a team setting. With this method, each person in the team is asked to share data publicly with the other team members. The data shared may not be as inclusive as data revealed in an interview, but each person feels responsible to own up to the information he or she presents to the group and to deal with the issue raised. To prevent forced disclosure, one good ground rule is to tell people that they should raise only those issues they feel they can honestly discuss with the others. They then generally present only the information they feel comfortable discussing; thus, the open sharing of data may result in less information but more willingness to "work the data." It may be helpful to systematically discuss barriers to effective team functioning that may exist in the other three Cs: team context, team composition, or team relationship and task competencies.

The kinds of questions suggested for the interview format are the same ones that people share openly at the beginning of the team-building session. Each presents his or her views on what keeps the team from being as effective as it could be or suggests reasons for a particular problem. Each person also describes the things he or she likes about the team, hindrances to personal effectiveness, and the changes he or she feels would be helpful. All of the data are compiled on a flip chart or whiteboard. (In another variation, data for a large team could be gathered and shared in subgroups.) Then the group moves on to the next stage of the team-building cycle, data analysis.

Diagnosis and Analysis of Data

With all of the data now available, the manager and the consultant work with the team to summarize the data and put the information into a priority listing. The following summary categories could be used:

A. Issues that we can work on in this meeting
B. Issues that someone else must work on (and identify who the others would be)
C. Issues that apparently are not open to change; that is, things we must learn to accept or live with

Category A items become the top agenda items for the rest of the team-building session. Category B items are those for which strategies must be developed by involving others. For category C items, the group must develop coping mechanisms. If the manager is prepared, he or she can handle the summary and sort the data into these three categories. If the manager feels uneasy about this, the consultant may function as a role model to show how this is done.

The next important step is to review all of the data and try to identify underlying factors that may be related to several problems. A careful analysis of the data may show that certain procedures, rules, or job assignments are causing several disruptive conditions.

Action Planning

After the agenda has been developed out of the data, the roles of the manager and the consultant diverge. The manager should move directly into the customary managerial role of group leader. The issues identified should become problems to solve, and plans for action should be developed.

While the manager is conducting the meeting, the consultant functions as a group observer and facilitator. Schein has referred to this activity as "process consulting," a function that others in the group also can learn to perform.[1] In this role, the consultant helps the group look at its problem-solving and work processes. He or she may stop the group if certain task functions or relationship functions are missing or being performed poorly. If the group gets bogged down or steamrolled into uncommitted decisions, the consultant helps look at these processes, why they occur, and how to avoid them in the future. In this role, the consultant trains the group to develop better problem-solving skills.

Implementation and Evaluation

If the actions planned at the team-building session are to make any difference, they must be put into practice. Ensuring that plans are implemented has always been a major function of management. The manager must be committed to the team plans; without commitment, it is unlikely that a manager can effectively hold people responsible for assignments agreed on in the team-building meeting.

The consultant's role is to observe the degree of action during the implementation phase and be particularly active during the evaluation period. Another data-gathering process now begins, for that is the basis of evaluation. It is important to see if the actions planned or the goals developed during the team-building sessions have been achieved. This again ultimately should be the responsibility of the manager, but the consultant can help train the manager to carry out good program evaluation.

The manager and the consultant should work closely together in any team development effort. It is ineffective for the manager to turn the whole effort over to the consultant with the plea, "You're the expert. Why don't you do it for me?" Such action leads to a great deal of dependence on the consultant, and if the consultant is highly effective, it can cause the manager to feel inadequate or even more dependent. If the consultant is ineffective, the manager can then reject the plans developed as being unworkable or useless, and the failure of the team-building program is blamed on the consultant. Managers must take responsibility for the team-building program, and consultants must work with managers to help them plan and take action in unfamiliar areas in which the manager may need to develop the skills required to be successful.

The consultant must be honest, aggressively forthright, and sensitive. He or she must be able to help the manager look at his or her own leadership style and its impact in facilitating or hindering team effectiveness. The consultant needs to help group members get important data out in the open and keep them from feeling threatened for sharing with others. The consultant's role involves helping the group develop skills in group problem solving and planning. To do this, the consultant must have a good understanding of group processes and be able to help the group look at its own dynamics. Finally, the consultant must feel a sense of pride and accomplishment when the manager and the team demonstrate their ability to solve problems independently and no longer need a consultant's services.

In Summary

The ability of a team to diagnose its own problems and initiate change is perhaps the distinguishing feature of high-performing teams. In this chapter, we have suggested that managing effective change in teams requires the following:

- The team must be able to accurately diagnose its problems and the underlying causes to those problems. The team-building checklist in Figure 5.1 can be used to do such an assessment.
- The team leader must recognize whether he or she will need the assistance of a consultant, set out in figure 5.2 or can manage the team-building cycle, set out in figure 5.3, alone.
- The manager (and the consultant if needed) should determine the most effective way to gather data about the team, whether through surveys, interviews, or open data sharing. The method used is often determined by the size of the team, the level of trust in the team, and what kinds of information are needed.
- Teams must have the ability to generate useful data with regard to team skills, processes, and performance; to determine what the data mean for the team; and to identify and prioritize the issues and problems that need to be addressed.
- Teams must be able to develop and implement their action plans, as well as evaluate the results. A process for assigning accountability and following through is also important.

6

BRINGING THE FOUR Cs TOGETHER

Designing a Team-Building Program

The goal of any team-building program is to help the team engage in a continual process of self-examination to gain awareness of those conditions that keep it from functioning effectively. In chapter 5, we identified a number of symptoms of unhealthy teams. Having gathered data about such problems, the team must learn how to use those data to make decisions and take actions that will change team context, composition, or competencies in ways that will lead to a growing state of team health. Team building in this sense is an ongoing process, not a one-time activity.

As we noted in chapter 5, team building often begins with a block of time, usually two or three days, during which the team starts learning how to engage in its own review, analysis, action planning, decision making, and action taking. Following the first meetings, the team may periodically take other blocks of time to continue the process, review progress made since the last team meeting, and identify what should be done to continue to improve the team's overall effectiveness. It is also possible that in time, the team will develop its skills for development to such a point that team members are always aware of areas that need improvement and will raise them at appropriate times with the appropriate people, thereby making it unnecessary to set aside a special meeting for such action.

There is no single way to put together a team-building program. The format depends on the experience, interests, and needs of the team members; the experience and needs of the team leader; the skills of the consultant (if one is needed); and the nature of the situation that has prompted the need for team building.

This chapter describes a range of design alternatives for each phase of a team-building program. Those planning such an activity may wish to select various design elements from among the alternatives that seem applicable to their own situations. Although the design of a team-building program generally follows the cycle described in chapter 5, in this chapter we outline some of the specific steps and actions that we take when designing a program.

Preparation

There are certain phases or steps in any team-building program. The first phase is describing the purpose of the program and introducing the team-building process to team members. We briefly describe the options available for team leaders as they begin to prepare their teams for team building.

Goals

The goals of this phase are to explain the purpose of team building, elicit agreement to work on certain problems, get commitment for participation, and do preliminary work for the team-building workshop. Any team-building program must be well conceived, and those involved must have indicated at least a minimal commitment to participate. Commitment will increase if people understand clearly why the program is being proposed and if they have an opportunity to influence the decision to go ahead with the program.

If this is the first time the team has spent some time together with the specific assignment to review their effectiveness and plan for change, they will likely be anxious and apprehensive. These concerns must be brought to the surface and addressed. Questions of deep concern probably will not be eliminated, but team members' concerns may be reduced as a supportive climate is established and as people test the water and find that plunging in is not very difficult. Experience will be the best teacher, and people will allay or confirm their fears as the session proceeds. Those conducting the session should anticipate such concerns and raise them prior to the first meeting to reduce any extreme anxiety by openly describing what will happen and what the anticipated outcome will be.

Alternative Actions

Among the possible actions that managers might take to get started are these:

1. Have an outside person interview each team member to identify problems, concerns, and the need for change.

2. Invite an outside speaker to talk about the role of teams in organizations and the purposes of team development. The speaker might discuss the Four Cs of team performance and how they might relate to the performance of that team.

3. Gather data on the level of team effectiveness. (See the team-building checklist in figure 5.1 and the other instruments presented in this book or online.)

4. Have a general discussion about the need for developing a team competency—which can emerge through a team-building program.

5. Invite a manager who has had successful team-building experiences to describe the activities and results in his or her unit.

Creating an Open Climate for Data Gathering

The second phase of the team-building program is creating a climate for gathering and sharing data. The goals for this phase and alternative approaches follow.

Goals

The goals of this phase are to create a climate for work; get people relaxed; establish norms for being open with problems, concerns, and ideas for planning and for dealing with issues; and present a framework for the whole experience. The climate established during the start-up phase influences the rest of the program.

Alternative Approaches to Data Gathering

There are several alternatives that the team can use for data gathering. These alternatives follow.

Alternative 1 The manager or team leader can give a short opening talk, reviewing the goals as he or she sees them and the need for the program, emphasizing his or her support, and reaffirming the norm that no negative sanctions are intended for any open, honest behavior. The role of the consultant, if there is one, can be explained by either the manager or the consultant.

WEB www.josseybass.com/ go/dyerteamassessments

Participants can share their immediate here-and-now feelings about the meetings by responding to questions handed out on a sheet of paper (figure 6.1). They call out their answers (to set the norm of open sharing of data), and the person at the flip chart records the responses.

The data can be gathered openly from team members and tabulated on a whiteboard or it can be gathered anonymously,

Figure 6.1 Attitudes About Change

Instructions: Answer the following questions on a scale of 1 to 5.

1. How confident are you that any real change will result from these meetings?

1	2	3	4	5
I am not confident at all.		I am somewhat confident.		I am highly confident.

2. To what degree do you feel that people really want to be here and work on team development issues?

1	2	3	4	5
People don't really want to be here.		People have some interest in being here.		People have high interest in being here.

3. How willing do you think people are to make changes that may be suggested?

1	2	3	4	5
People will be unwilling to change.		People have some willingness to change.		People are very willing to change.

4. How willing do you think you and others will be to express real feelings and concerns?

1	2	3	4	5
We are not very willing to express feelings.		We have some degree of willingness to express feelings.		We are very willing to express feelings.

with the results tallied (with high and low scores on each item and the mean score) and then presented to the team. After seeing the results, the team should be asked to discuss these questions: Why are the scores rather low (or high)? What could be done here to help people feel more positive about these meetings? If the team is large, subgroups should be created to discuss these questions for twenty minutes and report back to the entire team.

This alternative for beginning is to set the norm that the program is centered on data gathering, data analysis, open sharing, and trying to plan with data. This also allows group members to test the water about simple, immediate data rather than more sensitive work group issues to see how they will respond and react to the questions.

Alternative 2 After preliminary remarks by the manager, the team members could be asked, "For us to get a picture of how you see our team functioning, please take a few minutes to describe our team as a kind of animal or combination of animals, a kind of machine, a kind of person, or whatever image comes to mind." Some teams in the past have been described as:

- A hunting dog—a pointer. "We run around and locate problems, then stop and point and hope that somebody else will take the action."

- A Cadillac with bicycle pedals. "We look good on the outside, but there is no real power to get us moving."

- A centipede with several missing or broken legs. "Although the centipede can move forward, its progress is crippled by the missing and broken legs."

- An octopus. "Each tentacle is out grasping anything it can but doesn't know what the other tentacles are doing."

As people share the images and explain why they came to mind, some questions for follow-up are: What are the common elements in these images? Do we like these images of ourselves? What do we need to do to change our image? Discussion aimed at answering these questions becomes the major agenda item for subsequent group meetings.

Alternative 3 In this alternative, the team is asked, usually by a consultant or trained observer, to work on a major decision-making problem—such as an arctic or desert survival exercise, or Tinker Toy tower building—and to function under the direction of the team leader in a fashion similar to the way they have previously worked on problems.[1] The consultant acts as a process observer for the exercise. After the exercise, the consultant has the group members review their own processes and determine both their strengths and their deficiencies in solving problems. The consultant shares his or her observations with the group. In some instances, we have found it useful to videotape the team doing the exercise and then replay the videotape so team members can see how they performed.

As the exercise is reviewed, lists of positive and negative features are compiled. The agenda for the following session is set, based on the question, "How do we maximize our strengths and overcome deficiencies?" For example, if the process review indicates that the group is highly dependent on the leader, that some people are overwhelmed by the "big talker," and that the group jumps to decisions before everyone has a chance to put in ideas, the agenda would focus on how to reduce or change these negative conditions.

Group Data Analysis and Problem Solving

After the team understands the purpose of the team-building program and data have been generated regarding the team's functioning and performance, the next phase is to focus on analyzing the data and developing a plan of action to solve the team's problems.

Goals

One goal of this phase is to begin to take action on the problems identified in the previous phase. Assignments are made and dates set for completing the work. Another goal is for the team to practice better problem-solving, decision-making, planning, and delegation skills.

Whatever the start-up method or combination of methods used, this third phase usually has two parts: (1) the team begins to engage in the problem-solving process, and (2) a process consultant or observer helps the group look at its context, composition, and competencies in working on problems as an effective team as a prelude to improving its problem-solving capabilities.

The process consultant or observer usually tries to see to what extent the group is effective at both task activities and relationship-maintaining activities. Ineffective teams are often characterized by one or more of the following conditions, and the consultant should watch for evidence of these conditions:

- Domination by the leader
- Warring cliques or subgroups
- Unequal participation and uneven use of group resources
- Rigid or dysfunctional group norms and procedures
- A climate of defensiveness or fear
- A lack of creative alternatives to problems
- Restricted communications—not all have opportunities to speak
- Avoidance of differences or potential conflicts

Such conditions reduce the team's ability to work together in collective problem-solving situations. The role of the consultant here is to help the group become aware of its processes and begin to develop better group skills. Specifically, after becoming aware of a process problem, the group needs to establish a procedure, guideline, or plan of action to respond to the negative condition.

Alternatives for Data Analysis

There are several alternatives that the team can use to analyze the data that have been gathered and generate solutions to team problems. These alternatives follow.

Alternative 1 Following the opening remarks, the consultant, outside person, or team leader presents data that have been collected from the team members through observations, interviews, or instruments prior to the meeting. The team is asked to analyze the data. What do the data mean? Why do we respond the way we do? What conditions give rise to negative responses? What do we need to change to get a more positive response to our own team? The team might sort the data into the categories of context, composition, competencies, and change to identify the root causes of the team's problems.

This analysis can best be done in subgroups of three to four people and then shared with the whole group and compiled into a list of issues and possible change actions. The summaries form the basis for subsequent sessions. The team also puts the data into the A, B, and C categories described in chapter 5. Category A items, those that can be worked on now in the meeting, are the major work issues on the agenda.

Alternative 2 This design requires some extensive case analysis prior to the team-building sessions. A consultant or someone in management pulls together one or more studies, vignettes, or critical incidents that seem to represent recurring problems for the team. Another possibility is to have each member take a problem area for him or her and write it up as a short case. The group task is to look at the cases, try to discern the underlying conditions that trigger recurring problems, and then plan action steps for reducing the likelihood that such problems will reoccur.

Alternative 3 In this alternative, objective data gathered from records about the team are compiled and presented to the group members. Such information as production records, the grievance rate, absenteeism, turnover, lost time, budget discrepancies, late reports, cost increases, and so on are included in this feedback. The team's job is to conduct an in-depth analysis of the data, diagnose the causes of the negative trends, and then plan for improvement.

Alternative 4 Instead of presenting data from prior data collection methods to the team, data about the conditions or problems of the team can be raised at the team meeting. Each person is asked to come prepared to share his or her answers to the following questions:

- What keeps this team from functioning at its maximum potential?
- What keeps you personally from doing the kind of job you would like to do?
- What things do you like in this team that you want to have maintained?
- What changes would you like to see made that would help you and the whole team?

Team members or the leader may have other items they would like to put on the agenda.

Each team member takes a turn sharing information. The responses are listed and common themes identified. The most important issues are listed in priority, and they become the items for discussion.

Problem-Solving Process

By this point, regardless of the alternatives selected, the team should have identified a series of problems, concerns, or issues. It may be helpful in the problem identification stage of team building for the team leader or consultant to share with the team the Four Cs of team performance and then list the problems the team faces in the four categories: context problems, composition problems, competency problems, and change management problems. In this way, the team can determine which problems reside within the team and which are related to context issues that may not be under the team's direct control.

The team next moves into a traditional problem-solving process by engaging in the following actions:

1. Put problems in order of priority and select the five or six most pressing ones to address during the workshop.

2. Begin the classic problem-solving process: clearly define the problem, describe the causes of the problem, list alternative solutions, select the alternative to implement, develop an action plan, perform the action, and evaluate the results.

3. Conduct a force-field analysis.[2] Identify the existing level of team performance on a set of performance metrics, formulate a specific goal to improve performance, identify the restraining forces (the factors that are barriers to better performance) and driving forces (the factors that encourage high performance), and develop a plan to remove the restraining forces or add driving forces.

4. Begin role negotiation. Negotiate between people or subunits that are interdependent and need to coordinate well with each other to improve effectiveness.

5. Set up task force teams or subunits. Give each team a problem to work on. It should develop a plan of action, carry out the plan, and assess the results.

6. After all problems have been listed, the team can sort them into categories based on the nature of the problem: (A) we can work on the problem here within our team, (B) someone else must handle the problem (and identify who that is), or (C) we must live with this problem, since it appears to be beyond our ability to change.

7. Set targets, objectives, or goals. The group should spend time identifying short- or long-range goals it wishes to achieve, make assignments, and set target dates for completion.

The Appreciative Inquiry Approach to Team Building

Up to this point we've focused on using a problem-centered approach to team building: the team identifies the problems it faces and then engages in problem solving to improve its performance. An alternative team-building approach is to focus on the more positive aspects of the team in a process called appreciative inquiry (AI).[3]

The AI approach to team building starts with the assumption that every team has some positive characteristics that can drive it to high performance. The issue for the team is how to discover and tap into these positive characteristics. Rather than focus on the negative—the problems that the team experiences—this approach focuses on the positive characteristics of the team. To begin the team-building activity, the manager, team leader, or consultant asks team members to answer the following questions[4]

1. Think of a time when you were on a hugely successful team, a time that you felt energized, fulfilled and the most effective— when you were able to accomplish even more than you imagined. What made it such a great team? Tell the story about the

situation, the people involved, and how the team achieved its breakthrough.

2. Without being humble, what was it about you that contributed to the success of the team? Describe in detail these qualities and what you value about yourself that enables team success.

3. It is one year from today and our team is functioning more successfully than any of you imagined. What are we doing, how are we working together differently, what does this success look like, and how did we make it happen?

Members of the team pair up and share their answers to these questions. They then can move into larger subgroups and share their stories, or the entire team can be brought back together to report their stories and their feelings about the future of the team. Gervase Bushe, professor of leadership and organization development at Simon Fraser University, who uses the AI approach, explains how one team improved its performance through AI:

In one business team I worked with one member talked about a group of young men he played pick-up basketball with and described why they were, in his opinion, such an outstanding "team." He described their shared sense of what they were there to do, lack of rigid roles, [and] easy adaptability to the constraints of any particular situation in the service of their mission. But what most captured the team's imagination was his description of how this group was both competitive and collaborative at the same time. Each person competed with all the rest to play the best ball, to come up with the neatest move and play. Once having executed it, and shown his prowess, he quickly "gave it away" to the other players in the pick-up game, showing them how to do it as well. This was a very meaningful image for this group as a key, unspoken, tension was the amount of competitiveness members felt with each other at the same time as they needed to cooperate for the organization's good. "Back alley ball" became an important synthesizing image for this group that resolved the paradox of competitiveness and cooperation.[5]

By sharing such powerful images, a team may be able to envision a different way of functioning from its current pattern and create new values and beliefs that will enable it to plot a new course. The role of the team leader or consultant is to help the team identify images and metaphors that they can incorporate as they seek to improve team performance. The team members should ask and answer the following questions: (1) How can we as a team become like the high-performing teams that we've experienced in the past? and (2) How can I as a member of this team contribute to helping our team achieve its full potential? As the team and its members answer these questions, commitments are made to change the team in a positive direction. The team can use the images of team excellence to motivate the team to a higher level of performance.

The AI approach is often useful when team members tend to focus on the negative, continually bringing up negative images of the team and complaining about other team members. The positive approach of AI can give energy to an otherwise impotent and demoralized team. However, when using AI, the team should still be willing to confront important problems and not see the world completely through rose-colored glasses.

Using Feedback to Improve Team Performance

A major issue that often arises following the identification of problems is the sharing of feedback with individuals, subgroups within the team, or the team as a whole. Certain actions, functions, personal styles, or strategies on the part of one or more people may be hindering teamwork and preventing other team members from achieving their goals or feeling satisfied with the team. If this is the case, it may be legitimate to engage in an open feedback session.

Goals

The team should share feedback among individual team members in such a way as to help them improve their effectiveness and give feedback to the whole team with the same objective in mind. The goal of a feedback session is to share data about performance so that difficulties can be resolved. It is critical that a feedback session not slip into name calling, personal griping, or verbal punishing of others. All feedback should reflect a genuine willingness to work cooperatively. For example, one might say, "My performance suffers because of some things that happen in which you are involved. Let me share my feelings and reactions so you can see what is happening to me. I would like to come up with a way that we all can work more productively together."

Types of Feedback

Feedback is most helpful if it can be given in descriptive fashion or in the form of suggestions. Here are some examples.

Descriptive feedback: "John, when you promise me that you will have a report ready at a certain time, as happened last Thursday, and I don't get it, that really frustrates me. It puts me behind schedule and makes me feel very resentful toward you. Are you aware that such things are going on? Do you know what is causing the problem or have any ideas on how we could avoid this type of problem in the future?"

Suggestions: "John, let me make a suggestion that would really help me as we work together. If you could get your reports to me on time, particularly those that have been promised at a certain time, it would help my work schedule and reduce my frustration. Also, if I don't get a report on time, what would you prefer I do about it?"

Other possibilities: The following are some other ways group members might go about sharing feedback with one another:

- *Start-stop-continue activity.* Each person has a sheet of newsprint on the wall. Each team member writes on the sheets of other members' items in three areas: things that person should begin doing that will increase his or her effectiveness, things the individual should stop doing, and things he or she should continue to do. (More on this in chapter 7.)

- *Envelope exchange.* Each person writes a note to other team members with specific, individual feedback, covering the same issues as in the previous activity, and gives the notes to the other team members.

- *Confirmation-disconfirmation process.* Group members summarize how they view themselves and their own work performance—their strengths and areas that need improvement. Others are asked to confirm or disconfirm the person's diagnosis.

- *Management profile.* Each person presents the profile of his or her effectiveness from previously gathered data (there are a variety of profile instruments). The group confirms or disconfirms the profile.

- *Analysis of subunits.* If the team has subunits, each subunit is discussed in terms of what it does well, what it needs to change, and what it needs to improve.

- *Total unit or organizational analysis.* The entire department, division, or organization looks at how it has been functioning and critiques its own performance over the past year, identifying things it has done well and areas that need improvement. Group size is, of course, the main constraint with this option. Beckhard and Weisbord have developed approaches for working with large groups.[6]

- *Open feedback session.* Each person who would like feedback may ask for it in order to identify areas of personal effectiveness and areas that need improvement.

- *Prescription writing.* Each person writes a prescription for others: "Here is what I would prescribe that you do [or stop doing] in order to be more effective in your position." Prescriptions are then exchanged.

Action Planning

The end result of all the activities mentioned so far is to help the team identify conditions that are blocking both individual and team effectiveness so that the team can begin to develop plans for action and change. Action plans should include a commitment to carry the action to completion.

Goals

The goals of this phase are to pinpoint needed changes, set goals, develop plans, give assignments, outline procedures, and set dates for completion and review. Often the plan is a set of agreements on who is willing to take a specific action. All such agreements should be written down, circulated, and followed up later to ensure that they have been carried out.

Options for Action Planning

Following is a set of actions that are possible during this phase:

1. *Personal improvement plan.* Each person evaluates his or her feedback and develops a plan of action for personal improvement. This plan is presented to the others.

2. *Contract negotiations.* If there are particular problems between individuals or subunits, specific agreements for dealing with conflict issues are drawn up and signed.[7]

3. *Assignment summary.* Each person summarizes what his or her assignments are and the actions he or she intends to take as a follow-up of the team-building session.

4. *Subunit or team plans.* If development plans have been completed, they are presented and reviewed.

5. *Schedule review.* The team looks at its time schedule and its action plans. Dates for completion and dates for giving progress reports on work being done are confirmed. The next team meeting is scheduled. If another team development workshop or meeting is needed, it may be scheduled at this time.

Implementation, Evaluation, and Follow-up

Follow-up is an integral part of any team-building program. There must be some method of following up with team members on assignments or agreements and then some form of continuing goal setting for improved performance. These follow-up activities can be done by the whole team together, one-on-one between team members, or a combination of the two. Fortunately, some excellent research has been done that describes follow-up processes that have proved to be successful.

Wayne Boss of the University of Colorado became interested in the "regression effect" following a team-building session.[8] He observed, as have others, that during a two- or three-day intensive team-building activity, people become very enthusiastic about making improvements, but within a few weeks, the spark dwindles, and they regress to old behaviors and performance levels. Boss wondered whether there is a way to keep performance high following the team-building session and to prevent regression. He began to experiment with a one-on-one follow-up meeting he called the personal management interview (PMI). The PMI has two stages. First is a role negotiation meeting between team leader and subordinate (usually lasting one hour) during which both clarify their expectations of each other, what they need from each other, and what they will contract to do for each other.

Second, following the initial role negotiation session, the two parties meet regularly. Boss found that these meetings have to be held on a regular basis (weekly, biweekly, or monthly), but if they are held and follow the agreed-on agenda, performance stays high without regression for several years. States Boss, "Without exception, the off-site level of group effectiveness was maintained only in those teams that employed the PMI, while the teams that did not use the PMI evidenced substantial regression in the months after their team-building session."[9]

What goes on in these interviews that makes such a difference? Despite some variation, each interview tended to deal with the following issues:

- Discussion of any organizational or work problems facing the subordinate
- Training or coaching given by the supervisor to the subordinate
- Resolution of any concerns or problems between supervisor and subordinate
- Information sharing to bring the subordinate up to date on what is happening in the team and organization
- Discussion of any personal problems or concerns

These were common agenda items, but the first part of every meeting was spent reviewing assignments and accomplishments since the previous session. Time was also spent on making new assignments and agreeing on goals and plans to review at the next PMI. These assignments and agreements were written down, and both parties had a copy that was the basis of the review at the following meeting.

Boss has the following suggestions for conducting an effective PMI:

- The PMI is most effective when conducted in a climate of high support and trust. Establishing this climate is primarily the responsibility of the superior.

- The interviews must be held on a regular basis and be free from interruptions.

- Both parties must prepare for the meeting by having an agreed-on agenda; otherwise, the PMI becomes nothing more than a rap session.

- When possible, a third party whom both the supervisor and the subordinate trust should be present to take notes and record action items.

- Meetings should be documented by use of a standard form to make sure the key issues are addressed in a systematic way. Both parties agree on the form.

- The leader must be willing to hold subordinates accountable and ask the difficult "why" questions when assignments are not completed.

Boss has found that performance drops off if these meetings are not held but increase if meetings are started, even if they have never been held before or had been stopped for a time. Boss has tracked the use of PMIs in 202 teams across time periods ranging from three months to twenty-nine years.[10] His research indicates that regular PMIs can significantly decrease, and even prevent, regression to previous levels of team performance for as long as twenty-nine years with no additional interventions after the original team-building sessions. Certainly the evidence is compelling enough to indicate that this is an effective way to follow up on decisions made during a team-building session.

Boss's research does not discuss any further team sessions. Some units that have used the PMI have also reported having regular team meetings to deal with issues common to all, as well as additional team development sessions every three to six months. These later sessions identify any current problems or concerns and establish new goals for change and plans for improvement. And as we noted in chapter 3, Bain & Company has been successful by critiquing team performance monthly.

In the past, many teams have followed up a team-building session with additional team meetings to review progress. The advantage of the PMI is that it allows time to talk with each person on individually. If this were done in the presence of the whole team, it could be both inhibiting and extremely time-consuming.

Follow-up Team Sessions

We have known for many years, since the early research of Rensis Likert, that follow-up team sessions can also help to sustain high performance.[11] In his research on sales teams in sales offices from a national sales organization, Likert described the elements of follow-up team meetings that make a significant difference in the performance of members on the team. The top twenty sales units were compared with the bottom twenty to see what made the difference in their performance. Likert found the following to be the most important factors:

- The team leader (the sales manager) had high personal performance goals and a plan for achieving those goals. Team members saw an example of high performance as they watched the team leader.
- The team leader displayed highly supportive behavior toward team members and encouraged them to support one another.
- The team leader used participative methods in supervision. That is, all team members were involved in helping the team and the members achieve their goals.

The major process for achieving high performance was holding regular, well-planned meetings of the sales team for review of each person's performance. In contrast to Boss's PMI, a one-on-one follow-up, the units in the Likert research used team meetings as the follow-up process. Those team meetings had the following major features:

- The team met regularly every two weeks or every month.
- The size of the team varied but was usually between twelve and fifteen members. (Note that this is larger than the ideal team size discussed in chapter 3.)
- The sales manager presided over the meeting but allowed wide participation in the group. The main function of the manager was to keep the team focused on the task; push the team to set high performance goals; and discourage negative, nonsupportive, ego-deflating actions of team members.
- Each salesperson presented a report of his or her activities during the previous period, including a description of the approach used, closings attempted, sales achieved, and volume and quality of total sales.
- All of the other team members analyzed the person's efforts and offered suggestions for improvement. Coaching was given by team members to one another.
- Each salesperson announced his or her goals and procedures to be used, which would be reviewed at the next team meeting.

The researchers concluded that this form of team meeting results in four benefits:

1. Team members set higher goals.
2. They are more motivated to achieve their goals.
3. They receive more assistance, coaching, and help from their boss and peers.
4. The team gets more new ideas on how to improve performance as people share, not keep secret, their successful new methods.

It seems possible, then, to have either one-on-one follow-up meetings or a series of follow-up team meetings as a way of maintaining the high performance of team members. The key issue is that team building requires a continuous effort to monitor the team's ability to improve team performance. The key person is the team leader, who must build a follow-up procedure into the process.

The two most common follow-up methods are one-on-one interviews and follow-up team meetings. However, other follow-up procedures are available, depending on the nature of the team's problems and plans. For example, a follow-up data-gathering process can use a survey or questionnaire to see if the unit members feel the activities of the team have improved. Another approach is to have an outsider interview members to check on what has improved and what actions are still needed. Alternatively, an outside observer could be invited to watch the team in action and give a process review at the end of the meeting.

If a team has poor interaction at meetings, it is possible to follow up with a procedure to get reactions of people after each meeting or after some meetings. The team leaders could use a short paper-and-pencil survey or ask for a critique of the meeting verbally, posing questions such as the following:

- How satisfied were you with the team meeting today?
- Are there any actions we keep doing that restrict our effectiveness?
- What do we need to stop doing, start doing, or continue doing that would improve our team performance?
- Do we really function as a team, or are there indications that teamwork is lacking?
- Are we achieving our goals and using each person's resources effectively?

If your team discusses these questions, be sure to allot sufficient time for an adequate critique. If you use a written form, summarize the results and begin the next team meeting by reviewing the summary and discussing what should be done in the current meeting to make the team more effective.

In Summary

In this chapter we have described the basic elements of a team-building program:

- The purposes of the team-building program are described and any concerns or fears of team members are addressed. If a consultant is used, his or her role should be explained to the team.
- Data regarding the performance of the team are generated by examining archival data, observing the team as it performs a particular task, interviewing team members, or surveying members of the team. A variety of alternatives are available to generate such data.
- The team engages in a problem-solving process to come up with solutions to the problems that have been identified. An appreciative inquiry approach is an alternative to the traditional problem-solving model.
- The team develops and implements the action plans. Commitments generally are written down and assignments clearly communicated to team members.
- To ensure that changes in the team persist over time, team leaders should engage in regular personal management interviews with members of their team or conduct regular team meetings to review commitments made in the team-building sessions and to make changes as needed.

The next chapters explore some specific problems found in teams and some new team dynamics that often require the use of team building. We will outline some specific strategies for overcoming these problems to help a team be more effective.

Part Two

SOLVING SPECIFIC PROBLEMS THROUGH TEAM BUILDING

7

MANAGING CONFLICT
IN THE TEAM

One of the common problems found in teams is the presence of disruptive conflict and hostility. Feelings of animosity between individuals or between cliques or subgroups may grow to such proportions that people who must work together do not speak to one another at all. All communications, if any, are by memo or e-mail, even though offices are adjoining. Why do such conflicts occur, and how can a team resolve such differences?

In this chapter, we explore the basis of conflict in teams by discussing expectation theory and its application to teams. We outline the various conflict resolution methods and then focus on what to do when the manager or team leader is the problem, how to manage diversity successfully in a team, and how to deal effectively with a problem team member.

Expectation Theory of Conflict

Probably the most common explanation for understanding conflict is the theory of conflicting personalities. When two people do not get along, it is easiest to say that their "personalities clash." Underlying this explanation is a presumption that one individual's personality (a complex of attitudes, values, feelings, needs, and experiences) is so different from another's that the two cannot function compatibly. However, attributing team conflict to personality clashes is not helpful and in fact often makes things worse, since the only way to resolve the problem would be to get someone to change his or her personality (at a deep level, none of us wants to feel that we have personality flaws that need to be changed; as a result we will be very defensive when our "personality" gets attacked) or be removed from the team. Because personality is so deeply rooted by reached adulthood, it would seem impossible to improve the situation.

A more useful way to understand conflict is to view it as the result of a violation of expectations. Whenever the behavior of one person violates the expectations of another, negative reactions will result. If expectations are not clearly understood and met by individuals who must work together on a team, a cycle of violated expectations may be triggered. Negative feelings can escalate until open expressions of hostility are common, and people try to hurt or punish each other in various ways rather than try to work cooperatively.

Every person comes to a team with a set of expectations about himself or herself, the team leader, and the other team members. Their expectations of others can be described in terms of what is to be done, when it should be done, and how it is to be done. Frequently people may agree on the "what" conditions, but expectations in the other two aspects—expectations about when actions should be taken and how they should be taken—are more often violated.

To illustrate this concept, consider the following example of how violated expectations led to conflict between a newlywed couple (virtually all married people have their own stories of adjustment after they got married).

Ann leaves the apartment for her first day of work after the honeymoon. She can't wait to finish work so that she can rush home to enjoy a quiet and, she hopes, romantic evening with her new husband, John. Because John is a second-year MBA student who finishes class by 3:00 p.m., Ann guesses that he might surprise her by fixing dinner—something he did frequently while they were dating. Before she left, he had asked, "What do you think about spaghetti carbonara for dinner?" a favorite meal that he has made for her before.

At school, John discovers that he has a finance case analysis due tomorrow with his study team. The team decides that the only time they can all meet is from 4:00 to 7:00 p.m. John wants to be home to meet Ann when she returns at 6:30 p.m., so he suggests that the team meet at his apartment. After two hours of work, the case team begins to get tired and hungry. The analysis is more difficult than they expected, and they realize they will need more time. So they decide to order pizza and work until 8:00 p.m. When Ann arrives home, she finds a mess in the kitchen from the pizza and snacks. She also finds a mess in the family room where John's team has strewn papers everywhere. John gives Ann a quick kiss and tells her about the assignment but promises they should be done within an hour or so. He's sorry he can't make dinner for her—but he's saved a slice of pizza for her.

Ann surveys the mess. This is not what she was expecting. Couldn't he have called to warn her? But she decides to clean up the mess and patiently wait for John to finish the assignment. After all, she's brought home John's favorite cheesecake, a surprise she was hoping would be the icing on a quiet, romantic evening together. After an hour, John appears and says, "Sorry, this assignment is a bear; it's probably going to be another half-hour." After another hour, the study team finally leaves. John flops on a chair in the kitchen and says, "I'm exhausted."

Out of the corner of his eye, he spies the cheesecake, grabs a fork, and exclaims, "This is just what I need!" Shortly he is at the table shoveling in the cheesecake when something clicks in his awareness. Something is wrong, he senses. Ann is awfully quiet and is just picking at the piece of cheesecake he pushed in front of her.

"Anything the matter?" he asks. Ann says nothing, eyes fixed on the cheesecake.

Now he knows something is wrong and puts down the fork. "What's the matter, Ann?" he asks with real concern.

Tears start to well up in Ann's eyes as she thinks about the lost evening. John didn't call her to tell her he couldn't make dinner; he didn't clean up after his mess in the kitchen; he didn't thank her for the cheesecake; and worst of all, he hadn't paid her any attention.

"The honeymoon is definitely over," she says angrily. "Thanks for the cold pizza and for letting me clean up your friends' mess."

John is stunned. Where is this anger coming from? Hadn't he arranged to at least be home? Hadn't he at least thought to save her a slice of pizza? Doesn't she realize he needs good grades to get a good job?

"Well, thanks for your patience and support of my graduate work," he replies sarcastically.

And before they know it, Ann and John are embroiled in their first fight as a married couple.

Of course, Ann and John's experience is not unusual. Each had expectations that were violated. From Ann's perspective, husbands should call when plans change, they should pick up after themselves, and they should say "thanks" when their wives surprise them with their favorite dessert. From John's perspective, wives should be more flexible when plans change and patient when their husbands have important work to do, just as husbands should when their wives have important work to do. We see violated expectations leading to conflict all the time in all types of relationships, not only in teams.[1]

The bottom line is that violated expectations lead to conflict when they are not understood, discussed, and resolved. Most individuals, whether in a family or work team, do not knowingly violate the expectations of those with whom they must collaborate. The problem is that many expectations are implicit: we have them, and we may not even know we have the expectation until it is violated. Following are some common expectations that team leaders, subordinates, or peers on a team may violate.

Typical Ways That Team Leaders Violate Subordinates' Expectations

- Micromanaging their work (not giving them any autonomy to make decisions)
- Making decisions that affect the subordinate without asking for his or her input
- Letting some team members shirk their duties without any negative consequences
- Not giving praise or any rewards for a job well done
- Not recognizing that the subordinate has a life outside work that occasionally takes priority over work

Typical Ways That Subordinates Violate Team Leaders' Expectations

- Missing or being late to team meetings
- Not outwardly demonstrating commitment and support for the leader's agenda and priorities
- Not completing assignments in a timely manner so the team can complete its work
- Not letting the leader know when there are problems so that the leader isn't surprised

Typical Ways That Peers Violate Expectations

- Not sharing resources (or competing for resources)
- Not sharing credit for a job well done

- Not responding to voice mails or e-mails in a timely
  manner

As we have noted, our expectations of ourselves and others
are often implicit; they are held but not explicitly stated or
understood. By just surfacing the expectation, the conflict may
be resolved. Of course, in other cases, resolving conflict requires
compromise, the adjustment of expectations of others, or adjustment in behaviors so that expectations are met.

Expectation theory is useful in dealing with conflict because
it focuses on clarifying expectations of ourselves and others by
identifying specific behaviors that may violate those expectations. If team members can begin to identify the behaviors or
actions that violate their expectations, perhaps agreements can
be negotiated, so that the end result is greater mutual understanding and fewer conflicts.

Negotiating Agreements

In planning a team-building session to deal with conflicts, certain
agreements between the conflicting parties need to be met.

- It helps if people can agree that problems exist, that those
  problems should be solved, and that all parties have some
  responsibility to work on the issues.
- All parties must agree to meet and work on the problems.
- People may find it easier to deal with conflict if they can
  accept the position that the end result of the team-building
  session is not to get everyone to "like" one another but
  rather to understand one another and be able to work
  together. People do not need to form personal friendships,
  but group members at least should be able to trust one
  another and meet one another's expectations.

The disagreeing parties will work best together in the team-building session if they can adopt the position that it is not productive to try to unravel who is at fault or what led to the problems. Rather, they should accept the fact that differences exist and that they need to work out agreeable solutions.

Helping Teams in Conflict or Confusion: The Role Clarification Exercise

A particularly useful intervention for determining expectations is what we call the role clarification exercise. The role clarification model of team building is considered appropriate if several of the following conditions are prevalent in the organization or unit that is considering a team-building program:

- The team is newly organized, and no one has a clear understanding about what others do and what others expect of them.
- Changes and reassignments have been made in the team, and there is a lack of clarity about how the various functions and positions now fit together.
- Job descriptions are old and not consistent with current realities.
- Meetings are held infrequently and only for passing on needed directions.
- People carry out their assignments with very little contact with others in the same office. They generally feel isolated.
- Conflicts and interpersonal disruptions in the unit seem to be increasing. Coffee-break talk and other informal communications center on discussion of overlaps and encroachments by others on work assignments. People get requests they don't understand. They hear through the grapevine about what others are doing; it sounds as if

it's something they should know about, but nobody informs them.

- The boss engages primarily in one-on-one management. Team meetings are infrequent or primarily involve listening to the boss raise issues with one individual at a time while others watch and wait for their turn. Almost no problem solving is done as a team or between people. Issues are taken to the boss, and only then are needed people called together.

- People sit in their offices and wonder, "What is happening on this team? I don't know what others are doing, and I'm sure nobody knows [or cares] what I'm doing."

- A crisis occurs because everyone thought someone else was responsible for handling a task that was never completed.

Planning

The following sections describe the steps of a role-clarification team-building exercise. Over the years, we have found this to be one of the most useful exercises for a team to engage in, with generally very positive results.

Time Commitment For a team of eight to ten people, the minimum time needed for this type of team building is approximately one-half hour to one hour for each person, or a total of four to ten hours of meeting time, preferably in a solid block. With a training day from 8:30 a.m. to 12:00 p.m. and 1:00 to 4:30 p.m., this typically could be achieved in one day. It also would be possible to conduct this type of team-building session by taking one afternoon a week over a period of time. Our experience, however, indicates that spending the time in one block has more impact. Each time a group meets, a certain amount of settling-in time is required, which is minimized if only one session is held.

Resource Personnel If the ground rules, procedures, overall goals, and design elements are clear, a manager need not be afraid to conduct this type of meeting with no outside assistance from a consultant or facilitator. If certain realistic concerns suggest that an outside person would be helpful in facilitating the meeting, one could be included. This person may be someone from within the company but in a different department, such as a human resource or organization development specialist or a consultant from outside the company.

Regardless of whether an outside resource person is used, the entire team-building meeting should be conducted and managed by the team leader or boss. Team building is management's business; it is a supervisor building his or her team. It is not an exercise called by a staff person in human resources.

Program Design Goal The goal of a role clarification team-building program is to arrive at that condition in which all members of the team can publicly agree that they:

- Have a clear understanding of the major requirements of their own job
- Feel that the others at the team-building meeting also clearly understand everyone's position and duties
- Know what others expect of them in their working relationships
- Feel that all know what others need from them in their working relationships

All agreements in working relationships should be reached with a spirit of collaboration and a willingness to implement the understandings. Procedures should be established that permit future misunderstandings to be handled in more effective ways.

Preparation This part of the team-building activity can be done prior to the session or done first by each member of the team in private as the team session begins. Each person should prepare answers to the following questions:

1. What do you feel the organization expects you to do in your job? (This may include the formal job description.)

2. What do you actually do in your job? (Describe working activities and point out any discrepancies between your formal job description and your actual job activities.)

3. What do you need to know about other people's jobs that would help you do your work?

4. What do you think others should know about your job that would help them do their work?

5. What do you need others to do in order for you to do your job the way you would like?

6. What do others need you to do that would help them do their work?

Meeting Design

Managing the role clarification meeting is an important role for the team leader or consultant. Following are the goals, ground rules, and steps in role claification.

Goals The goals of the team-building meeting should be presented, clarified, and discussed. Everyone should agree on the goals or hoped-for outcomes of the sessions.

Ground Rules Ground rules should be developed by the team, written on a sheet of paper, and posted for all to see. Some suggested ground rules are as follows:

1. Be as candid and open as possible in a spirit of wanting to help improve the team.

2. If you want to know how another person feels or thinks about an issue, ask that person directly. If you are the person asked, give an honest response, even if it is to say, "I don't feel like responding right now."

3. If the meeting becomes unproductive for you, express this concern to the group.

4. Every member should have an opportunity to speak on every issue.

5. Decisions made should be agreeable to all those who are affected by the decision.

Role Clarification

Each person will have an opportunity to be the focal person and will follow these steps:

1. The focal person describes his or her job as he or she sees it. This means sharing all information about how the focal person understands the job: what is expected, when things are expected to be done, and how they are expected to be done. Other team members have the right to ask questions for clarification.

2. All others indicate that they understand what the focal person's position entails after this person's description: what is to be done, when things are to be done, and how they are to be done.

3. If the focal person and others have differences in expectations about the focal person's job, they should be resolved at this point, so that there is a common agreement about what the focal person's job entails.

4. After agreement has been reached about the nature of the job, the focal person talks directly to each person on the

team, identifying what he or she needs from the other in order to do the job as agreed on.

5. The others then have the opportunity to tell the focal person what they may need in return or what additional help the focal person might need from them so that the focal person can accomplish the demands of the position.

At the end of the role clarification session, it is often important to get feedback about how people are feeling. To get such feedback, team members might be asked to respond to the following questions:

1. How have you felt about the role clarification exercise?
2. What were the best parts for you?
3. What should be changed or improved in the future?
4. Do we need other sessions like this? If so, what should we discuss? When should we meet again?

This type of team development meeting is one of the easiest to manage and one of the most productive of all design possibilities for improving team effectiveness. Most groups of people slip into areas of ambiguity in their working relationships. Expectations about performance develop that people do not understand or even know about. For example, during a role clarification exercise with one company's executive committee, the members of the president's management group were outlining their jobs as they saw them and identifying what they felt they needed from one another in order to carry out their jobs more effectively. When the personnel manager's turn came, she turned to the president and said, "One of the actions I need from you is a chance to get together with you a couple of times a year and review my performance and see what things you feel I need to do to improve."

The president asked in surprise, "Why do you need to get together with me?"

Responded the personnel manager, "When I was hired two years ago, it was my understanding that I was to report directly to you."

"Nobody ever cleared that with me," stated the president. "I thought you reported to the executive vice president."

The personnel manager had been waiting for two years for a chance to get directions and instructions from the person she thought was her direct superior, but that relationship had never been clarified until the role clarification session. Although most work teams do not have misunderstood expectations to this degree, the periodic clarification of roles is useful for any work team.

Another role clarification session we facilitated had a dramatic impact on the team and team leader. During the course of the session, the team members and the team leader—the company CEO—reached an impasse. The CEO believed his role was to make most of the decisions for the team, and the team members' role was mostly to follow his orders. Those on the team, the company vice presidents, reacted strongly against this view: they thought that decisions should be made more by consensus and that the role of the CEO should be to facilitate, not make, team decisions. The role clarification ended without resolution.

After the meeting, the vice presidents met and made a decision: either the CEO would need to rethink his role or they would quit. A few of the vice presidents, as representatives of the team, met with the board of directors, described the role conflicts between them and the CEO, and issued an ultimatum: "Either the CEO goes or we go." The board decided to "promote" the CEO to serve on the board and appointed one of the vice presidents to serve as the new CEO. As a result, the new management team with new clarity about the role of the CEO began to perform at a much higher level than before.

Although the goal of such a team-building session is not to get the team leader fired or removed, a role clarification session encourages the team to focus on the problems the leader has caused. Thus, the leader can respond in an affirmative way and agree to make some changes or, as in this case, stonewall the team and refuse to negotiate a new set of roles and behaviors. Either way, the exercise forces the team to confront some difficult issues and creates energy for change, which can lead to a more positive outcome for the team. Of course, this case also illustrates the risks involved when clarifying the roles of team members.

The Start-Stop-Continue Exercise

In some cases a team in conflict may not have the time to conduct a role clarification exercise, or it may prefer a team-building session that focuses more on what the team needs to change in order to minimize conflict and improve performance. In these cases we recommend the "start-stop-continue" exercise.

In this team-building exercise, each person lists what the team as a whole needs to (1) start doing, (2) stop doing, and (3) continue doing in order to reduce conflicts and improve performance. This process typically clarifies how each team member expects the team to behave. Starting at the team level is a way to work down to the individual level within the team. This may work well when team conflict is not high and when team conflicts are general in nature and not focused on specific individuals or subgroups. Of course, when there are multiple parties in conflict, be it individuals or subgroups in the team, it can be helpful for each party to build a list for the other. Each person lists the things he or she would like to see the other individual or group start doing, stop doing, and continue doing if expectations are to be met and positive results achieved. The parties then share their lists.

With the lists of things that each party wants from the other on display for all to see, a negotiation session ensues. Subgroup or person A agrees on what it will do in return for a similar behavioral alteration on the part of subgroup or person B. Such agreements should be written up because signing an agreement may increase the commitment to making the change. This process puts the formerly warring factions into a problem-solving situation that requires them to try to work out solutions rather than spend time finding fault or placing blame.

The design of a conflict-reducing meeting can vary widely. It may be desirable to precede the session with a presentation of expectation theory and a description of the negative consequences of continued hostility. Another possibility is to have each team member try to predict what the other team members think about them and what they think the other members want from them. These guesses are often surprisingly accurate and may help in reaching an agreement.

A similar design may also be used to negotiate agreements between individuals. If a manager feels that the thing most divisive on the team is conflict between two people, the two may be brought together for a problem-solving session to begin to work out agreements with each other. If there are disagreements among team members at any point, it is often best to stop and work out a negotiation and come to an agreement.

Negotiation often involves compromise: each party gives up something to receive something of similar value from the other. Too frequently, however, conflicts are handled by people engaging in the following activities:

- *Ignoring*—trying to pretend that no disagreement exists.
- *Smoothing*—trying to placate people and attempting to get them to feel good even though an agreement has not been reached.

- *Forcing*—getting agreement from a position of power. If the more powerful person forces the other to agree, the result may be public agreement but private resistance.

When an effective team experiences conflict, the team takes time to identify the cause of it. The team identifies the conflict as a problem to be solved and takes problem-solving actions.[2] The facilitator (usually team leader) must be perceptive enough to ensure that ignoring, smoothing, or forcing behaviors do not occur during the team-building session. Otherwise the problems will not be resolved and conflict will quickly reemerge.

The Manager as the Center of Conflict

It is rather common to find that the center of conflict is the manager or team leader. Sometimes the problem is between the manager and the whole group and sometimes between the manager and one or two members of the group. In either case, unless the superior is aware of the situation and is willing to take steps to remedy the problem, it is difficult for team members to open up the issue and deal with it. It is also not uncommon for the superior to be totally or partially unaware of the extent of the emotional breach that has occurred. In power relationships, subordinates learn to become quite skilled at masking negative feelings and pretending everything is going well when in fact there are problems. Sometimes feelings are not completely masked, and instead a form of passive-aggressive resistance occurs that the superior may see but not understand.

When any of the major symptoms of team difficulties (as listed in chapter 5) emerge, the team leader should ask, "Is it possible that I am at least partly responsible for these problems?" How does a team leader get an honest answer to this question?

1. *Ask the team members.* Either in a team meeting or in an interview with each of the team members, the team leader might

say something like this: "I want you to level with me. I know that things have not been going well in our team. [He or she then describes some of the symptoms.] I want to know if I am responsible for creating some of these problems. I would appreciate it if you could let me know either openly now or in a memo later what things I am doing that create problems and any suggestions you have that would improve matters."

In asking for feedback, it is often useful if the leader can identify some things that have already come to mind—for example, "I think that I sometimes come to meetings with my mind already made up and then put pressure on people to agree with me; then when I get the forced agreement, I pretend that we have reached a consensus. Do you see this behavior in me? [The leader waits for a response.] If you do, what suggestions do you have that will help me avoid this kind of problem?" If there is a lack of trust in the team or in certain team members, this direct asking may not elicit any real data or at best only hidden messages. This means that the leader may then need to resort to other means of getting data.

2. *Use an outside resource.* A common method of getting information to the leader is to find an outside person, either outside the team but in the organization (usually a human resource or organization development specialist) or an external consultant. A skilled outside resource can interview team members and try to elicit information about the involvement of the team leader in team problems. This information can then be fed back to the leader and a strategy devised for using the information with the team.

3. *Use survey instruments.* Currently a wide variety of survey instruments is available for gathering data, anonymously if necessary, from subordinates about their perceptions of the leader. A human resource person is useful for handling this task and then seeing that the data are summarized and returned to the superior. Then a method for using this information with the team needs

to be devised. A recommended method is for the manager to present a summary of data to the group, indicate acceptance of the data, announce some preliminary actions that will be taken, and ask the team members to suggest other appropriate changes.

4. *Undertake laboratory training.* A method used more often some years back than today is for the manager to go to a training program that features giving feedback to all participants on their interpersonal style. The manager then brings a summary of this feedback to the team, checks with the members about its validity, and works out a program of improvement.

Although the superior wishing to find out if his or her performance is causing conflicts in the team may take a variety of actions, a more difficult issue remains if the leader is unaware of his or her impact or does not seem to want to find out. In such a situation, here are some ways for team members to get data to the leader:

1. *Suggest a role clarification session.* This session could allow the team members to identify actions they need from the team leader or changes they feel would improve activities in the team.

2. *Give direct feedback.* One possibility is for team members to find an opportunity to give direct, albeit unsolicited, feedback to the leader. Despite the inherent risks, the team—either all together or through representatives—could say to the leader, "We have a dilemma. There are problems in the team that we feel involve you. Our dilemma is we think we should share this information with you, but we do not want to disrupt our relationship with you. Do you have any suggestions as to how we might deal with this dilemma?" This approach usually results in the leader's asking for the data in a far different atmosphere than the one that results from confronting the leader unexpectedly with tough feedback.

3. *Use an outside person.* It is possible for the team to go to an appropriate internal resource person and ask for assistance. Often the outside person can then go to the leader and suggest a set of alternative actions or behaviors that will improve team performance.

Diversity as the Source of Conflict

Diversity is another common source of conflict for teams today. Diversity in teams is the result of several forces. More and more, various groups once considered minorities in business (women, African Americans, Hispanics, Native Americans, the aged, and others) are being represented on decision-making teams. Also, businesses are becoming more international to capture foreign markets. This means more multicultural planning and policymaking groups. Factions formerly in adversarial positions are now trying to work together collaboratively: management, labor, government, environmental groups, consumer groups, and the media, among many others. Along with these types of groupings is a wide range of social groupings that may contribute to diversity in teams: age, race, ethnic origin, social status, sexual orientation, education, religion, political affiliation, gender, family status, regional identification, personal style, personal experiences, and so on. All of this means that when any people come together as a team, there is a range of diversity that leaders should recognize as a great strength and not a drawback to effective work. Most of the research on groups that use diversity productively shows that these groups are innovative and creative; members are more sensitive and appreciative of others who are different and have different skills and personal resources.[3]

When diversity is not managed effectively, differences can split people apart, cause endless arguments and bickering, and result in bitter feelings, resentment, and less productive work.

The issue is how to make diversity work in a positive way to capitalize on the richness of difference that is in every team.

When team members have obvious differences, one of their goals should be to achieve a level of constructive controversy. Used in this context, *controversy* is defined as the willingness to explore all sides of every issue. Achieving controversy is therefore a desired goal, not something to avoid. Here are some of the key ingredients for building constructive controversy into the team:

- *Common goals or vision.* If people with diverse backgrounds can all commit themselves to a common set of goals or a shared vision of what they can accomplish together, they may be able to combine their richness of difference in new and more innovative ways. Thus, teams characterized by diversity must spend time coming to agreements about what they want to accomplish together.

- *Diversity as a value.* Team members must understand and accept as a shared value that diversity of background and experience is a positive ingredient. They need to discuss what controversy is and see controversy as the willingness to explore all facets of all issues before any decisions or plans are concluded. People on the team might describe their own differences so others can understand where they are coming from when they express ideas and opinions.

- *Guidelines for work.* Assuming that members of the diverse team have a commitment to common goals and accept diversity as a value, developing a set of guidelines for work is immensely useful. Even a diverse group will have deadlines to meet and goals that need to be achieved. The following guidelines might be helpful:

  ○ Every team member who has some experience with an issue is expected to share his or her own best thinking on that issue.

○ A team member who agrees or disagrees with another member should share that position with the group.

○ The team might adopt the golden rule of diverse communications: discuss issues with others as you would like them to discuss issues with you, and listen to others as you would like them to listen to you.

○ Before any decision is finalized, the leader or a group member should ask, "Have we heard every idea, suggestion, or argument about this proposal?"

○ Any person who disagrees with another should be able to repeat back to the other person's satisfaction the other's position to make sure that the first person disagrees with what the other person meant, not what was heard.

○ It should be completely accepted that every member of the team is a person of worth and intelligence and that every person's opinions, ideas, and arguments therefore should be listened to with respect.

○ The following might be a team slogan: "Controversy, when discussed in a cooperative context, promotes elaboration of views, the search for new information and ideas, and the integration of apparently opposing positions."

- *Critiquing.* Every team, especially a diverse team, should take the time to critique its own processes and performance. How well has the team followed its own guidelines? What has hindered it from being as creative as possible? Has the team used controversy constructively? What do team members need to do to become a more effective team and use their diversity more productively?

The Problem Member

One of the most common questions we hear is, What do you do when one member of the team continually disrupts the rest of the team? This person may always take a contrary point of view, vote against proposals everyone else supports, take a negative or pessimistic position on everything, and frequently miss meetings or not follow through on assignments.

The obvious question in response is, Why do you keep a person like that on your team? Usually the answer is that this person has some needed skill, that he or she is a long-time employee, or that terminating or transferring someone has a lot of built-in problems. As Bob Lutz, who engineered numerous innovations as president of Chrysler, observed, "Disruptive people can be an asset . . . Some (repeat some) disruptive people are very much worth keeping. They're more asset than cost. They're the irritating grains of sand that, in the case of oysters, every now and then produce a pearl. Disruptive people can pre-cipitate breakthroughs, sometimes by forcing an uncomfortable reexamination of comfortable assumptions."[4] However, Lutz acknowledges that in some cases disruptive people are just plain disruptive, and they have to go.

If a manager or supervisor is trying to build a team and one person won't buy into the process, some method of removing that person from the team (such as transfer, reassignment, or even firing) may be necessary. The following actions have also been found to be successful in some cases:

- *Direct confrontation between the team leader and the problem person.* This may give the supervisor an opportunity to describe clearly the person's problem behaviors and the consequences if such behaviors do not change.

- *Confrontation by the group.* If only the boss deals with the problem person, the conflict may be perceived by that person as just the personal bias of the boss. In such a case, it would be better for the group to deal directly with the problem member collectively in a team meeting. The team members must be descriptive in their feedback, not evaluative (e.g. "Why do you do such stupid things?").

They must describe the problem behaviors and identify the negative consequences of the behaviors—all without punitive, negative evaluations of the individual personally.

- *Special responsibility.* For some difficult people, giving them a special role or responsibility on the team increases their commitment to the team process. The person might be asked to be the team recorder, the agenda builder, or the one to summarize the discussion of issues. One team even rotated the difficult member into the role of acting team leader with the responsibility for a limited time of getting team agreement on the issues at hand.

- *Limited participation.* In some rare cases, it may be necessary to limit the participation of the problem member. One team asked the problem person to attend team meetings, listen to the discussion but not participate in the team discussion, and then have a one-on-one session with the team leader. If the leader felt that the member had some legitimate issues to raise with the team, the leader would present them to the team at the next meeting. This intervention forced the problem team member to listen and take some time to think through his ideas before commenting (this is especially useful for individuals who react quickly and emotionally to arguments and who blurt out their thoughts without listening to others or carefully thinking through what they plan to say). This intervention generally is not a palatable solution in the long run, for it essentially ostracizes the person from the group, but it may have some short-term benefits when a particular assignment needs to be completed quickly.

- *External assignment.* At times it may be possible to give the problem person an assignment outside the activities of the rest of the team. The person may make a contribution to the work unit on an individual basis, whereas the bulk of the work that requires collaboration is handled by the rest of the team.

All of these suggestions are useful when the person is a serious obstruction to the working of the group. One must always be careful, however, to differentiate the real problem person from someone who sees things differently and whose different views or perspectives need to be listened to and considered with the possibility that this may enrich the productivity of the team. Teams can get too cohesive and isolate a person who is different. As a result, the team may lose the innovative ideas of a person who thinks differently.

However, the most likely reason for failure to take action in the face of a disruptive team member is the team's inability to openly confront such a problem. In one MBA class, a student group was asked to complete a group assignment and then write individually about their experience in the group. As the instructor read the group's individual papers, he found that several students gave a very negative assessment of one woman in the group. The criticisms were so stinging that the professor decided to meet with the group (initially without the woman present) to make sure that he understood the problems accurately. When he met with the group, each member reviewed the problems he or she had with this particular woman. She was overbearing and forced her opinion on others. Moreover, she agreed to do the bulk of the work on the group assignment and then failed to come through with her part on time. This caused the group to finish its project late and produce a rather mediocre product.

As the professor explored what could have been done to solve the problem, he asked the students, "Why didn't you discuss the problems you were having with this woman?" One student replied, "We couldn't do that. She'd think we didn't like her!" Of course, the problem was that the group members didn't like her, and their relationship with her hurt group performance. The group members felt that since this was just a class assignment, they could get through it as best they could, take their grade, and move on to the next class. What they didn't learn was the skill of how to confront and work with a difficult team member.

In Summary

Overcoming unhealthy conflict is one of the objectives of all team leaders. We have found that thinking of conflict as the result of violated expectations is a useful way to identify the source of many conflicts and to take action. We've outlined how teams can reduce conflict and confusion by engaging in role clarification or using the start-stop-continue format. We've also presented some concrete suggestions for how teams can deal with conflicts with the boss, issues of diversity, and the recalcitrant team member. Over the years, we have seen many teams improve their performance significantly by implementing these team-building strategies.

8

OVERCOMING UNHEALTHY AGREEMENT

Imagine working on a team for which you have high regard and respect for every member. In an attempt to be an agreeable and easy colleague to work with, you respond positively to the first suggestion that another team member makes. Everyone else on the team follows the same pattern or tries to be agreeable and positive. Problem solving happens quickly because everyone goes along with the first solutions that are offered. However, while the team initially may avoid conflict by following such a pattern, decisions are made that haven't been carefully scrutinized or don't really have the full support of the group.

This condition, which we call unhealthy agreement, is one of the more vexing problems facing teams and can lead to poor decision making and poor team performance. Teams achieve extraordinary performance by drawing on the complementary skills and knowledge of team members. However, this cannot happen unless team members are willing to listen, challenge, and debate each other as they jointly pursue optimal solutions to the problems they are addressing. In this chapter we explore this problem and discuss team-building activities that have been used successfully to prevent unhealthy agreement.

Unhealthy Agreement

Jerry Harvey popularized the concept of what he called the "Abilene paradox," the now-famous analysis of groups of people who make public decisions that seem to reflect total agreement, although few, if any, of the team members feel that the decisions are appropriate. At times teams make poor decisions not due to open conflict but because people pretend to agree when in fact they do not. We continue to use the following story in this edition of *Team Building* because it illustrates an all-too-common problem: too many teams are still taking a "trip to Abilene."[1]

The Abilene Paradox

July Sunday afternoons in Coleman, Texas, are not exactly winter holidays. This one was particularly hot—104 degrees as measured by the Walgreen's Rexall Ex-Lax Temperature Gauge located under the tin awning that covered a rather substantial "screened-in" back porch. In addition, the wind was blowing fine-grained West Texas topsoil through what were apparently cavernous but invisible openings in the walls.

"How could dust blow through closed windows and solid walls?" one might ask. Such a question betrays more of the provincialism of the reader than the writer. Anyone who has ever lived in West Texas wouldn't bother to ask. Just let it be said that wind can do a lot of things with topsoil when more than thirty days have passed without rain.

But the afternoon was still tolerable—even potentially enjoyable. A water-cooled fan provided adequate relief from the heat as long as one didn't stray too far from it, and we didn't. In addition, there was cold lemonade for sipping. One might have preferred stronger stuff, but Coleman was "dry" in more ways than one; and so were my in-laws, at least until someone got sick. Then a teaspoon or two for medicinal purposes might be legitimately considered. But this particular Sunday no one was ill; and anyway, lemonade seemed to offer the necessary cooling properties we sought.

And finally, there was entertainment. Dominoes. Perfect for the conditions. The game required little more physical exertion than an occasional mumbled comment, "shuffle 'em," and an unhurried movement of the arm to place the spots in the appropriate perspective on the table. It also required somebody to mark the score; but that responsibility was shifted at the conclusion of each hand so the task, though onerous, was in no way physically debilitating. In short, dominoes was diversion, but pleasant diversion.

So, all in all it was an agreeable—even exciting— Sunday afternoon in Coleman; if, to quote a contemporary radio commercial, "You are easily excited." That is, it was until my father-in-law suddenly looked up from the table and said with apparent enthusiasm, "Let's get in the car and go to Abilene and have dinner at the cafeteria."

To put it mildly, his suggestion caught me unprepared. You might even say it woke me up. I began to turn it over in my mind. "Go to Abilene? Fifty-three miles? In this dust storm? We'll have to drive with the lights on even though it's the middle of the afternoon. And the heat. It's bad enough here in front of the fan, but in an un-air-conditioned 1958 Buick it will be brutal. And eat at the cafeteria? Some cafeterias may be okay, but the one in Abilene conjures up dark memories of the enlisted men's field mess."

But before I could clarify and organize my thoughts even to articulate them, Beth, my wife, chimed in with, "Sounds like a great idea. I would like to go. How about you, Jerry?" Well, since my own preferences were obviously

(Continued)

out of step with the rest, I decided not to impede the party's progress and replied with, "Sounds good to me," and added, "I just hope your mother wants to go."

"Of course I want to go," my mother-in-law replied. "I haven't been to Abilene in a long time. What makes you think I wouldn't want to go?"

So into the car and to Abilene we went. My predictions were fulfilled. The heat was brutal. We were coated with a fine layer of West Texas dust, which was cemented with perspiration by the time we arrived; and the food at the cafeteria provided first-rate testimonial material for Alka-Seltzer commercials.

Some four hours and 106 miles later, we returned to Coleman, Texas, tired and exhausted. We sat in front of the fan for a long time in silence. Then, both to be sociable and also to break a rather oppressive silence, I said, "It was a great trip, wasn't it?"

No one spoke.

Finally, my mother-in-law said, with some slight note of irritation, "Well, to tell the truth, I really didn't enjoy it much and would have rather stayed here. I just went along because the three of you were so enthusiastic about going. I wouldn't have gone if you hadn't all pressured me into it."

I couldn't believe it. "What do you mean 'you all?'" I said. "Don't put me in the 'you all' group. I was delighted to be doing what we were doing. I didn't want to go. I only went to satisfy the rest of you characters. You are the culprits."

Beth looked shocked. "Don't call me a culprit. You and Daddy and Mama were the ones who wanted to go. I just went along to be sociable and to keep you happy. I would have to be crazy to want to go out in heat like that. You don't think I'm crazy, do you?"

Before I had the opportunity to fall into that obvious trap, her father entered the conversation again with some abruptness. He spoke only one word, but he did it in the quite simple, straightforward vernacular that only a life-long Texan and particularly a Colemanite can approximate. That word was "H-E-L-L-L."

Since he seldom resorted to profanity, he immediately caught our attention. Then he proceeded to expand on what was already an absolutely clear thought with, "Listen, I never wanted to go to Abilene. I was sort of making conversation. I just thought you might have been bored, and I felt I ought to say something. I didn't want you and Jerry to have a bad time when you visit. You visit so seldom, I wanted to be sure you enjoyed it. And I knew that Mama would be upset if you all didn't have a good time. Personally, I would have preferred to play another game of dominoes and eaten the leftovers in the icebox."

After the initial outburst of recrimination, we all sat back in silence. Here we were, four reasonable, sensible people who, on our own volitions, had just taken a 106-mile trip across a Godforsaken desert in furnace-like temperatures through a cloudlike dust storm to eat unpalatable food at a hole-in-the-wall cafeteria in Abilene, Texas, when none of us really wanted to go. In fact, to be more accurate, we'd done just the opposite of what we wanted to do. The whole situation seemed paradoxical. It simply didn't make sense.

At least it didn't make sense at that time. But since that fateful summer day in Coleman, I have observed, consulted with, and been a part of more than one organization that has been caught in the same situation. As a result, it has either taken a temporary side-trip, and occasionally, a terminal journey to Abilene when Dallas or Muleshoe or Houston or Tokyo was where it really wanted to go. And for most of those organizations, the destructive consequences of such trips, measured both in terms of human misery and economic loss, have been much greater than for the Abilene group.

This story illustrates the following paradox: teams (and team members) frequently take actions in contradiction to what they really want to do and therefore defeat the very purposes they are trying to achieve. It also deals with a major corollary of the paradox, which is that the inability to manage agreement can be a major source of dysfunction in organizations from the team level up to the total organization.

When a team gets lost in such a cloud of unrecognized agreement, it frequently manifests behavior that leads one to believe, mistakenly, that the team is caught in a dilemma of conflict. For that reason, it takes a different type of team building—one involving agreement management—to develop more functional behaviors.

Symptoms of the Problem

Because the surface symptoms (that is, conflict) of both agreement and disagreement are essentially similar, the first requirement is to be aware of the symptoms of an agreement-management dilemma. Harvey has identified two sets of symptoms.[2] The first set can most easily be identified by someone outside the team under scrutiny. In effect, being free of the blinding forces of action anxiety, negative fantasies, and unrealistic risk, all of which contribute to the pernicious influence of the paradox, the outsider can frequently observe symptoms hidden by the dust that is all too familiar to residents of Abilene. The second set, more subjective in character, can be more easily recognized by team members.

Symptoms More Easily Observable to Outsiders

Outsiders, whether detached laypeople or professional consultants, can be relatively sure that the team is on a trip to Abilene if they observe the following symptoms:

- Team members' nonverbal cues suggest that they are not satisfied with team functioning (they demonstrate apathy, use sarcasm, and so on). Team members may be passive-aggressive, and while they outwardly seem to support or go along with decisions, inwardly they feel frustrated and powerless.

- Members agree privately, as individuals, as to the nature of the problems facing the team.

- Members also agree, privately, as individuals, on the steps required to cope with the problems.

- Team members blame each other for the condition the team is in.

- The team breaks into subgroups of trusted friends to share rumors, complaints, fantasies, or strategies relating to the problem or its solution.

- In collective situations (group meetings, public memoranda), members fail to communicate their desires and beliefs to others accurately. In fact, they sometimes communicate just the opposite of what they really mean.

- On the basis of such invalid and inaccurate information, members make collective decisions that lead them to take actions contrary to what they personally and collectively want to do. This leads to even greater anger, frustration, irritation, and dissatisfaction with the team.

- Members behave differently outside the team. In other situations (with families, at church, in other work units), they are happier, get along better with others, and perform more effectively.

Symptoms More Easily Observable to Insiders

Some symptoms, stemming primarily from team members' subjective experiences within the team, are more easily identified by the team members themselves who are caught up in the problem of mismanaged agreement. For example, if you experience the following feelings within your team, you may be pretty sure that you are lost in a dust storm of agreement and are on a trip to Abilene:

- You feel pained, frustrated, powerless, and basically unable to cope when trying to solve a particular problem.

- You frequently meet with trusted associates over coffee, clandestine lunches, or in the privacy of your home or office to discuss the problem, commiserate, and plan fantasized solutions that you would attempt "if only the conditions were right." (Fortunately, or unfortunately, depending on your point of view, they seldom are.)

- You blame others—the boss, other divisions, or those "unperceptive people in unit X"—for the dilemma. The boss, in particular, frequently gets an unequal share of the blame and is described with such statements as "He's out of touch," "She's lost control of the unit," or "He sure isn't as good as Ms. Watson in dealing with problems like this."

- In collective meetings at which the problem is discussed, you are frequently cautious, less than candid, and vague when discussing your ideas regarding the problem and its solution. Stated differently, you frequently try to determine what others' positions on the issues are without clearly revealing your own.

- You repeatedly find that the problem-solving actions you take, both individually and collectively, not only fail to solve the problem but also tend to make it worse.

- You frequently hold fantasized conversations with yourself on what you might have done—or should have done: "When he said . . . , I wish I had said . . ."

- You frequently look for ways to escape by taking sick leave or vacation time, traveling, or scheduling other, "more important" meetings on days when the problem is going to be discussed.

Only when someone on the team becomes aware of either or both sets of symptoms does it become possible to design a problem-solving process to break out of what is ultimately a self-defeating process.

Team Building Around the Crisis of Agreement

Because an essential cause of unhealthy agreement is that team members are afraid to own up to their basic concerns, coping with hidden disagreement in teams is especially difficult.[3] That difficulty stems from three essential dilemmas: (1) it involves risk and takes skill for an individual to own up to his or her true feelings and beliefs about an issue when other members of the team have publicly taken different or contrary positions—people want to be seen as team players; (2) it involves risk and takes skill for others to own up to their similar private feelings and beliefs because of their negative fantasies of the consequences that might occur if they reveal them in an unequivocal manner; and (3) it is very difficult to learn the individual and collective skills required, even if one is willing to accept the risks.[4]

In summary, the possibility that a team could exhibit public equanimity and private turmoil and could perform ineffectively is one compelling reason for teams to hold periodic team reviews and development sessions when symptoms of the Abilene paradox are present. Another reason is that the team might be able to do something constructive about the problem, even though the skills required for success in such a session may not be easy or comfortable to learn.

Format Possibilities for Agreement-Management Team-Building Sessions

A number of possible formats exist for taking action to solve the Abilene paradox. Generally they are gathering data, sharing theory, and taking action. Data gathering may be conducted by insiders or outside consultants.

Data Collection by a Consultant

To bring hidden unhealthy agreements to light, it may be useful to have an outside consultant interview people in the team. (An outside consultant is someone who is not a part of the blinding, collusive anxiety system that facilitates the hidden-agreement syndrome and knows the theory and practice of agreement management; he or she may be a competent professional, friend, or colleague.) Such a consultant might ask the following questions, based on the theory of agreement management:

1. *What problem does this team have that you have a hard time accepting, facing, or discussing?* The question assumes that the respondent knows the nature of the problem and can state it.

2. *What decisions have been made or actions taken recently that you have not really agreed with?* The question helps determine whether there are consistent discrepancies between private beliefs and public actions, a key symptom of an agreement-management dilemma.

3. *What actions or decisions do you feel would produce the best results for the team over the long term?* The question assumes that the respondent knows an effective solution to the problem.

4. *What will happen if you don't discuss your concerns, feelings, beliefs, and suggestions with all members of the team who are involved with the problem? What will happen if you do?* The questions assume that fantasized consequences will either help or hinder the individual's making a decision to discuss the issue with others in such a way that the problem might be solved.

Having gathered the data through interviews, the outside consultant then presents a summary of team members' responses to the team in a group problem-solving session, designed and "contracted" for, essentially, in the manner described by Dick Beckhard, Warner Burke, and Ed Schein.[5]

Data Collection by Members of the Team

It is also possible that within the team, people who are part of the problem could share data and, by exhibiting such behavior, encourage others to do so as well. In this case, an outside interviewer would not be needed. Again, such data are most effectively shared in a group meeting involving all people key to the problem. In such a meeting, the person who called the meeting explains his or her desire to own up and expresses a wish to know others' beliefs and feelings about the issue—for example: "I have some data I want to share with you. I'm anxious about doing it because I may find I'm the only one who sees the problem this way, and I don't like to feel alone. But here it is. I really don't think we are going to succeed on project X. It's important for me to know how others feel about it, though. I would appreciate your letting me know what you think." Despite the competence and good intentions of the person making such a statement, the fear element might still be so strong that other members of the team would be unwilling to reveal their true beliefs and feelings. It is also possible

that at least one person would own up to his or her concerns and the logjam would be broken. In the absence of such
owning statements, the probability of the problem being solved
is reduced.

Sharing the Theory and Taking Action

In addition to collecting and sharing data, another important
element of problem-solving sessions is for all members of the
team to know the theory of agreement management. To accomplish the goal of communicating theory, the story of the Abilene
paradox could be a reading assignment for each team member,
or the team could watch a half-hour video, *The Abilene Paradox*.[6]
Each person could then discuss whether he or she had ever
experienced or observed any situation in which the team was,
or might be, in danger of taking a trip to Abilene, that is,
doing something that no one really wants to do or not doing
something organization members really want to do. At the
problem-solving meeting, each person could be asked to discuss
the Abilene paradox and his or her observations of its relevance
to the team.

Because the reactions of authority figures set the parameters
for other responses in any type of confrontation meeting, it is
helpful if the team leader can begin the process and own up to
personal concerns about any trips to Abilene that he or she has
observed, participated in, led, or may foresee leading. Once the
team has discussed the theory of unhealthy agreements and has
shared information about any potential agreements that they
may be incorrectly treating as conflicts, it is important to come
to valid public agreement about the nature of the true conditions, make action plans based on the reality of such truths,
and then take steps to reduce the probability of future trips to
Abilene.

In Summary

Unhealthy agreement can put a team on the road to Abilene—a place where no team member wants to go. In this chapter we have described some of the symptoms of this condition (e.g., team members blaming each other for the team's failures or team members' feeling powerless) and have outlined how team building can be used to overcome this crisis of agreement. To the extent that the team leader and team members are aware of the Abilene paradox and its negative consequences, they are more likely to diagnose the problem and take corrective action to avoid an unhappy detour to Abilene.

9

REDUCING CONFLICT
BETWEEN TEAMS

Thus far we have focused on designs and methods for increasing team effectiveness within a work unit. But often a major organizational problem is the lack of teamwork between work units. In fact, teams that become too cohesive and too self-involved may be ineffective in their working relationships with other groups with which they must coordinate.

Because of the importance of dividing labor into various organizational units to promote efficiency, such units are, and should be, different from each other.[1] Thus, context, the first of the Four Cs of team performance, often drives conflict between teams since such teams often have differing tasks, goals, reward systems, time constraints, and structures. These differences related to the organization's context naturally cause these teams to function differently. The key issue for organizational and team leaders is how to develop processes and a culture that encourage these different work units to work together effectively. One strategy for bringing greater integration between work units is an interteam development program.[2]

In this chapter, we explore the causes of interteam conflict and discuss various team-building options that have been used successfully to reduce conflict and promote cooperation between teams.

Diagnosing the Problem

An interteam development program may be appropriate when two or more teams that must collaborate for each to achieve its own objectives experience one or more of the following conditions:

- The mutual product or end result that both teams are working toward is delayed, diminished, blocked, or altered, to the dissatisfaction of one or both parties.
- One team does not ask for services or information that it needs from the other team.
- One team does not satisfactorily perform services that the other team needs.
- Team members blame the other team for many of their problems and feel resentment as a result of interaction with the other team.
- Team members feel frustrated, rejected, or misunderstood by members of the other team with whom they must work.
- Team members spend more time complaining about or avoiding interaction with the other team than they spend working through mutual problems.

Designing the Solution

If one of the team's managers sees dysfunctional interteam interaction and is willing to contact the other team's manager, he or she may propose an interteam development program. It is necessary to get the agreement of both teams to conduct an interteam-building program. If the managers of the two teams agree to this process but do not get the commitment of their team members, team members are likely to put up a great deal of resistance to the program.

The goal of the team-building program is to develop a problem-solving process that will reduce the existing dysfunctional interaction and allow future problems to be solved before a breakdown in team interaction occurs. A number of design strategies can be used for planning and conducting the proposed program.

In preparation, managers (or an outside facilitator or consultant) should explain the purpose and format of the program to members of both teams. In so doing, the managers should make it clear what the team interdependencies are (see our discussion on the need for teamwork and the nature of interdependence in chapter 2) and why it is important for the teams to collaborate effectively. Members of both teams should agree to participate.

Managers should set aside a block of time to get the appropriate people from both teams to work on the interface problems. If the two teams are small, it may be possible to involve all team personnel. If teams are larger, it may be necessary to have representatives of the two teams work through the problem areas. The following designs describe some options for an interteam-building program.

Design A

1. Appropriate members from the two teams meet to work out a more functional method of operating. Members are introduced, and the plan, purpose, and schedule of the program are reviewed.

2. Ground rules are established. One essential ground rule is for people to adopt a problem-solving stance. The goal is to work out a solution, not to accuse or fix blame. Participants should agree to look at the behavior of their own group members and identify times when their own members are trying to accuse, fix blame, or defend a position rather than solve the problem.

3. Team members in their own groups answer the following questions and record their answers:

   - What actions does the other team engage in that create problems for us? List them.

   - What actions do we engage in that we think may create problems for them? List them.

   - What recommendations would we make to improve the situation? In particular, since context variables (e.g., reward systems, structures, goals) are often the cause of the problems rather than merely interpersonal differences between members of the different teams, the teams should focus on how the organization's context may be undermining teamwork between the teams and therefore make recommendations for changes in the context. Because this often requires the agreement and support of upper management, recommendations may need to be made not only to the other team but to managers who have the power to make changes in the teams' context.

4. Each team brings its written answers and gives them to the other team to review.

5. Time is allotted for each team to review the work of the other team and ask questions for clarification. Agreements and disparities in the two lists are noted.

6. Members of the two teams are now put into mixed teams composed of an equal number of members from both teams. Each mixed team reviews the lists and comes up with a list of the major problems or obstacles that they think keep the two teams from functioning together effectively. Each mixed team presents its list of problems to the whole group, and the results are tabulated. The whole group then identifies and lists what they think are the major problems.

7. Members return to the mixed teams, which are asked to work out a recommended solution to one of the problems identified. Their recommendation should include what the problem is, what actions should be taken, who should be responsible for what actions, what the time schedule should be, and how to keep the problem from reoccurring.

8. Mixed teams bring their solutions back to the whole group for review and to seek agreement, particularly from those who must implement the actions. At this stage senior managers may need to be brought into the discussion to get their input and support if they are needed to help implement any solution.

The next design is similar to design A, but is a fishbowl design. Instead of the two teams doing their work alone and then presenting to each other, each team discusses the problems in front of the other group.

Design B

1. Group X sits together in a circle. Group Y sits outside and observes and listens. Group X members discuss the three questions listed in item 3 of design A. A recorder writes down the points of discussion.

2. Group Y now moves into the center circle and repeats the process while group X observes and listens.

3. Following the fishbowl discussions, mixed teams are formed, and they perform the same tasks as in design A.

A variation on designs A and B is to have the teams discuss different questions from those in design A. The designs for interaction are the same, but the questions are different.

Design C

1. How do we see the other team? What is our image of them?

2. How do we think the other team sees us? What is their image of us?

3. Why do we see them the way we do? The teams might review the Four Cs, which often determine how one group sees another.

4. Why do we think they see us as we think they do?

5. What would a more positive relationship between our two teams look like? How might we interact with, help, and support one another in the future to achieve our mutual goals?

6. What would have to change so we would have a more positive image and interaction with each other?

With this design, the teams should follow the principles of appreciative inquiry outlined in chapter 6. Members of both teams should be asked to envision what a positive working relationship would look like in the future between the two teams. As the teams describe this new, more positive working relationship and the benefits that would come out of it, both teams can begin to commit themselves to new ways of interacting with one another and develop plans for change.

Another approach involves the following steps.

Design D

1. An outside facilitator interviews members of both teams privately prior to the team development session. He or she tries to identify the problems between the teams, the source of the problems, and potential solutions proposed by team members.

2. The facilitator summarizes the results of these interviews at the interteam meeting. The summaries are printed or posted for all to see.

3. Mixed teams from both teams review the summary findings and list the major areas they believe need to be resolved. Major ideas are agreed on by the whole group.

4. Mixed teams devise recommended solutions to the problems assigned to them.

The final design involves selecting a task force composed of members from both teams. The job of the task force is to review the interface problems between the teams and then recommend solutions to the problems for both groups to consider and agree on.

Design E

1. Representatives of the task force are selected in the following manner: team X lists all of its members the group feels could adequately represent them on the task force and gives this list to team Y. Team Y then selects three or four members from team X. Both teams engage in this listing and selecting process. The result is a mixed task force composed of members agreeable to both teams.

2. The task force may wish to interview people from the other teams or invite a facilitator to work with it. Whatever the working style, the task force is asked to come up with the major conditions blocking interteam effectiveness, what actions should be taken, who should be responsible for what actions, a time frame, how these problems can be prevented from occurring again, and what method will be used for solving other problems that may arise.

Choosing an Appropriate Model

Given the variety of interteam-building models available, what determines which model would be most appropriate? One factor to consider is the confidence and competence of the team managers to conduct the program alone, without the help of an outside facilitator. If they choose to conduct the session alone, it would be wise to select an alternative that is simple, is easy to communicate to others, and has minimal chance for slippage in implementation. Design E (selection of an interteam task force) is the most traditional way to work on interteam problems and is probably the easiest alternative to implement without help. It is also the design with the least involvement of all the members of the two groups and may have the least impact, at least initially.

Design A probably is the most straightforward problem-solving format, with the least possibility of bringing conflicts and issues to the surface that could erupt into an unproductive rehash of old grievances. The fishbowl design may create reactions to individuals by the observers that may be difficult to handle without a trained facilitator. Similarly, approaching the issue through an examination of mutual images (design C) may also give rise to feelings and reactions that may be disruptive to one not used to handling such concerns. However, in design C, the manager might also elect to skip over the first four questions directed at exploring the images the teams hold of each other and focus only on positive images for change (questions 5 and 6).

Follow-Up

What happens if the two teams have new or recurring problems in the future? There needs to be some method for dealing with new concerns as they arise. It is possible to go through one of the five designs again. It is also possible to establish a review board made up of members of both groups that reviews progress and takes any necessary corrective action. This may take the form of a weekly or monthly meeting to track progress. To maintain the momentum for change, these follow-up interteam meetings are just as important as the personal management interviews and follow-up team meetings that we discussed in chapter 6.

Case Studies of Interteam Conflict Resolution

To illustrate how to use the various approaches to manage interteam conflict, we present two cases: ElectriGov and ExactCorp (all names are disguised). Although each case concerns interteam conflict, the methods used to manage the conflicts differ rather significantly.

Case One: ElectriGov

ElectriGov is a government agency whose mission is to supply electric power to various locations in the United States. To accomplish this task, the organization has three line crews of five to ten men whose job it is to install high-voltage power lines. Each crew is highly cohesive, led by a foreman. Moreover, crew members have worked together for many years and have an established pattern for doing their work and solving problems. The work is hard, dirty, and dangerous. Almost all of the men have had a friend who has been seriously injured or killed while on the job.

The crews typically work independently, but when there are large projects to complete, they must work together. This can create serious conflicts, since the crews often don't agree with each other's approaches to organizing and managing a particular job, and none of the three foremen wants to be subservient to the others. Thus when line crews do large projects together, they tend to compete with one another rather than cooperate. On one project, the conflict became so nasty that one crew failed to inform another crew that the wires were hot at a certain section of the project. This serious safety breach was reported to senior management, who immediately launched an investigation. We, as consultants, were initially asked to serve as part of the team investigating the causes of the safety violations.

After the initial investigation, we were asked by ElectriGov's senior management to "clean up the conflicts" between the crews. The approach we used to help the crews reduce their conflicts was a variation on design A. All three crews were brought together in one room, and the need for an interteam development program was discussed. Each crew was asked to commit to solving the conflicts between themselves and the other crews and to agree to give the program a chance. Once we had their agreement, each crew was then asked to meet separately to list their perceptions of the other crews and the specific problems that they had in working with the others. After meeting separately, the teams came back together and each reported its perceptions of the other crews.

In our consulting role, we facilitated the discussion, making sure that each crew's perceptions were made clear and that each crew described the problematic behaviors of the other crews in concrete, specific terms. As a ground rule, crews were asked to be descriptive and to avoid using emotionally laden language when critiquing the other crews. After each crew presented its perceptions, the other crews could ask questions to clarify points, but the crews were not allowed to debate the validity of the other crews' perceptions.

After each crew aired its views, the crews, together in an open session, were then asked to come up with recommendations to improve the relationships. Their suggestions were listed on large poster boards in the room. The crews discussed how they might do more advanced planning on the larger projects to determine who would do what and who would be in charge of the project. They also considered rotating crew members to improve relationships between crews. Most important, the crews agreed on a common goal: avoiding accidents at all cost.

At the end of this interteam-building session, each crew made a public commitment to change its behavior and implement the recommendations. As a result of this intervention, the crews now have a new approach to working with each other on large projects that minimizes the conflicts that they had in the past.

Case Two: ExactCorp

ExactCorp is a large retail organization with sales of over $1 billion per year. The company has grown rapidly since its inception and is operating in over thirty countries around the world. ExactCorp has been highly successful, largely due to its aggressive sales force, which is paid almost entirely on commission. Salespersons are encouraged to "always serve the customer" and think of unique ways to encourage sales. Salespersons believe they have wide latitude in offering incentives and discounts to customers in order to meet their sales targets.

ExactCorp's marketing department sets out the overall marketing strategy for the company. It also provides the product information, marketing materials, and promotional campaigns designed to help the company increase its worldwide sales. In other words, the marketing department provides the "ammunition" for the sales force to achieve its goals.

One day we received a call from the director of ExactCorp's U.S. sales force, Paul Jones, who expressed some frustration with the relationship between his sales force and the marketing department. Recently he had been reprimanded by a senior manager because his sales force was not "following the guidelines" for product promotions and incentives that Phil Snyder, senior director of marketing, had outlined. Paul had called Phil to express his concern that marketing was being "inflexible" and undermining his sales efforts. Phil responded that his role was to be a watchdog for the company and that sales was often "giving away the store." Phil believed the problem lay with Paul's department, not with his.

As Paul described his problem to us, it became clear that some type of interteam intervention would be helpful. In this situation, Paul's sales force was composed of over thirty salespeople, and Phil had over forty people in the marketing department. Thus, an intervention that included all the sales and marketing employees would not likely be workable. Initially we decided to meet with Paul, Phil, and Phil's assistant to see how we might get marketing and sales to work more effectively together.

Included in this initial meeting was also a senior vice president who was interested in having the two departments work more effectively together. It was the vice president who contacted Paul and Phil and got them to agree to work on improving their relationship. Although we served in a facilitator role in the meeting, the vice president was clearly in charge. This was a management problem, and our role was to facilitate the process, not to solve the problem for them.

In the initial meeting, which lasted about an hour, both Paul and Phil outlined their positions. Neither would budge. As we listened to them, it became clear that what was needed was a clear set of goals that both could agree to and then a process to achieve those goals. At the end of this initial meeting we decided to use design E: set up a task force with members of both departments to clarify the problems and make plans to solve them. The task force members would include Paul, Phil, and four people from each department. In addition, we agreed to serve on the task force as consultants, and the senior vice president also decided to be a member of the task force, at least for the first few meetings.

In the initial task force meeting, team members took a few minutes to describe themselves and their backgrounds. This was the first time that many of them had even met someone from the other department. The next agenda item was to determine the mission and purpose of the task force. Immediately the task force identified three objectives: improve communication and coordination between marketing and sales, develop programs jointly to increase sales, and develop metrics to measure their progress.

Moreover, the task force agreed to have two representatives from marketing attend the weekly sales meeting to give input to the sales force regarding their plans and to solve any conflicts between the departments. The task force agreed to meet monthly for several months to work on their three objectives.

Initial results have been very positive: both marketing and sales are working together more effectively to increase sales, and sales incentives are being coordinated more effectively than in the past.

In Summary

Interteam problems raise questions about the definition of *team*. In organizations today, it is not enough to build intense loyalty into the work team or department, particularly at the expense of the larger organization. People in different departments must collaborate, see the larger picture, and understand that the team must contribute to the whole, in order to avoid unhealthy interteam conflicts. Team-building sessions between teams can be conducted before serious problems occur to cement relationships and establish working guidelines. We have found that it is important to get work teams together and iron out difficulties using one or more of the designs described in this chapter to help managers and their organizations achieve their goals.

10

LEADING INNOVATIVE TEAMS

We now turn to a key question for all managers or team leaders: Do you have what it takes to create an innovative team? Most managers spend little time thinking about this question because they're too busy playing to their strengths and focusing full attention on execution: delivering results through the current strategy, business model, processes, and product mix. In the short run, this may work, but in the long run, it will not differentiate you or your company. An organization's most valued leaders are those who lead innovative teams—teams that generate and implement valuable new product, process, and strategy ideas.

So what are the characteristics of leaders—and teams—who excel at innovating? Research by Jeff Dyer, Hal Gregersen, and Clayton Christensen, some of it published in *The Innovator's DNA*, suggests that innovative teams typically have these qualities:[1]

- A leader with strong innovation skills who leads by example (contributes directly to innovation) and creates a safe space for others to shine instead of dominating them
- Team members who possess a complementary mix of innovation and execution skills, as well as complementary expertise in multiple functions and knowledge domains
- Team processes that explicitly encourage, support, and even require team members to engage in questioning, observing, networking, experimenting, and associational thinking as

they hunt for creative solutions to problems (these are the skills of innovators as identified by the research)

When a team has all of these qualities, it has the capacity to become an innovation lighthouse for an organization. To realize this role, though, requires a leader fully capable of leading an innovative team.

Who Are You as a Leader?

As a first step to leading an innovative team, team leaders (usually the manager, although some teams are led not by a formal manager but by a designated team leader for a particular project) must take a look at those who report to them (if you are a manager), their peers, and their manager. The leader might ask questions of the team like these: How would they describe me as a leader? Would they describe me as innovative? How creative do they feel in my presence? Do I build a team culture that lets others' innovation lights glow, or do I snuff them out? Answering these questions requires that you look hard at yourself and ask another question: Where do I typically spend my time at work?

When we ask executives this final question, we suggest that they divide their core tasks into two categories: discovery activities and execution activities. Discovery focuses on innovation and includes spending time actively engaged in questioning, observing, networking, and experimenting in search of innovative ideas to change or improve products, services, or processes. Execution is all about delivering results, analyzing, planning, executing, and implementing strategies.

Team leaders need to look at their calendars for a typical workweek and ask: "What percentage of my time do I personally spend on discovery versus execution activities? Is innovation a priority for me and my team?" Table 10.1 will help them

Table 10.1 How Do You Spend Your Time at Work?

Leadership Task	Today	Tomorrow	Gap
Discovery			
Execution			
Total	100%	100%	

figure this out. Leaders should make their best guess about what percentage of time they currently spend on discovery and innovation and put this in the "Today" column. Then they should record their best judgment about where they think they should spend their time (the "Tomorrow" column), given the team's purpose and the company's strategy. Third, they should calculate the difference between "Today" and "Tomorrow" for each category, and add that to the "Gap" column.

Now they should focus on the gap calculated for discovery time. Is it negative, positive, or neutral? If the gap is zero, they're spending the time and energy that they think they should on discovery. However, if they calculated a negative gap, this reflects a need to spend more time on discovery activities to improve their ability to become a discovery-driven leader. According to some of our research, CEO founders of innovative companies spent roughly 33 percent of their typical week on discovery activities as compared with about 15 percent for a typical CEO. So leaders who aren't spending a large percentage of their time on discovery probably aren't leading a very innovative team.

Develop Your Discovery Skills

After reflecting on where the leader typically spends his or her time (discovery versus execution, in particular), it's time to get a more refined, specific sense of the leader's innovation skills. Dyer, Gregersen, and Christensen's long-term research project on business innovators suggests that particular skills separate business innovators like Jeff Bezos (Amazon.com), the late Steve Jobs, and Marc Benioff of Salesforce.com from ordinary managers. They refer to these as the five skills of disruptive innovators and describe them as follows:

1. *Questioning* allows innovators to challenge the status quo and consider new possibilities.

2. *Observing* helps innovators detect small details in the activities of customers, suppliers, and other companies that suggest new ways of doing things.

3. *Networking* permits innovators to gain radically different perspectives by talking to individuals with diverse backgrounds.

4. *Experimenting* prompts innovators to try out new experiences, take things apart, and test new ideas through pilots and prototypes.

5. *Associational thinking* is a cognitive skill of finding connections among questions, problems, or ideas from unrelated fields. It is triggered by new information brought in through questioning, observing, networking, and experimenting and is the catalyst for creative ideas.[2]

Team leaders should ask themselves, To what extent do I question the status quo, engage in observations of customers or companies for new insights, network far and wide with diverse people to spark new ideas and get different perspectives, and experiment by learning new skills, taking apart products or processes, or launching a pilot or creating a prototype? If leaders find that they aren't engaged in these behaviors frequently, they probably aren't triggering lots of new creative ideas for the problems that face their teams.

After assessing the leader's strengths and weaknesses on these discovery skills, the next step is to find a specific, current innovation challenge or opportunity so that the leader can practice these skills with the team. This challenge might be creating a new product or service, reducing employee turnover, or coming up with new processes that reduce costs by 5 percent in the business unit. With this innovation challenge clearly in mind, the leader and the team together develop a plan to practice some of the discovery skills as the team searches for creative solutions.

We propose working on questioning skills first, since innovation often starts with a compelling question and innovative teams have a culture that supports questioning. The leader, perhaps with the team, should write down at least twenty-five questions about the team's innovation challenge. This will help them identify the key questions that need to be addressed in the search for a creative solution. It will also help create a safe space for others on the team to ask questions. The team should identify the top three to five questions that need to be answered in order to come up with a creative solution to its challenge.

After setting out the key questions to answer, identify some ways that the team could generate ideas that might be relevant to its innovation challenge. For example, identify some observations the team could do—of customers, end users within the company or other companies—that might provide useful insights. Identify some individuals the team should talk to about its innovation challenge to get their perspective. Finally, have the team run an experiment (e.g., create a prototype) to answer some of those key questions. Try to devise some experiments that might answer "what if" questions about the team's innovation challenge. The team leader (or team consultant) should involve the team as much as possible in observing, networking, or experimenting as it searches for a solution to its challenge. Finally, the team leader, both with and without the team, should engage in frequent brainstorming sessions to practice associational thinking—with the hope of producing an innovative solution.

The team and team leader should then repeat the process again and again and again. Improving discovery skills requires building new habits, which takes time, practice, and self-discipline. So start with realistic expectations and allocate time to improving team discovery skills. This sends an important signal to the team about the importance of innovation. Innovative leaders are often very conscious that they set the example by modeling behavior for others. A. G. Lafley, former chairman and CEO of Procter & Gamble, recognized the need to be an innovative leader. "Lafley always gets out in market places and wants consumer interactions," says Gil Cloyd, a member of his top management team and former chief technology officer. "He's genuinely curious about it. This becomes important because it's not just role modeling of something you'd like, but it's an infectious curiosity to discover how we can provide an ever more delightful experience for our consumers, improving lives in yet another way."

By simply watching Lafley's everyday actions and noticing how much time he personally spent generating new ideas, his team (and organization) "got it" about innovation. Lafley also showed that innovation is not an individual game but a powerful team effort. "You remember the times when nobody knew what to do and you came through with something that people didn't think you could come through with or when you create something that people didn't think could be created," he observed. "When this happens in our company, it's never one person. It's always a group . . . Getting everybody in the same boat, rolling in the same direction, that is really what's fun. Especially when you win."

Create a Safe Space for Others to Innovate

Having the team leader know his or her own personal skill set and leading by example lays the foundation for what is arguably the most difficult part of leading innovative teams:

creating a safe, encouraging space for others to innovate. Researchers call this creating "psychological safety," a condition where team members are willing to express opinions, acknowledge mistakes, and have confidence that they can engage in risky, learning-related behaviors without punishment.[3] Leaders of innovative teams possess a rare talent: they establish a sense of psychological safety so that people feel empowered to produce insights with impact. "If you foster an environment where people's ideas can be heard," says AZUL and JetBlue founder David Neeleman, "things naturally come up." When people feel safe enough to generate and share new ideas, they also feel compelled enough to translate those ideas into action.

Leaders who create a safe space for others to innovate begin by inspiring team members to show the courage to innovate by asking for game-changing ideas. Just ask! Asking people to be creative legitimizes the generation of original—even wild and crazy—ideas. We've seen this firsthand when watching graduate student teams come up with solutions to a business problem facing a company. In most cases, the only way to cultivate more innovative solutions is to give the assignment and say: "Be creative in your solution. I'm looking for something innovative." We get far more innovative solutions when we ask for them than when we don't.

Second, creating a team culture that encourages questions can make a big difference in establishing psychological safety. At Southwest Airlines, Herb Kelleher created an innovation safe space by soliciting challenging questions from direct reports and others. "I just watch, I listen," he says. "And I want them to ask me tough questions." Another senior executive who successfully led innovative teams worked to create a culture to encourage "everybody to ask why" from the top down. He's found it easier sometimes to elicit such questions from young people because "veterans stop using their minds; they've moved into this execution mode and they stop asking questions." So he strives to encourage both newcomers and seasoned employees to ask tough questions.

Third, encouraging and supporting team members to engage not only in questioning but also in observing, networking, and experimenting activities helps establish psychological safety. This means not only giving team members time to engage in those activities but applauding what they learn by doing so. Building psychological safety happens interaction by interaction, moment by moment, one-on-one as well as with the entire team. Leaders should ask themselves honestly whether they applaud and support others' innovative behaviors or whether they shut down their innovative actions through disinterest, lack of support (not giving them time to think about doing things in a new way), or even criticism ("Why did you spend your time doing *that?*"). Research shows that out of sixty new product ideas that are generated, only about one or two of them will eventually get to market. Because failure is a common experience of teams that are trying to innovate, the leader must continually encourage, challenge, and support those who try new ideas, even when they are not successful. Of course, the leader needs to help team members understand when the failure is a "smart failure"—the team did the best it could under the circumstances and learned a lot from the experience—versus "dumb failures" where team members failed to do their homework or properly collaborate.

Unfortunately, many leaders think they create an environment that encourages others to engage their discovery skills, but in reality coworkers don't see it that way. On average, according to the research by Dyer, Gregersen, and Christsensen, team leaders thought they were significantly better at encouraging discovery activities than their managers, peers, or direct reports did. (See figure 10.1.)

These data suggest that most leaders show room for improvement in creating a more supportive innovation space. The findings are similar to research that shows that over 90 percent

Figure 10.1 Leading Innovation:
Perceptions of Leaders Versus Others

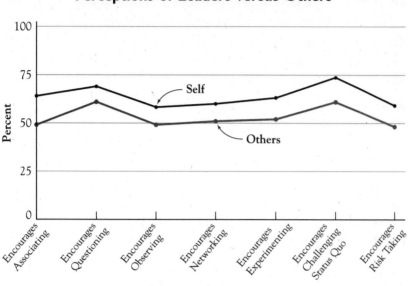

of males in the United States think they are in the top 50 percent in athletic ability. We often judge ourselves as doing better than we really are.

Occasionally we run across managers who personally excel at being innovative but can't lead an innovative team. At the core, the problem is that they don't value others' innovative skills and outputs as much as they do their own. These managers like to see their own innovative ideas come to fruition more than they like to see others' ideas get traction and succeed. This challenge for leaders is not uncommon. In fact, Dan Ariely's research in *The Upside of Irrationality* shows a simple cognitive bias that we all have.[4] Ideas that are "not invented here" are always suspect because people tend to discount or ignore evidence from sources they don't know or trust. This is especially true if the idea contradicts an existing belief or something they already favor. This creates a real leadership challenge that requires biting our tongues and genuinely trying to welcome new ideas from new quarters.

In our work with executives around the world, we often ask large groups, "Do you get as excited about others' ideas and achievements as you do about your own?" More often than not, about half of the hands go up in the room. Then we ask a tougher version of the question: "Do you get more excited about others' ideas and achievements than you do about your own?" Far fewer hands go up in answer to this question. Yet enthusiasm for others' ideas remains a fundamental condition for our teams to feel safe in our presence. "One of the best things we can do for creative men and women," said John Gardner, one of the most influential leadership thinkers of the twentieth century, "is to stand out of their light." Leaders of innovative teams not only value others' ideas as much as their own, but they work to create a safe, trusted environment where others' ideas flourish.

Build a Team with Complementary Skills and Expertise

Innovative teams work best when their members have complementary skills in two areas. First, the team needs complementary innovation and execution skills to generate novel ideas as well as implement them. Second, it helps immeasurably if team membership reflects a complementary set of functional skills—that is, different types of expertise. Innovation design firm IDEO's substantial experience designing innovative teams recommends the importance of complementary expertise among members in understanding human factors (the desirability of an innovative idea), technical factors (the technical feasibility of an innovative idea), and business factors (the business viability and profitability of an innovative idea).

Complementary Innovation and Execution Skills

Effective leaders of innovative teams not only understand their personal strengths and weaknesses with regard to innovation and execution, but they also strategically balance their own weaknesses with other people's strengths. For example, during the highly successful run at Dell Computer from 1990 to 2005, Michael Dell engaged in a frequent tug of war between discovery and delivery with Kevin Rollins, president of the company at that time. Dell recalled:

> Kevin gave me a toy bulldozer driven by a little girl with a huge smile on her face. Sometimes I'll get really excited about an idea and I'll just start driving it. Kevin put the bulldozer on my desk, and it's a signal to me to say, "Wait a second, I need to push it a little more and think through it for some others and kind of slow down on this great idea that I'm working on." I gave Kevin a Curious George stuffed animal. The Curious George is for Kevin to ask questions, to be a little more inquisitive. We don't use them that much, but they're subtle little jokes between us.

Similarly, Pierre Omidyar, cofounder of eBay, was aware that he was strong at discovery but weak at execution. Identifying this need for stronger execution skills on his team, he invited Jeff Skoll, a Stanford MBA, to join him. "Jeff Skoll and I had very complementary skills," Omidyar told us. "I'd say I did more of the creative work developing the product and solving problems around the product while Jeff was involved in the more analytical and practical side of things. He was the one who would listen to an idea of mine and then say, 'Okay, let's figure out how to get this done.'" Omidyar grasped the power of complementary skills when building a top management team at eBay.

The message from these stories is that teams that innovate successfully need both the ability to generate novel ideas and execute on those ideas. Smart leaders know this and consciously think about team composition, making sure the team is balanced enough in terms of discovery and delivery skills. Figure 10.2 shows discovery and delivery skills temporarily in balance on a team. But sometimes discovery skills should weigh more heavily

Figure 10.2 Balancing Innovation and Execution Skills in a Team or Company

The Balancing Act

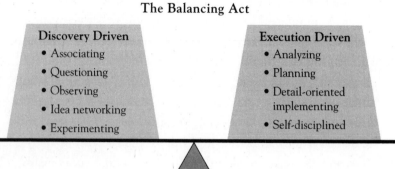

Discovery Driven
- Associating
- Questioning
- Observing
- Idea networking
- Experimenting

Execution Driven
- Analyzing
- Planning
- Detail-oriented implementing
- Self-disciplined

on a team or throughout an organization, particularly during the founding stage of an organization or if the team is charged with product development or other business development tasks. At other times, delivery skills are relatively more important and should be given greater weight on the team, typically during the growth or mature stage of a business or in functional areas related to operations and finance. The key is knowing who has what skills and then figuring out how to combine those complementary strengths within a team to generate great ideas that have positive impact.

Complementary Human, Technical, and Business Expertise

Making sure that innovative teams possess complementary innovation and execution skills matters, but we learned that making teams multidisciplinary—with individuals who have deep expertise in different disciplines—matters even more when it comes to innovation. To illustrate this idea, consider how IDEO, the hottest innovation design firm in the world (it has won twice as many Industrial Design Excellence Awards as any other firm) staffs innovation design teams.

In general, IDEO tries to create multidisciplinary teams with individuals who are "T" shaped in terms of expertise: deep in at least one area of expertise with shallow expertise in multiple knowledge domains. The deep area of expertise often falls in one of three domains that they call "human factors," "technical factors," or "business factors." First, they like to have a human factors expert on a product or service design team—someone with a background in one of the behavioral sciences like cognitive psychology or anthropology. This person's role is to provide insight into the desirability of a new product or service from the user's perspective. The human factors person orchestrates in-depth observations of customers to understand customers' latent needs and wants and to acquire deep user empathy. For example, when designing a product or service for people in wheelchairs, the human factors person might make sure that folks on the team spend a day a week in a wheelchair, experiencing the world as someone confined to a wheelchair. By gaining insight and empathy into the user experience, the human factors person brings insight into the desirability of an innovative new design. This perspective is particularly important in early stages of designing a new product or service.

The technical factors person brings deep expertise in various technologies that the team might employ in the design of a new product or service. This person likely has an engineering or science background. This expertise is important for the team to understand what technologies are feasible for use in a particular new product or service design. Technical expertise is particularly critical after the user's needs have been clearly identified (the "job to be done") and the team is searching for and deciding which technologies might provide the optimal solution.

Finally, the business factors person brings the business expertise necessary to figure out whether an innovative new product or service design will prove viable in the market. This person likely has a business background, such as a master's degree in business administration with expertise in operations, marketing, or finance. Naturally this expertise becomes critical in the later stages of the innovation process, when a team must figure out the optimal way to manufacture, distribute, promote, and price the product for profitability.

Effective innovation teams at IDEO possess the necessary complementary expertise to figure out how to create a product or service that is desirable, feasible, and viable. This requires multifunctional expertise within the innovation team. Most organizations attack problems within functional silos, which means those on the team bring limited perspectives to the problem. Teams are much more likely to generate innovative solutions to problems when those on the team are diverse in background, expertise, and perspective.

Use Team Processes That Encourage Innovation

The final piece of the team innovation puzzle is having team processes that encourage—even require—team members to question, observe, network, and experiment in search of new ideas. *The Innovator's DNA* research on successful innovators shows that they engage in those four behaviors much more than noninnovators do.[5] Not surprisingly, the same is true for innovative teams. Beyond diverse team composition, IDEO founder David Kelley attributes IDEO's success at innovating to its team processes. "We're experts on the process of how you design stuff," he says. "We don't care if you give us a toothbrush, a tractor, a space shuttle, a chair; we want to figure out how to innovate by applying our process."[6]

So what team processes does IDEO rely on to innovate? Not surprisingly, IDEO teams start with a questioning process, move to observing and networking processes to gather data about their initial questions, and conclude with an experimenting process where innovative ideas emerge and evolve through rapid prototyping. These processes stood out in the now famous *Dateline TV* episode that shows an IDEO team that is redesigning a shopping cart.[7] Today IDEO takes the same approach in its quest for more innovative products and services with a variety of clients. For example, these processes formed the core of IDEO's recent work with Zyliss, a maker of kitchen products, to completely redesign its kitchen gadget line, from cheese graters, to pizza cutters, to mandoline slicers.

Process 1: Questioning

The IDEO project team begins its quest for an innovative cheese grater (or anything else) by asking a series of diverse questions to better understand the problems associated with using traditional cheese graters. What are the problems with cheese graters? What don't people like about those on the market now? How important is safety? What other things do people want to grate with a cheese grater? Who are the "extreme users" of cheese graters (highly skilled and highly unskilled users), and how do their needs differ? As far as kitchen gadgets go, extreme users are cooks and chefs (those using kitchen gadgets for hours each day), as well as those who are first-time or rare users of kitchen gadgets, such as college students, children, or the elderly.

This initial process has been referred to by Dyer, Gregersen, and Christensen in *The Innovator's DNA* as QuestionStorming, a method to ensure that teams ask questions about a problem before jumping in to offer solutions.[8] Those at IDEO start a project by asking lots of questions to better understand what to look for as they move to the data-gathering phase of observing and networking. They then put these questions on small sticky notes so they can easily rearrange and prioritize them. As Matt Adams of IDEO told us, "By having the right questions, it becomes clearer how you might go about answering those questions." Then IDEO teams have a much better sense of what to ask, how to ask it, and what kinds of people to ask as they move to the next processes: observing and then networking.

Process 2: Observing

In this phase, the IDEO design team goes out into the field where they observe and document the customer experience firsthand. "Our process is to go in and try to really understand the people that you are designing for," says Kelley. "We try and look for a latent customer need, a need that's not been seen before or expressed in some way." So the Zyliss team spent hours and hours observing various product users, particularly extreme users, in Germany, France, and the United States, trying to intuit what they were thinking and feeling. They took photos and videos of customers using kitchen gadgets to document what they had noticed.

Through observations, the team captured many problems with using traditional kitchen gadgets. For example, they saw that traditional cheese graters easily clogged, were hard to clean, and often required considerable dexterity to be used safely. They noticed that the mandoline slicer, well beloved by advanced cooks, presented severe safety hazards due to extremely sharp blades that were often exposed.

During these observations, they look for ways to optimize ergonomics (ease of use), cleanability, and functionality. For example, to optimize ergonomics, they carefully observed hand and arm movements so they could make subtle adjustments in handle shape or tool angle for tremendous ergonomic benefit.

Process 3: Networking

As IDEO team members observe, they also talk to as many product users as they can about the kitchen gadgets they are using. In particular, they visit with users while they are using the gadget because this is when users are most likely to offer ideas or insights about things they like and hate about it. They especially like to talk to "experts" (such as chefs and home cooks) because they are the most demanding and difficult-to-please users who often have great suggestions for product improvements.

Through these unscripted conversations, IDEO team members gain critical insights into designing novel kitchen gadgets. They're trying to develop deep empathy to the point that they can champion a particular user, such as a chef. They come to understand what she loves, what her challenges are, and what's important so they can share that person's story later with other team members. Peter, a project leader at IDEO, says that during the observing and networking phases, IDEO teams "go out to the four corners of the earth and come back with the golden keys of innovation."[9] Those keys, observation and idea networking, help unlock the doors to innovative ideas.

Process 4: Brainstorming Solutions and Associating: The Deep Dive

The next phase is to bring all of the insights acquired through observation and interviews back to a brainstorming session that IDEO calls a "deep dive." During the deep dive, everyone openly shares all of the knowledge acquired during the data collection phase (they call this "downloading"). It's basically a storytelling session with lots of details about individual lives where they capture insights, observations, quotes, and details and share photos, videos, and notes.

The team leader facilitates the discussion but there are no real titles or hierarchy at IDEO because status comes from presenting the best ideas and everyone gets an equal opportunity to talk. After the ideas are shared, the team starts to brainstorm design solutions to the problems they've observed. To support associational thinking during the brainstorming phase, IDEO maintains a "tech box" at every office (full of a range of unrelated things, from model rockets to a Slinky). Many items are often spread in view of the team to stimulate creative thinking as they brainstorm innovative product designs.

Five Traps for Teams When Brainstorming

All teams, and especially diverse teams, face numerous challenges on the road to innovation success. Here are the most common traps that we have observed and tips for avoiding them.

Trap 1: The fewer-ideas-generated problem. On average, a team of people generates far fewer ideas than individuals doing the same thing on their own. A primary reason is that people in a group simply have less time to share ideas because they have to wait for everyone else to share their ideas. The net result is that everyone has less time to share ideas when they have to wait for others before sharing. One approach is to have people generate ideas on their own first and then quickly share them with the team, which then decides which ideas warrant team discussion and brainstorming.

Trap 2: The "first-idea-in-line" problem. In teams, it's easier to fixate on a particular topic or idea than when we're working as individuals. Of course, the value of the team is the ability to consider an idea from multiple angles and build on others' ideas. However, in some cases, the first ideas offered get undue attention. Quantity matters in getting great ideas, but quantity all centered on the same topic is not likely to generate great ideas. For a host of reasons, fixation on early ideas offered happens unless the team leader or facilitator keeps the team generating new and different ideas.

Trap 3: Failure-to-listen problem. Another reason for productivity loss is that everybody may end up talking rather than listening. If we're trying to remember our own ideas, we don't listen very well to others' ideas and don't build on them. This is a bigger problem on diverse teams because it may be harder to listen to, and understand, the perspective of someone who is different from us. One way to address this problem is to have people brainstorm and write down ideas on their own before bringing them together as a group. This will help everyone feel comfortable that their ideas at some point will be seen by the group and will increase the quantity of ideas for the team to work with.

Trap 4: The intimidation problem. In some cases, team members are reluctant to contribute to group discussion because they feel intimidated, either by the leader or other members of the team. This is particularly the case when discussing controversial issues where people have strongly held opinions. Moreover, in a diverse team, others are more likely to disagree with a perspective. Clearly, when people feel that they are being judged, they are reluctant to share new ideas. In these situations, building trust and psychological safety is paramount to having a productive group conversation.

Trap 5: The free-rider problem. Fewer ideas may emerge in a group due to free riders. As teams get larger and more diverse, members may feel that their perspective won't be valued, so they might as well stay quiet. One way to avoid this problem is to rotate from member to member, asking each for ideas and contributions. This makes it harder for any single person to hide and not contribute. Of course, it also helps if team members contribute to the performance reviews of others on the team.

Process 5: Prototyping (Experimenting)

The final phase is rapid prototyping when designers build working models of the best kitchen gadget ideas that emerge from the brainstorming session. Kelley argues that a prototype is critical to the innovation process: "You know the expression 'a picture is worth a thousand words.' Well if a picture is worth a thousand words, then a prototype is worth about a million words . . . Prototyping is really a way of getting the iterative nature of this design going through feedback from others. If you build a prototype, other people will help you."[10]

IDEO takes its kitchen gadget prototypes to a variety of product users—from chefs to college students to children—for feedback. For example, the new cheese grater design has a large drum to grate cheese as it rolls and can grate more cheese (or chocolate or nuts) with less cranking. An optimized, clog-resistant tooth pattern provides maximum grating with minimal resistance for older users and people with small hands. The fold-able and opposable hand crank makes for more efficient drawer storage and for easier use by both right- and left-handed users. These innovations are refined with each new prototype because they "build to think and think to build," as Matt Adams put it. Taking the prototype out for a test drive is the fastest way to get great feedback on new product ideas.

Finally, IDEO teams follow a set of guiding principles that give them the courage to innovate. Among these philosophies, which are posted in their work spaces, are "Fail often to succeed sooner," "Encourage wild ideas," and "Build on the ideas of others." "You have to have some wild ideas," claims Kelley. "And then you build on those wild ideas to build a really innovative idea."

A critical step in leading an innovative team is to ask them to be creative. By asking for creative and wild ideas, you legiti-mize this process. That way people don't have to worry about being shot down for a wild idea. IDEO's guiding principles and team processes encourage, support, and expect innovation from everyone on the team (human factors, technical factors, and business expertise combined). It is no surprise, then, that John Foster, head of talent and organization at IDEO, believes that "leadership is a group outcome," especially innovative leadership.[11]

In Summary

Mahatma Gandhi once suggested that each of us "be the change you want to see in the world." If you are the team leader or a member of the team, do others see you contributing to innovation? Or do they see you mostly admonishing others to innovate? When it comes to innovation and creating highly innovative teams, doing what innovators do gains much greater traction than talking about it.

Without question, the most effective leaders of innovative teams are good at questioning, observing, networking, and experimenting. They lead by example and can mentor and coach others because they are capable innovators. But even team leaders who aren't particularly skilled at innovating can lead an innovative team if they understand the people, processes, and philosophies on an innovative team. This requires that they select team members with complementary discovery and execution skills (as well as multidisciplinary expertise) to ensure that novel ideas can be generated and executed. It requires establishing processes that encourage and support team members in questioning, observing, networking, and experimenting. Finally, it requires establishing a culture and philosophies that create psychological safety on the team—where team members trust that they can throw out wild ideas, experiment, and take risks without retribution. Creating a climate of trust and safety is the role of the leader, and it is critical to leading innovative teams.

The authors wish to acknowledge and thank Hal Gregersen and Clayton Christensen, coauthors with Jeff Dyer of *The Innovator's DNA*, for their contributions to this chapter.

Part Three

TEAM BUILDING IN DIFFERENT TYPES OF TEAMS

11

MANAGING
THE TEMPORARY TEAM

The use of temporary teams, often called ad hoc committees, task forces, or project teams, is common in most organizations. This collection of people must come together and, in a relatively short time (usually from six weeks to a year), come up with a work plan, make decisions, develop recommendations, or take specific actions that are carefully thought through and useful. To accomplish these goals with people who already have full-time assignments elsewhere in the organization, the team must quickly coalesce and be productive almost immediately—which is not easy given that developing the appropriate team context, composition, and team competencies typically takes considerable time. How to start and manage these types of teams is the focus of this chapter.

Preliminary Conditions for Temporary Teams

Temporary teams are by definition together for a short duration, and consequently team members feel that there is little time or need for team development activities. Therefore, they often feel under pressure to dive immediately into the work at hand and are reluctant to spend the time needed to get acquainted, plan how the group will work together, develop measurable performance goals, and build some commitment to one another—in other words, become a real team.

A story of two groups, each appointed to function for about a year, highlights the importance of team formation to the group's later functioning. One group was a high school science curriculum committee asked to coordinate a unified curriculum for all the science classes in the school. The other was the Atomic Energy Committee under the direction of David Lilienthal, which was given the charge to develop guidelines for the control and use of atomic energy in the United States following the blasts over Hiroshima and Nagasaki in World War II. At the end of one year, the high school curriculum committee had nothing to show for its efforts and declared the problem too complex for a committee to solve. In contrast, the Atomic Energy Committee completed an extensive document that outlined the policies for the use of atomic energy for the nation, and this report became the basis of national policy in this area.

This example showed that the two teams differed in major ways in the attention they paid to building team competencies at the beginning of the project. The curriculum team plunged immediately into work and struggled for a year because it did not develop processes for dealing with different ideas, opinions, and recommendations and found itself riddled with conflict almost from the beginning. They had spent little time getting acquainted, discussing how to resolve disputes or disagreements, or developing a process for consensus or majority vote decision making.

The atomic energy team started differently. During the first several meetings, members spent time getting acquainted with one another and developing some guidelines for working together. This group adopted as one of its important operating principles the notion that all of its members were intelligent, committed, productive people. Therefore, if any group member said that he or she did not understand something, did not agree with something, or felt lost or confused, all members said, "We are therefore all confused or not in agreement or not fully understanding, and we must review everything again." The group did not want to have subgroups forming because of different ideas and especially did not want members to belittle someone by saying, in essence, "Why are you so stupid you can't understand? You are holding us up. Get on board and agree so we can move ahead." In other words, to achieve the goal of becoming a productive temporary team, team members need to agree that they will spend enough time preparing to work before they start the work.

An important contextual condition is to give the temporary team adequate resources and authority to get the work done. A few years ago, a major U.S. automobile company found itself behind its competitors in important design features. An analysis showed that temporary design teams made up of people from several basic functional departments (engineering, R&D, production, and so on) took as much as a year longer than competitors to come up with new designs. Further analysis also disclosed that most team members were told by their superiors in their functional departments, "Don't you make any final decisions until you come back and check with me." This meant that decisions in the design team were continually being postponed while team members checked back with functional bosses. These delays continued until the design teams were given authority to make key decisions without checking back with departments.

While having the proper amount of authority to make decisions is important, temporary teams are typically acting at the request of senior managers in the organization, and it is senior management who often has the final word when it comes to the decisions or actions that the team takes. Hence, it is important for the team to keep senior managers or anyone else who is sponsoring the team activities aware of the progress the team is making and what decisions have been or will be made.

Unfortunately, many temporary teams have been derailed because after they complete their work, senior managers complain, "We didn't know that's what you were doing. Who authorized you do to that?" Moreover, if implementation of the temporary team's decisions requires the support of other stakeholders—people, departments, or groups—outside the team, it is important to include people representing those stakeholders on the team or have a liaison to report team progress to those stakeholders so they will be supportive of the team's decisions when implementation of the team's decisions is needed. One solution to this problem is to identify what types of decisions will need to be made and then clearly specify who has the authority to sign off on those decisions (we describe in chapter 14 the strategic decision-making template process that Eli Lilly uses).

One temporary committee at a university was tasked with redesigning the college's curriculum and spent an entire semester meeting each week to come up with a new set of classes. However, the committee failed to keep the faculty (who would need to implement the changes) informed of the team's ideas and progress. When the committee presented its recommendations to the faculty for a vote, the faculty turned down the recommendations. Why? Because little had been done to make sure that the committee's actions had the support of key stakeholders, namely the faculty. After the vote, the curriculum committee was disbanded, leaving team members discouraged and feeling that the entire effort was a waste of their valuable time.

The major tasks facing the temporary team are basically the same as for more permanent teams. Team members must build relationships, establish a supportive emotional climate, and work out methods for (1) setting goals, (2) solving problems, (3) making decisions, (4) ensuring follow-through and completion of tasks, (5) establishing open lines of communication, and (6) ensuring an appropriate support system that will let people feel accepted and yet keep issues open for discussion and disagreement. One advantage the temporary team has over an established unit in a team-building situation is that it does not have to break down any barriers, bad habits, useless or harmful stereotypes or attitudes, inappropriate working relations, or procedures that have been formed and are sometimes set rigidly in the concrete of human habit. Generally the new team can start its activities by asking, "How can we set in motion the kinds of actions that will allow us to work together and get our goals accomplished and leave us feeling good about ourselves and one another?"

Design for a Temporary Team

When a temporary team is being formed, its members must first meet long enough to get acquainted and set guidelines and procedures for work. The design of a new temporary team consists of several distinct steps.

Step 1: Developing a Realistic Priority Level

Often people who are put together on a new team, frequently by assignment, have slightly different levels of priority or commitment to the work of the team. Some may see it as a highly significant assignment and worthy of a great deal of time and energy. Others may see it as important but lower on their personal priority list, and yet others may see it as low in both importance and priority. To come to grips with the priority issue, team members can do the following:

1. Using the scale shown in figure 11.1, have each person draw a vertical line that represents his or her total work requirements and priorities. Each person marks the point that represents where this team assignment ranks as a priority activity.

2. Have each person write down the amount of time he or she is willing to commit to the work of the team over a month.

3. Summarize the priority rankings (see figure 11.1) and the time commitments. Note the range of times and priorities and also the averages for the two dimensions.

Figure 11.1 Team Members' Priority Rankings

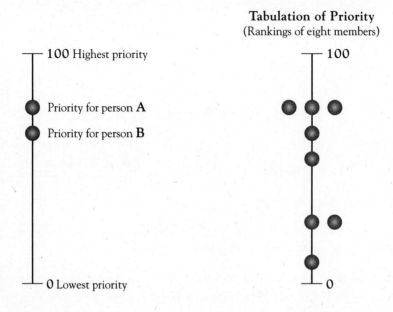

4. In the group, let each person who desires explain his or her priority and time rankings and then come to agreement as to a realistic amount of time and energy that can be expected of the team as a whole. Those with a higher priority and team commitments may be allowed to accept heavier assignments. Making this decision openly reduces the resentment some have for doing more work and the guilt of others for letting them.

Step 2: Sharing Expectations

Give the team five minutes for each person to think about and get ready to respond to the following questions:

- What worries you most or is your biggest concern about working on this team?

- How would this team function if everything went just as you hoped?
- What do you expect to be the barriers to effective team functioning? What will likely prevent the team from achieving its goals?
- What actions do you think must be taken to ensure the positive outcomes?

Each person should be given an opportunity to share reactions, and everyone should respond to each question in turn. Try to identify the major concerns people have, and list them on a whiteboard or flip chart. These concerns should become items on a planning agenda as conditions to take into consideration in order to ensure a positive outcome.

Step 3: Clarifying Goals

Having established priority and commitment levels and identified positive and negative expectations, the new team is ready to clarify its goals and objectives. The team should discuss and then write down what members agree is the team's core mission—a statement of the basic function or "reason for being" for that group, committee, or team. All plans and actions should be evaluated against the core mission. The question to ask continually is "If we continue the activities already outlined, will we accomplish our core mission?" Extending from the core mission are the subgoals and specific objectives for a given period of time.

For example, the Edgemont Company (we have disguised this case) formed a task force to review all training and development activities in the company and make recommendations for a coordinated training and development effort. The task force met and established its core mission: "The mission of this task force is to ensure that the Edgemont Company has appropriate and effective programs in management and organization development."

Subgoals were then identified. The team agreed to try to accomplish the core mission by (1) reviewing all ongoing training and development programs; (2) assessing the effectiveness of these programs; (3) determining if there were any overlaps or major gaps in training and development; (4) constructing a model of an effective program; (5) making recommendations to the executive committee as to the type of program needed; (6) assisting, if needed, in implementation of the recommendations; and (7) assisting in evaluating the consequences or results of the implemented recommendations.

Once the core mission and specified subgoals have been set, the task force can make specific assignments to its members.

Step 4: Formulating Operating Guidelines

The new team needs to establish guidelines for how it will work. Provisions also need to be formulated for changing the guidelines if they prove to be dysfunctional or inappropriate as conditions change. The guidelines should clarify actions and roles and reduce any ambiguity or mixed expectations of people as to how things ought to function, which is the basis of a great deal of conflict in a working group. The following questions indicate some of the areas for which guidelines may be useful.

How Will We Make Decisions? It is useful for the new team to talk about its decision-making procedures. Do members want to make all decisions by majority vote or team consensus, or do they want to leave some decisions to subgroups that are assigned to do the work?

If the group opts to make decisions by consensus, all should realize that this does not mean unanimity (everyone thinking alike). A consensus is a decision hammered out by permitting everyone to participate. Consensus is reached after discussion, give-and-take, and compromise—when people can honestly say, "This is a sound decision—one that I am willing to support and implement. It is not exactly what I personally want, but given the range of opinions, the time factor, and the kinds of personalities involved, it is a good working decision."

Unless everyone can take that position, a consensus has not been reached. Discussion would need to continue, and adjustments or compromises or new alternatives would have to be explored until a solution is found that results in team consensus.

What Will Be Our Basic Method for Work? The team should decide what it feels will be the most efficient way to get work done. Should the total group consider all items? Should people do individual work that is then submitted to the group? Or should subcommittees do the initial work? All of these methods may be used, depending on the nature of the work to be done. However, the method of work should be decided at the outset.

How Do We Make Sure That Everyone Gets a Chance to Discuss Issues or Raise Concerns? If a team is to be effective, members need to feel that they can discuss and have others consider the issues or concerns they deem important. How will the team ensure this condition? It may be agreed that any members can put any item of concern on the agenda for the next meeting. An open meeting might be scheduled periodically to allow discussion of any topic or issue. Time could be reserved at the end of certain meetings for an open discussion. Members could be asked to distribute a memo or e-mail identifying the issue they want discussed.

How Will We Resolve Differences? Any working group will have times when individuals or subgroups disagree. If not handled or managed, disagreements can, at the least, waste time and may even split the group into warring factions.

A guideline for dealing with differences can be useful. If two people or subgroups disagree, it may be more useful to have a guideline stating that they get together (sometimes with a mediator) outside the meeting of the whole group to work out their differences rather than holding up the work of the entire team. A third person or subunit could be appointed to listen to both sides of the issues and recommend possible compromises or new alternatives. Time limits for the open discussion of differences might expedite reaching a conclusion (or might be a frustrating hindrance). A majority voting procedure might be appropriate if the group can honestly adopt a "loyal opposition" position that allows the people the right to disagree or vote differently but still support and implement actions. Whatever the method for discussing, understanding, and resolving issues, a guideline will provide a beginning for coping with the sensitive problem of differences that may occur.

How Will We Ensure Completion of Work? One of the major problems in working in groups (particularly of a committee or a task force) is the frustrating experience of some people coming unprepared or failing to complete assignments. How can the team face that issue constructively?

The guidelines may state that no one will be given or will accept an assignment if the person honestly knows that he or she will not invest an appropriate amount of energy in its preparation. This means that there must be a realistic level of priority building and a climate of trust so that people will feel free to state their honest preferences and reactions to assignments. This guideline may outline a procedure for having the chairperson or other designated leader remind everyone with an assignment (typically by e-mail) at a suitable time prior to the next meeting. An action summary of every meeting will clearly identify all

Table 11.1 Action Summary for Tracking Assignments

Decision	Who Is to Do What	Date for Completion	Date to Report Progress
1. A training seminar for all supervisors will be held on June 15.	1. John Hicks will make all physical arrangements.	June 10	Next meeting— May 20
	2. Ann Stewart will contact the three possible resource people.	May 24	Next meeting— May 20

assignments and dates for report and completion, as illustrated in table 11.1.

The action summary can be used in place of or in addition to regular narrative minutes, but it should clearly pinpoint assignments and times for completion. The guideline may suggest an appropriate action, such as a personal visit by the chairperson, a report and explanation to the committee, or some other review mechanism, if a person fails to complete an assignment.

How Will We Change Things That Are Not Producing Results? There should be some guidelines for reviewing the way the committee or team has been working and a method for making changes when guidelines or procedures or even people in certain positions are no longer achieving results. This guideline may suggest a periodic evaluation session at which the team honestly looks at its own work, reviews its successes and failures, and asks, "What changes would make the team more effective?" If team guidelines have been operating effectively, many issues will have been covered, but the team may need to agree on a periodic review and evaluation meeting or may decide that any person may call for such a meeting when he or she feels that conditions warrant it.

Again, the success of such a meeting depends on members' feeling free to express their honest views about the team's effectiveness and to make recommendations for improvement. A fearful, defensive group will find it difficult to plan useful changes. Temporary teams that are functioning poorly may also decide to engage in more extensive team-building activities by using one of the designs outlined in chapter 6.

How Can We Keep Key Stakeholders Informed? The temporary team should generate a list of key stakeholders—senior managers, department heads, clients, and so on—who will pass judgment on the team's final product. Next to each name on the list, the team should note when the stakeholder needs to be informed of a team decision or activity or whether the stakeholder must approve the decision or activity. In this way, as the team sets out a timetable for its work, it can identify when to get stakeholders involved at appropriate milestones to ensure their support and avoid an unpleasant surprise like the one experienced by the college curriculum committee described earlier.

In Summary

Managing a temporary team creates certain challenges for such a team given the short time frame in which it has to do its work. Upfront planning and sharing of expectations are often the keys to successful temporary teams. The team also needs to set clear priorities and goals, establish operating guidelines for how to make decisions, keep the work on schedule, solve problems, and keep key stakeholders informed.

12

CREATING EFFECTIVE CROSS-CULTURAL TEAMS

One of the more dramatic changes in teams in recent years has been the increasing number of them composed of members from different cultural backgrounds. Various studies of cross-cultural teams present contradictory findings. Some studies indicate that cross-cultural teams can be highly creative and high performing, while others show that such teams have significant conflicts and low performance.[1] When a team is composed of individuals who have different norms, values, language, and experiences, the likelihood of creative problem solving is enhanced, but the chances for misunderstandings, mistrust, and miscommunication also increase.

Because members of a cross-cultural team may lack specific information about each other, they often form stereotypical expectations of each team member based on their prior experience or history with people from that particular country, ethnicity, or culture of origin. For example, because Javier is from Mexico or Jean François is from France, team members will expect them to behave according to the stereotypes they have of people from Mexico or France. Such stereotypes often undermine the team's ability to perform at a high level since they create the mismatched expectations and unwanted conflicts that were discussed in chapter 7.

One senior executive in discussing cross-cultural teams in his organization said: "In my company, we are having great difficulties with such groups. We've had strategic plans suffer and careers derail because of complications arising from multinational groups.

Just last month we killed a global product development project because the team had taken so long that the competition had already sewn up the market."[2]

In order to better understand how to create and manage effective cross-cultural teams, we examine in this chapter what culture is and how it influences team performance, along with how team leaders can use the Four Cs of team performance to improve the performance of cross-cultural teams.

What Is Culture?

In any discussion of cross-cultural teams, the team and team leader need to have a basic understanding of culture in order to identify potential cultural problems in working together as a team. Culture is often thought of as being monolithic—for example, American versus Japanese cultures—but there are also ethnic cultures, regional cultures, organizational cultures, and even team and family cultures. And we sometimes find greater cultural differences between groups within nations rather than between nations. Thus, we are not just focusing on teams composed of individuals from different countries, but any team with individuals who come from significantly different cultural backgrounds. Our focus is especially on teams whose members have not been exposed to the cultural backgrounds of the other members of the team. We define *culture* as socially acquired and shared rules of conduct that are manifested in a group's artifacts, norms, values, and assumptions.[3] We'll discuss each of these four levels of culture in turn.

Cultural Artifacts

Artifacts are the tangible aspects of culture—the behaviors, language, dress, and other overt manifestations of cultural rules. These are the things we can see, hear, or touch and reflect a group's rules of conduct. For example, when entering a traditional Japanese home, a visitor will slide open the door, step into the *genkan* (the area where family members and visitors leave their shoes), and then yell into the home, "*Gomen kudasai*" ("Please excuse my interruption"). The alerted homeowner will then go to the *genkan* to greet the guest.

In the United States, if someone were to open a homeowner's front door, walk in, and start calling out, they might be greeted with a hail of bullets. Entering a Japanese home manifests certain physical artifacts (the door and the *genkan*), a behavioral artifact (opening the door and walking in), and a verbal artifact (calling out, "*Gomen kudasai*) that reflect a cultural rule in Japan: it's acceptable to open the door, walk into the *genkan*, and yell a greeting. In the United States and many other countries, this would be deemed unacceptable behavior.

Cultural Norms

Cultural norms are the rules that are reflected in a group's cultural artifacts and used by individuals to act appropriately in specific situations. For example, in the United States, we commonly greet a new person by shaking his or her hand. In a similar situation in Japan, one would bow when greeting and not shake hands.

These situation-specific rules or norms guide team behaviors such as where team members sit, who calls a team meeting to order, how a disagreement is handled, and so forth. Of course, there can be some variance in what might be considered appropriate behavior in a specific situation. For example, a professor teaching a class may decide to sit in a chair and teach the class, may walk back and forth in front of the class while lecturing, or stand behind a podium—all behaviors that most people would deem acceptable and consistent with norms around appropriate teaching behavior for a professor. But if the professor decided to teach a class while lying down on the floor in the middle of the classroom, the students would recognize this behavior as inconsistent with the rules that are supposed to govern appropriate behavior for a professor while teaching (and they also might want to find the professor a good therapist).

Similarly, in the United States, students at the college level typically feel comfortable, and may even be encouraged, to question what the professor has said. However, in South Korea and Japan, among some others, it would not be appropriate—and in fact would be viewed as disrespectful—if students openly questioned what the professor said in class. These norms may be unwritten and tacit in nature, or rules could be written down and codified by a group in a formal procedures manual.

Cultural Values

Cultural values are more general rules that represent the collective feelings of a group about what's good, proper, valuable, and right. Unlike norms, values are broader rules that can be found across various situations. These values may be articulated in statements of philosophy or beliefs. For example, the Scout Law of the Boy Scouts states that a boy scout is "trustworthy, loyal, helpful, friendly, courteous, kind, obedient, cheerful, thrifty, brave, clean, and reverent." The notion behind this statement of values is that a boy scout will follow and apply these values (rules) in a variety of situations.

Similarly, IDEO, the highly successful innovation design firm, has its values plastered all over the walls: "One conversation at a time," "Encourage wild ideas," "Fail soon to succeed sooner." These values encourage individuals at IDEO to engage in these behaviors, thereby creating a culture of innovation. One organization that we worked with had a phrase that management commonly used: "Do what's right." The story accompanying this phrase was of a manager who didn't know the right course of action to take, so he asked his boss what to do. The boss listened carefully and then said: "You've thought this through; now do what you think is right." The manager wanted more direction, so he went to a number of other higher-level managers for more direction on what to do. In each case, they told him to "do what's right." Finally, the manager found himself in the company president's office asking for direction and got the same answer: "Do what's right."

The value expressed in "do what's right" is that your superiors should not be expected to give you the answers to all your questions. You should study the problem and then take action rather than waiting for your superiors to tell you what to do. This value, which was used in a variety of situations, encouraged innovation and creativity in the organization and was a large part of the company's success.

Shared Assumptions

Assumptions are the basic beliefs that underlie artifacts, norms, and values. These are the fundamental beliefs about whether people can be trusted, the nature of relationships, the nature of the world around us, and so forth. Hofstede identified four basic assumptions along which country cultures tend to differ: individualism versus collectivism, power distance, uncertainty avoidance, and task or relationship (long term versus short term) orientation.[4] Table 12.1 briefly explains these dimensions and identifies some of the potential issues that may arise in multicultural teams.

Since such assumptions are often tacit and not articulated by members of a particular cultural group, they generally must be inferred as we look at a group's artifacts, norms, and values. For example, when examining the culture of a classroom in the United States, we generally see certain artifacts: students are seated, they raise their hands, the teacher is speaking more often than anyone else, and students tend to focus their attention on the teacher. Certain norms such as raising one's hand when a student has a question or broader values of respect and order may

Table 12.1 Cultural Variables That Influence Multicultural Teams

Variable	Implications for Multicultural Teams
Individualism versus collectivism *Individualism*: prefer to act and be recognized as individuals rather than as members of groups (the United States, France, the United Kingdom, Germany) *Collectivism*: prefer to act as members of groups (China, Japan, Indonesia, West Africa)	❖ Individualistic team members will voice their opinions more readily, challenging the direction of the team. The opposite is true of collectivists. Collectivists prefer to consult colleagues more than do individualists before making decisions. ❖ Collectivists don't need specific job descriptions or roles but will do what is needed for the team, ideally together with other team members. Individualists will take responsibility for tasks and may need reminding that they're part of the team. ❖ Individual-oriented team members prefer direct, constructive feedback on their performance tied closely to their individual performance. Collectivists might feel embarrassed if singled out for praise or an individual incentive award. ❖ Collectivists prefer face-to-face meetings. Individualists prefer to work alone, not needing face-to-face contact.
Power distance *High distance*: prefer and accept that power is not distributed equally (France and Russia) *Low distance*: prefer and accept that power is distributed more equally (Netherlands, the United States)	❖ Team members from cultures that value equality (that is, low power distance) expect to use consultation to make key decisions, and subordinates are more likely to question and challenge leaders or authority figures. ❖ A team leader exercising a more collaborative style might be seen as weak and indecisive by team members from a high-power-distance culture. ❖ Members from high-power-distance cultures will be very uncomfortable communicating directly with people higher in the organization.

Uncertainty avoidance
High-uncertainty-avoidance cultures: prefer more structured tasks and avoid ambiguity (France, Japan, Russia)
Low-uncertainty-avoidance cultures: have a high tolerance for ambiguity and risk taking (the United States, Hong Kong)

❖ In a culture in which risk taking is the norm or valued, team members tend to be comfortable taking action or holding meetings without much structure or formality. Members who are more risk averse need a clearer, prepared meeting structure, perhaps with a formal presentation by all members of the team. They're unlikely to take an active part in brainstorming sessions.

❖ Members from lower-uncertainty-avoidance cultures do not respond well to micromanagement. They may also be more willing to use new technologies.

Task or relationship orientation
Long-term orientation: China, Japan
Short-term orientation: the United States, Russia

❖ Team members from long-term-oriented cultures want to spend extra social time together, building trust, and may have problems interacting smoothly with short-term-oriented members. They also like opportunities to work toward long-term goals.

❖ Individuals from long-term-oriented cultures demonstrate greater concern for relationships, whereas those from short-term-oriented cultures demonstrate greater concern for task completion.

Source: Adapted from G. Hofstede, *Culture's Consequences: International Differences in Work-Related Values* (Thousand Oaks, CA: Sage, 1980).

be a part of the classroom culture. This classroom culture reflects the basic assumptions that the teacher knows more than the student, and the teacher has the power to reward or punish students (by giving grades). These assumptions form the foundation for the artifacts, norms, and values in the class.

Of course, there can be some variance in classroom cultures depending on whether the teacher assumes the students can be trusted to read the material and do the assignments and whether the class assumes that learning can come from others in the class, not just the teacher. For example, if the assumption of a class was that no one knew more than anyone else, then the class would likely rotate who would teach and the class members might set their chairs in a circle (rather than the standard format) so that all could participate equally. Assumptions are the underlying drivers of the more overt artifacts, norms, and values.

Using the Four Cs in Cross-Cultural Teams

This discussion of culture helps to clarify why cross-cultural teams often have difficulty. First, people from different cultures interpret artifacts differently. From one cultural perspective, a certain act, a word, or an object may be entirely appropriate, but from another cultural perspective, it may be highly offensive. Furthermore, team members from different cultures often have norms, values, and assumptions that are different, thus leading to miscommunication and conflict. To remedy these problems, we find that using the Four Cs of team performance can help to ensure the success of a cross-cultural team.

Context

Creating the right context for a cross-cultural team is critical. Significant upfront, face-to-face time needs to be spent to help the team succeed. The agenda for the initial team meeting should be similar to that for temporary teams described in chapter 11.

The team members need to discuss the importance and priority of the team; share their expectations for the team; clarify the goals of the team; and formulate operating guidelines for issues regarding decision making, work assignments, raising concerns, resolving conflicts, and so forth. Also, the discussion in chapter 7 on team diversity suggests some agenda items for an initial meeting for a cross-cultural team.

To help build mutual trust and understanding, some cross-cultural teams have found it valuable to administer an online version of the Myers-Briggs Type Indicator, the widely used personality assessment tool that places people in one of four personality dimensions. (See humanmetrics.com for an online version of the test.) All team members should understand what each member brings to the team. At the team kickoff meeting, the team can review each team member's personality profile and background, and the team leader can encourage members to share some information about their country, culture, or personal background that might be useful knowledge for other team members. It sometimes helps if team members agree to remind each other of their own personality styles when they speak. For example, someone from a culture that values verbal expression might say, "As you know, I tend to think out loud," or, "Please remind me not to take up too much airtime." These kinds of conversations prove to be invaluable for helping team members view each other as individuals. Naturally this is critical to the formation of trust among team members.

Another way to build trust and mutual understanding is through a teamwork activity as part of the team's first meeting. One such activity is the "desert survival" activity, in which the team must work together to figure out how to survive in the desert. Try to make the activity fun, interesting, and interactive rather than competitive.

After the exercise, the team leader should consider asking team members to say something about their country and culture and how it tends to influence their work style. Team members can use concrete examples from the exercise just completed to help others understand their approach to teamwork and problem solving. At the end of the exercise, each team member could list on a whiteboard some of the questions, puzzles, or conflicts they had with other team members. The team could then explore how to help each team member understand what cultural rules (or other factors) may have caused the discomfort and discuss what be done in the future to avoid such problems.

Another approach to clarify cultural differences would be to have the team engage in an appreciative inquiry team exercise described in chapter 6. As team members describe their most productive team experiences and the role they played on the team, cultural differences can be identified and clarified by team members whose experience in productive teams may be quite different. We often see individuals from Asian countries describe their successful teams as ones where the team leader makes most of the decisions and there are clear roles and assignments. Americans, in contrast, often cite teams where there was a lot of freedom and little structure as being their best team experience. Such differences in expectations need to be reconciled for a cross-cultural team to perform effectively.

Composition

Creating a successful cross-cultural team requires several important things regarding the composition of the team. First, the team leader needs to be sensitive to cultural differences and attuned to the fact that his or her own cultural values may be inconsistent with those of other members of the team. Second, team members should be selected on the basis of their ability to share a common language. Certainly it's possible to use interpreters, but the process can be slow and unwieldy. Case studies have shown that inadequate proficiency in a common language can be a serious problem, and those who are less proficient are often deemed by team members to be less competent and thus less able to contribute to the team.[5] Thus, clarifying what language will be the primary language for the team—Chinese, French, English, or something else—and making sure each team member is proficient in the language is important. If the team leader and other team members are multilingual, so much the better, for they can help clarify misunderstandings that may occur. Furthermore, finding team members who have lived and worked in other countries or have previously worked on cross-cultural teams is often important for team success.

Competencies

One of the advantages of cross-cultural teams is that team members bring a diverse set of experiences, values, and beliefs that can be helpful to team performance. In some sense, the cross-cultural team gives the team the opportunity to create a unique culture, composed of cultural rules that fit the particular task of the team. Early on in the team's development, the team leader should lead a discussion of each of the competencies listed in chapter 4 and discuss how each team member feels such competencies might be developed in the team.

A discussion of these competencies also creates opportunities to talk about and clarify cultural differences. For example, a discussion in the team regarding how a team meeting should be run would likely raise a number of important issues to be resolved as team members from different cultures who have experienced different meeting styles begin to work together. Moreover, the focus on developing these competencies needs to be done early on in the development of the team. Goodman emphasizes the importance of early, competency-building activities on cross-cultural teams: "Those who work on global teams need to go through a cross-cultural teambuilding program in the formative stages of team development to avoid misunderstandings and to establish team trust. It is critical that team members explore the cultural nuances that often undermine global team effectiveness.

This includes: team members' mutual perceptions; setting global standards of roles, responsibility, and accountability; leadership and management styles; discussion of virtual and face-to-face communication styles; and the development of a communication plan. Other relevant topics to be covered should include the cultural tendencies of all relevant countries and how these impact teamwork."[6] A wise leader of a cross-cultural team will help the team develop such competencies before launching into significant work by the team and will typically need to spend significant one-on-one time with team members as they may have issues and concerns that they are unwilling to share with the team; moreover, the team leader can help interpret the issues and dynamics of the team to team members individually.

Change

Early in their development, cross-cultural teams need to regularly assess how they are performing and make any needed course corrections. This could be as simple as taking time after each meeting to critique the meeting's effectiveness or having a weekly or biweekly start-stop-continue team-building session to identify problems on the team. Role clarification can also be a useful team-building activity before the team begins its work and, more important, a few weeks after the team has been working together.

How to Manage Violated Expectations in Cross-Cultural Teams

Violated expectations as a result of different cultural rules are often the cause of conflict in cross-cultural teams. In chapter 7 we suggested that such unmet expectations need to be managed effectively for a team to succeed. In the case of cross-cultural teams, there are three primary ways that expectations tend to be violated:

- Communication behaviors
- Decision-making processes
- Conflict resolution behaviors and processes

Communication behaviors are the typical behaviors of team members for communicating and achieving the team goals. The specific potential areas of conflict include how quickly to respond to other team member requests, what communication vehicle to use for different types of information, and how to communicate sensitive information. It is important for the team to establish expectations at the beginning of the project with regard to these issues. Otherwise, it is easy for conflict to arise when communication norms or expectations are violated. It is not unusual for team members to have different expectations with regard to how quickly to respond to a particular request from another team member.

In one cross-cultural team, the leader had a team member who stopped communicating for three weeks. The leader sent repeated e-mails requesting information, to which the member did not reply. Rather than get angry at him, thinking maybe there were extenuating circumstances, the team leader consciously made an effort to keep the lines of communication open. She telephoned him and said, "Please tell me if I have offended you." He said, "Well I'm a Yorkshire man, and we go quiet when we are thinking." The team leader was astounded. She felt like saying, "I don't care if you come from Mars, I need the stuff." However, using proper restraint, she thanked him for explaining and then described her expectations of him with regard to communicating with her. But she also asked him what he expected from her, which opened the door for a mutual sharing of expectations.[7]

This team leader realized that it would have been helpful if she had established expectations clearly at the beginning of team formation that members should expect to respond to each others' e-mails or requests within a specific time period (within one week is a typical expectation unless the nature of the task requires faster—or allows for slower—responses).

A second area for which it is important to establish expectations is decision-making processes. It is important for all team members to clearly understand how decisions will be made, as well as their role in the process. In some cultures and organizations, the leader of the team usually makes the decision after listening to the issues that team members raise. In more collectivist and egalitarian decision-making cultures, decisions are made by consensus after a series of discussions between team members. The team leader plays an important facilitator role in this process, ensuring that all voices are listened to and that the team comes to an agreement on a decision. It is often helpful at the beginning of the project for the team to discuss and agree on the processes that will be used for decision making. It is especially important to anticipate how final decisions will be made if there is disagreement among the team as to what the decision should be.

A third area for which it is important to establish expectations is conflict resolution behaviors and processes. The basic idea is to establish some ground rules in case of disagreements among team members or with the team leader with regard to how those differences of opinion will be handled and resolved. Some individuals feel perfectly comfortable expressing differences of opinion with other members of the team and engaging in direct disagreements and dialogue with regard to those disagreements. Others feel very uncomfortable openly disagreeing with other members of a team and prefer to use more subtle processes for expressing disagreements. For example, in the United States, individuals tend to prefer to confront a problem directly with another individual, even if it is the team leader. In most Asian cultures, direct confrontation is avoided at all costs. When a subordinate wants to give feedback to a boss, this is typically done only in a roundabout way through the grapevine (other members of the team), usually when the team is out at night together drinking. This allows conflicts to be resolved in more subtle, informal ways without direct confrontation during team meetings or discussions.

Again it is extremely helpful if the team leader can establish expectations and ground rules at the time the team is formed. A role clarification exercise (as described in chapter 7) may be a useful way for team members to share what they expect from themselves and other team members. The team-building activities on setting priorities and expectations for temporary teams found in chapter 11 also can be a useful starting point. By acknowledging that disagreements will arise among team members, the team leader can legitimize that it is okay to disagree as team members work together to achieve team goals. However, these disagreements need to be managed carefully so as not to result in resentful feelings among team members.

In Summary

Cross-cultural teams will continue to be an increasing part of organizations. Moreover, to avoid the problems that are inherent when team members come from different cultural backgrounds with different cultural rules, it is important to pay attention to the team context, composition, competencies, and change. Time is needed at the start to create the context for discussing and clarifying cultural differences among team members, team members should be able to communicate proficiently in the language of the team, and ideally they should have had some experience in working with individuals from different cultures. The team should work through the list of team competencies to create their own, unique culture as they work together. And the cross-cultural team should engage in regular team-building activities to make sure that it is not going off course and that any cultural misunderstandings are addressed and clarified.

By so doing, members of cross-cultural teams might find out that they are not so different from each other. Remember the differences between Americans and Japanese when entering a home that we described at the start of the chapter? It just so happens that the underlying rule is the same in both cultures: no one can enter another's house without permission. However, in Japan, a guest who is standing inside the door but still in the *genkan* is considered to be outside the house. In the United States, the moment a visitor enters the door, he or she is inside another's home.

13

HIGH-PERFORMING
VIRTUAL TEAMS

A decade ago, virtual team were rare. Today they are common-place. What changed? First, companies are increasingly global, with office locations in numerous countries, which means that many teams cannot be colocated. Second, advances in commu-nication technology have dramatically lowered the costs of coordinating across distances, thereby making it more cost-effective to create and manage virtual teams. Finally, companies face increasingly complex business problems that require the contributions of people with varied knowledge who reside in different locations and time zones. Research by the Gartner group has shown that in the future, more employees will be spending their time working on virtual teams than ever before.[1] This trend suggests that a company's ability to manage virtual teams effectively will be critical to success.

In this chapter, we address important questions on how to manage virtual teams effectively:

- How does a virtual team differ from a traditional team?
- What are the common problems of managing virtual teams?
- How do you do team-building in a virtual team?

How Virtual Teams Differ from Traditional Teams

Virtual teams differ from traditional teams in at least three ways:

1. Greater diversity in work norms and expectations
2. Greater reliance on technology as a vehicle for communication
3. Greater demands on the team leader

Unlike traditional colocated teams, virtual teams are assembled with individuals from different locations with much greater diversity of cultures, languages, and business functions (e.g., sales and engineering). Because a virtual team is typically composed of members with much greater individual diversity, there is much greater diversity in team work norms and expectations. Naturally this is more likely to lead to group conflict (see chapters 7 and 12 on the problems and strengths of diversity and cultural differences).

To illustrate, when Daimler-Benz merged with Chrysler in 1998, it was necessary for the two companies to create a variety of integration teams with executives from Daimler in Germany working with executives from Chrysler in the United States. It should come as no surprise that these teams faced numerous difficulties integrating operations because Chrysler and Daimler-Benz had different corporate cultures that were reflective of their country cultures. A senior DaimlerChrysler executive (an American from Chrysler) claimed that the joint DaimlerChrysler teams faced significant conflicts and challenges as a result of differences in work norms and expectations. He described these differences to us using the following analogy.

Our different approaches to problem solving are illustrated by how we would each respond to opening a new board game at Christmas. The Americans at Chrysler would open the game, and while someone started reading through the instructions, the others would set up the board and the game pieces. After getting about halfway through the instructions, the group, eager to get started, would decide to start play and then figure out the game as they went along. In contrast, the Germans at Daimler would open the game and before setting up the board, they would carefully read all of the instructions at least once and carefully examine the board and game pieces. Then, after running some simulation games for a couple of days, they would be ready to start play.

This quote illustrates how very different the work norms and expectations were at Daimler-Benz and Chrysler. The obsession of Daimler's engineers for detail and careful upfront planning clashed with the desire of Chrysler's engineers to jump quickly into a problem and figure it out as they went along. Differences in language and time zones exacerbated the communication problems associated with managing the differing work norms and expectations that existed on these virtual integration teams. Not surprisingly, these teams experienced tremendous conflicts due to violated expectations that contributed to the exodus of many former top Chrysler executives within a year of the merger.

The second major difference between virtual and traditional teams is that virtual teams cannot rely on face-to-face meetings and must communicate using a much wider variety of technologies. The members of a virtual team can choose from a range of communication technologies to coordinate team activities, including e-mail, electronic displays or whiteboards, bulletin boards or web pages (including team calendars and chat rooms), teleconference (audio or video), or multipoint multimedia technology (a combination of full-motion video, whiteboard, and audio links).

Naturally the potential for miscommunication is much greater when team members do not meet face-to-face and must rely on electronic technologies to communicate. Moreover, the fact that all team members must be trained on all available communication technologies presents additional challenges to the virtual team. Not only must team members know how to use the various technologies; but they must also know when a particular communication technology is appropriate for a particular task. For example, e-mail and web pages are good for exchanging data and revising work plans and documents, whereas multipoint multimedia technology (videoconference with whiteboard) is best for brainstorming, debating options, drawing concepts, or displaying and diagramming complex data.

By now it should be somewhat obvious that the demands on the team leader are much greater on a virtual team. In addition to the team leader skills described in chapter 4, virtual team leaders must have enough cross-cultural and cross-functional experience to be aware of potential conflicts in work norms and expectations. Moreover, they not only must be aware of the areas of potential conflict but must also educate team members with regard to these differences and help the team establish a set of commonly understood and agreed-on work norms and expectations. Team leaders must also be proficient with the use of a variety of communication technologies, knowing how to use them all and when to use which technology. In addition, they must put in extra time preparing, and making sure team members are prepared for, team meetings so that team interactions can be as productive as possible. Finally, they must communicate frequently on an individual basis with each team member. These side conversations are critical to resolving disagreements, negotiating compromises, and making sure each member feels understood and heard by the leader.

Common Problems in Virtual Teams

We have found three common problems that afflict virtual teams more than colocated teams. The first problem of violated expectations and misunderstandings that can occur when individuals from different cultural backgrounds work together was discussed in chapter 12. In this chapter, we examine two additional problems that virtual teams often face: a lack of training and effective use of communication technologies and the lack of effective team leadership.

Lack of Training and Effective Use of Communication Technologies

Virtual teams must communicate long distance, which means team members must understand how and when to use particular communication technologies. The majority of effective virtual teams use technology to simulate reality by creating virtual work spaces that are accessible to everyone at any time. These are more than networked drives with shared files. Rather they are work spaces where the group is reminded of its mission, work plan, decisions, and working documents.

A good example of a virtual team work space is one that was set up at Shell Chemicals by team leader Tom Coons, who led a project to develop a companywide cash-focused approach to financial management.[2] The team's virtual work space, essentially a website accessed on an intranet, prominently displayed the project's mission statement on its home page, as well as the photographs and names of team members in a clocklike arrangement. The home page also had links to other tabs, or "walls," each devoted to a particular aspect of the project. The tab labeled "people," for instance, kept not only individuals' contact information but also extensive profiles that included their accomplishments, areas of expertise, and interests, as well as information about other stakeholders. On a tab labeled "purpose" was a hierarchical listing of the mission statement, the goals, and the tasks for meeting the goals, indicating how close each task was to completion. The "meeting center" wall contained all the information needed to manage the teleconferences: notices of when they were being held, who was supposed to come, agendas, and minutes. Yet another wall displayed the team's entire work product, organized into clearly numbered versions, so that people would not inadvertently work on the wrong one. The team room kept information current, organized, and easily accessible. This type of virtual work space creates a team identity, generates commitment to the team, and helps the team stay organized.

The Shell team created these tools internally. But an increasing number of collaboration tools like this are relatively inexpensive or even free. For example, Salesforce.com offers Chatter, software that creates collaboration tools for teams and organizations. Chatter takes the best of Facebook and Twitter and applies it to enterprise collaboration. It uses new ways of sharing information like "feeds" and "groups" so that without any effort, people can see what individuals and teams are focusing on, how projects are progressing, and what deals are closing. It can change the way teams collaborate on product development, customer acquisition, and content creation by making it easy for everyone to see what everyone else is doing. At companies using Chatter, e-mail inboxes have shrunk dramatically (by 43 percent at Salesforce.com) because the majority of communications are now status updates and feeds in Chatter. "Employees now follow accounts and updates are automatically broadcast to them in real-time via Chatter," Salesforce.com founder Marc Benioff told us. "This is the true power of Chatter—bringing to light the most important people and ideas that move our companies forward. I call this social intelligence, and it's giving everyone access to the people, the knowledge, and the insight they need to make a difference."

Some studies have found that these types of virtual work spaces are far better than e-mail as a way to coordinate virtual teams.[3] Indeed, many virtual teams have found that e-mail is a poor way for teams as a whole to collaborate. Trying to do the main work of the team through one-to-one exchanges between members can cause those not included to feel left out. To avoid this mistake, some teams have adopted the practice of copying everyone on every e-mail exchange between members, and soon everyone in the team is drowning in messages. To cope, many team members simply resort to deleting the e-mail without reading it. Over time this can create significant communication problems among team members when some have communicated information that others have not read or understood. A virtual work space tends to be a far better way to organize team meetings and work. A key benefit of the virtual work space is that it maintains an ongoing record for the team that enables virtual team members to understand the context of information as they see other members sharing the information. It also keeps an ongoing record of decisions, tasks completed, and progress toward the team's final deliverable.

A virtual work space helps the team members exchange data, revise working documents, and stay organized, but it is not the best method for coordinating more complex team interactions, such as brainstorming, debating and prioritizing options, or developing a common understanding of complex concepts, process flows, or scenarios. For these more complex tasks, the group must rely on audio- or videoconferences (table 13.1 provides a summary of the types of tasks virtual teams face and the communication methods available to the team).

Audioconferences are much better than e-mail, web pages, or bulletin boards for brainstorming, defining problems, prioritizing and voting on ideas, stating and discussing opinions, and reaching simple compromises. But audioconferences are also difficult to facilitate because the team leader must be very sensitive to not only what is being said but also how it is being said. Indeed, effective team leaders typically follow up with individual team members after the conference call to make sure they felt listened to and understood.

In some cases, the team members must discuss and debate complex concepts that may involve diagrams of process flows, sketches of products or blueprints, or other visual data. The more complex the task and the greater the interdependence of team

Table 13.1 Matching Virtual Team Tasks and Communication Methods

Communication Modes, Listed from Least Expensive to Most Expensive	Generating Ideas and Plans and Collecting Data	Benefits of and Problems With Answers	Benefits of and Problems Without Answers	Negotiating Technical or Interpersonal Conflicts
E-mail, web pages, and bulletin boards (data only)	*Good for*: exchanging data; revising plans and documents; commenting on ideas, products, polling, and so on *Not good for*: brainstorming, prioritizing, voting on ideas, reaching consensus	*Good for*: defining problems, transmitting data, and analyzing data *Not good for*: reaching consensus on problems, prioritizing data, or discussing the data analysis	*Good for*: identifying options *Not good for*: debating options, prioritizing options, making decisions or judgments	*Good for*: stating opinions *Not good for*: discussing opinions, reaching compromises, resolving conflicts, deciding alternatives
Audioconference	*Good for*: brainstorming, prioritizing and voting on ideas, reaching consensus *Not good for*: depicting complex concepts, process flows, scenarios, or sketches	*Good for*: defining problems, prioritizing options, making straightforward decisions *Not good for*: displaying and diagramming data, performing in-depth and complex analysis	*Good for*: discussing options, making assignments *Not good for*: making judgments about ambiguous topics	*Good for*: stating and discussing opinions, deciding among straightforward options or solutions, reaching simple compromises *Not good for*: resolving interpersonal conflict or disagreement
Videoconference	*Good for*: brainstorming, sketching ideas, drawing concepts, gaining agreement on complex concepts, process flows, scenarios or sketches	*Good for*: displaying and analyzing data, discussing trends	*Good for*: listing options, debating and prioritizing options, making decisions	*Good for*: discussing opinions, reaching compromises, deciding among alternative solutions, resolving simple interpersonal disagreement *Not good for*: resolving complex interpersonal conflict or disagreement

Source: Adapted from D. L. Duarte and N. T. Snyder, *Mastering Virtual Teams*, 3rd ed. (San Francisco: Jossey-Bass, 2006).

members, the more important it is to use videoconferencing technology such as Skype to simulate face-to-face interactions. For a simultaneous video- or audioconference, along with the ability to display data or graphics on a computer, WebEx conferencing has become a popular tool for coordinating the work of virtual teams. Finding the right technology for the job (task) that needs to be done by the team is critical for ensuring that a virtual team is completing its tasks as efficiently and effectively as possible.

Lack of Effective Team Leadership

The demands of managing a virtual team exceed the demands of traditional teams for the reasons described in the first section of this chapter. This means that the role of team leader is crucial and is much more challenging than this person's role in traditional teams. Although team membership may be part time, team leadership is often more than full time. A rule of thumb that we suggest is that the team leader should allocate 50 percent more time to the project than he or she would be spending managing a colocated team working on a similar problem. There are two primary reasons that team leaders must spend significantly more time managing virtual teams. First, the team leader (or assistant) must organize all team meetings and team activities electronically. This tends to be more time intensive because these communications must be clearly spelled out, often through written communication.

Second, effective virtual team leaders have frequent phone conversations with individual members to probe into their real feelings, questions, and suggestions for more effective team functioning. This gives the team leader an opportunity to keep his or her finger on the pulse of the team. Effective virtual team leaders know they must devote extra time to monitoring the morale of team members and concerns they may have with other team members or the team leader.

Team Building in Virtual Teams

The logistics of managing a virtual team make traditional team-building approaches somewhat more difficult to implement. However, there are several approaches to improving team performance that virtual teams can use:

- Assess the context and composition of the team as the team is formed. To a large extent, the context of a virtual team is not particularly conducive to effective teamwork: the structure, communications networks, reward systems, and so on might not encourage collaboration. Moreover, individuals on virtual teams often have different cultural backgrounds that can make teamwork challenging. Thus, if possible, the team should engage in some of the development activities designed for cross-cultural teams described in chapter 12. By so doing, the team should be able to recognize the context barriers that could make teamwork difficult and develop plans of action to respond to those barriers. For example, the team might discover that it needs additional communications technologies listed in table 13.1 for it to communicate effectively and complete its work, and thus it might need to request those resources from senior management.

- The virtual team should periodically assess its performance by filling out the team-building checklist in chapter 5. Data from the checklist can then be shared with the team online or by videoconferencing, and the team can then identify the problems it faces.

- After identifying and prioritizing the team's issues and problems, the team leader might select one of the team-building techniques presented in previous chapters, recognizing that the format would likely need to be adapted to a virtual team (although we encourage face-to-face team-building sessions when possible). One exercise that is likely to be helpful for a virtual team is role clarification. Before discussing team members' roles, each team member should answer the six questions regarding his or her role and what help they might need and also might give to others on the team (see chapter 7). In summary, the questions are:

1. What do you feel the organization expects you to do in your job?

2. What do you actually do in your job?

3. What do you need to know about other people's jobs that would help you do your work?

4. What do you think others should know about your job that would help them do their work?

5. What do you need others to do in order for you to do your job the way you would like?

6. What do others need you to do that would help them do their work?

The answers to these questions could be communicated by e-mail or some other electronic format. After receiving and reviewing the answers to these questions from other team members, the team can then interact via videoconferencing or some other online format to clarify roles and expectations and make agreements. Doing this or other exercises using technology is likely to take longer than it would for teams that can interact face-to-face. Thus, the team leader needs to make sure that enough time is set aside for the team to work through the exercise successfully.

In Summary

In today's global economy, virtual teams are becoming a necessity for organizations to be competitive. Such teams can experience significant problems: lack of trust and commitment, conflicting expectations of the team members, poor communication and decision making, lack of training on communications technologies, and lack of effective team leadership. Virtual teams may not function well for tasks (such as complex problems) that require highly interdependent relationships on the part of team members. Still, we have found that team leaders who understand the problems associated with managing virtual teams and use the strategies for team effectiveness and team building outlined in this chapter can indeed be successful in a virtual environment.

14

MANAGING INTERORGANIZATIONAL ALLIANCE TEAMS

In one of his final articles, management guru Peter Drucker noted that "the greatest change in corporate culture—and in the way business is being conducted—may be the accelerating growth of relationships based not on ownership but on partnership; joint ventures; minority investments cementing a joint marketing agreement or an agreement to do joint research . . . alliances of all sorts."[1] Indeed, just as the growth in virtual teams has exploded, one of the most important trends in the global business environment over the past twenty years has been the explosion of alliances between companies. Consider the fact that the percentage of revenues derived from alliances from the top one thousand U.S. public corporations grew from 3 percent in 1975 to almost 30 percent by 2000, an astounding growth rate that is expected to continue. Research suggests that within the top one thousand U.S. public corporations, alliances now account for roughly 35 percent of revenues.[2]

The growth in alliances is driven by organizations that are outsourcing activities and focusing on a narrower set of core competencies as they team with other companies with complementary skills. This has been possible because advances in communication technologies have allowed more effective interorganizational coordination across firm boundaries. However, this has created a complicated situation in which two companies are trying to create synergies by combining their diverse skills. To achieve those synergies, the partnering organizations must create an interorganizational alliance team to coordinate the efforts of both companies. Thus, these teams are being formed in greater numbers than ever before. The challenges that these teams face are formidable. Indeed, most studies on alliances show that 30 to 50 percent fail to meet the objectives outlined by the alliance team at the beginning of the alliance.[3]

Why the high failure rate? According to a Pricewaterhouse-Coopers study of alliances in the pharmaceutical industry (mostly between large pharmaceutical companies and biotechnology companies), the top four reasons for alliance failure were (1) differences in partner cultures, (2) incompatible partner objectives, (3) poor alliance leadership, and (4) poor integration processes.[4] Each of these is related to a failure in managing the alliance team rather than a "failure in technology" or "changes in the business environment" (two other top reasons), two factors that clearly can derail an alliance but are largely beyond the control of the partners. In short, the number one reason that alliances fail is an inability to manage the alliance team effectively.

In this chapter we address important questions related to how to manage alliance teams effectively:

- How does an alliance team differ from a traditional team?
- What are some processes that have been found to be effective in improving the functioning of alliance teams?
- How can team building be done on a regular basis to solve problems in the alliance team and keep the alliance on track?

How Alliance Teams Differ from Internal Teams

Alliance teams differ from typical internal teams in at least four important ways.

Organization Culture Clashes

The alliance team is composed of individuals from dissimilar organization cultures, meaning different contexts for teamwork and the composition of team members. As a result, team members often have differing values and beliefs, and they come to the team with different norms regarding decision-making processes, communication, work styles, and reward systems. As a result, interorganizational teams face problems similar to those associated with culture clashes after an acquisition.

Lack of Trust

Alliance team members not only must worry about value creation (increasing the size of the pie) but must also simultaneously be concerned about value appropriation (making sure their company gets a fair share of the pie). Because each company is trying to appropriate maximum value from the relationship, the dynamic is that alliance team members feel that they must cooperate and compete at the same time. Building trust is more challenging because each company is trying to capture its fair share of the pie. As a result, coordination is more difficult to achieve because knowledge does not flow as freely between team members due to lack of trust and the wish to prevent undesirable spillover of knowledge or intellectual property.

Shared Decision Making

Alliance teams often have more than one level of management involved from each partner, and significant decisions typically must be approved by key decision makers within each partner organization, sometimes by those not part of the alliance team. Lack of complete control over decisions is a challenging dimension of alliance execution.

Team Size and Expertise Duplication

Alliance teams are often larger than an internal project team because functional expertise is often duplicated on alliance teams to ensure that each partner's knowledge is fully used in completing tasks and making decisions. For example, internal cross-functional teams typically include a representative from key functional areas such as research and development, engineering, manufacturing, logistics, marketing, sales and distribution, and so on. However, in most alliance teams, each partner wants a voice in the product development, marketing, distribution, pricing, and branding plans, so that they feel comfortable that the alliance plans fit their own company's strategic objectives. As a result, there are often two people from marketing on the alliance team (one from each partner), two from logistics, two from research and development, and so on. Of course, some duplication is necessary in order to achieve the desired synergies and ensure that the alliance uses each partner's expertise. But it also makes the team large, complicates communication, and often leads to conflicts due to differing perspectives across the partner organizations.

Managing Alliance Teams: Lessons from Eli Lilly and Company

Eli Lilly and Company is among a small number of companies that have distinguished themselves as leaders in the management of strategic alliances.[5] Lilly has been featured in numerous articles and has received the Corporate Alliance Excellence Award from the Association of Strategic Alliance Professionals for having "achieved dramatic success in its alliance programs through excellent alliance management."

Lilly has been engaged in alliances at least since the 1920s, when it began working with University of Toronto scientists Frederick Banting and Charles H. Best, who had isolated insulin and demonstrated its value in managing insulin-dependent diabetes. They identified the molecule; Lilly had the capabilities to optimize its production and market it. Since then, much of Lilly's success in diabetes care has been partnership based. For example, Genentech Inc. cloned and then licensed to Lilly recombinant human insulin (Humulin), which, with Lilly's own modified analog molecule (Humalog), accounts now for almost 100 percent of Lilly's total insulin sales.

In the mid-1990s, Lilly recognized that alliances with biotech companies would be critical to accessing a new pipeline of drugs. Consequently, in 1999 it established the Office of Alliance Management (OAM) and made a commitment to being the premier partner in the pharmaceutical industry.

During the due diligence visit to each potential partner, an OAM team member conducts a cultural assessment of the partner before the alliance is established. The team member also assigns an alliance manager to each newly formed alliance to act as an "honest broker" and help manage the complexities of the alliance relationship (the alliance manager supports the alliance leader, the Lilly person who is responsible for managing the alliance team with the partner's alliance leader on a day-to-day basis). The OAM has developed a tool kit, or set of processes, specifically designed to help manage the idiosyncratic features of alliance teams. The alliance manager's job is to become proficient with that tool kit. In the following sections we describe some of the processes that have helped Lilly become a leader in managing alliance teams.

Cultural Assessment: The Due Diligence Team

After establishing hundreds of alliances, Lilly has learned that "differences in partner cultures are the number one reason for alliance failure."[6] As a result, after identifying potential partners, Lilly tries to assess whether they will be able to work together effectively on an interorganizational team.

Lilly has developed a process of sending a due diligence team to the potential alliance partner to do a systematic evaluation of the partner's assets, resources, and processes and to assess the partner's culture. The team (between two and twenty people depending on the size and complexity of the partner) visits the potential partner for two to three days to assess the partner's financial condition, information technology, research capabilities, quality, health and safety record, and culture.

During the cultural assessment, the team examines the potential partner's corporate values and expectations, organization structure, reward systems and incentives, leadership styles and decision-making processes, human interaction patterns, work practices, history of partnerships, and human resource management practices. Lilly can identify potential areas of conflict if it can understand the following:

- Differences in corporate values, such as different priorities placed on growth, revenues, profitability, and innovation
- Differences in organization structure, such as whether the partner has a centralized or decentralized management approach
- Differences in decision-making styles, such as whether the partner values fast decision-making processes versus slower consensus-building processes or whether the partner values disagreement and debate
- Differences in leadership styles, such as whether the partner tends to rely on autocratic versus more nurturing leadership styles
- Differences in reward systems, such as whether the partner rewards high-performing employees with stock options or bonuses or promotions or bigger offices and titles

Nelson Sims, Lilly's former executive director of the OAM, claims that the due diligence process and cultural evaluation is used as both a screening mechanism and a valuable tool to assist Lilly in organizing, staffing, and governing the alliance team. States former Lilly alliance manager David Haase:

> The assessment is extremely valuable in helping us to select a
> person to lead the alliance team. We want someone who we think
> can work well with the particular partner . . . In one case we found
> that a potential partner had a culture that fostered very quick
> decision making, which was not particularly compatible with
> our decision-making processes that tend to be slower. In this case,
> we were able to design the governance arrangement and structure
> to give more autonomy to our alliance leader, and to empower him
> to make quicker decisions.

In short, Lilly's cultural assessment helps it understand why an alliance team may fail even before it is formed. By understanding what factors may throw the team off track, it can educate team members so that they are aware of potential conflicts and can staff and govern the team in a way that will increase the probability that the team will work well together.

Strategic Futures Exercise

Once an alliance team is formed, Lilly conducts a strategic futures exercise to make sure all members of the alliance team are clear on the strategic intent of the alliance relationship. During this exercise, all team members have the opportunity to describe what they think are the key objectives of the alliance team. Each member responds to two questions:

- What specifically are the alliance team's goals and objectives next year and three years from now?
- How does each team member prioritize those goals?

After identifying and discussing the team's goals, the team engages in a discussion to identify what they think will be the key barriers to achieving those goals. These could be technological challenges, regulatory challenges, marketing or distribution challenges, or simply specific challenges associated with working together effectively. After identifying the key barriers, the team discusses strategies for overcoming those barriers. This discussion is critical because by anticipating the barriers to goal achievement and devising some initial strategies to respond to those barriers, the team is able to avoid the problems that often beset alliance teams early in the relationship. Moreover, this discussion helps the team identify the operating principles by which they are going to make the relationship work. Finally, this discussion helps build trust among team members by helping them see that they are committed to common goals.

Strategic Decision-Making Template

After completing the strategic futures exercise, Lilly's alliance teams develop a decision-making template in a two-step process to assist the team with the intricacies of shared decision making:

1. Identify the key decisions or types of decisions that the team will need to make.
2. Identify which persons or organizational unit is responsible for making each type of decision (for example, steering committee, operating committee, task team, functional pairs of individuals).

The team usually starts by identifying the most important and challenging decisions and then works down to the less critical decisions. It then typically assigns responsibility for making those decisions to the cochairs of one of the alliance team's three (sometimes more) decision-making units (steering committee, operating committee, or task team) or to a functional pair of individuals. There should be clarity regarding who signs off on changes in the project budget or allocation of funds; who makes decisions about licensing jointly developed intellectual property; who makes decisions about product pricing; who decides on the wording, content, and timing of press releases; and so on:

- *The steering committee* is the highest-level decision-making body and typically comprises senior executives from both organizations. This committee signs off on the most critical strategic decisions, such as the project budget, capital investments, deployment of intellectual property, and the product development plan.

- *The operating committee*, a step below the steering committee, comprises senior managers from both sides who are involved in the day-to-day activities of the alliance. It typically is charged with making resource allocation and personnel decisions and approves specific work plans for the team.

- *Task teams* typically are subteams within the larger alliance team that are charged with performing specific tasks, such as developing the manufacturing, marketing, or distribution plans, or working with government bodies to get regulatory approval.

Finally, within the alliance team, Lilly typically forms functional pairs, or individuals within the same function from both organizations who must make specific decisions about development, marketing, distribution, manufacturing, finance, and so on.

It is often the case that the alliance team will form a functional pair in marketing and give primary responsibility for key marketing activities to an individual at one of the partner organizations (the "lead"). This individual may then develop plans to target specific decision makers with a particular marketing pitch through particular media. However, before making the final decisions with regard to the marketing plan, the individual must get the input and sign-off on these decisions from his or her "functional pair" from the partner organization. This is important because the functional pair understands how marketing is done at the partner organization and will know whether the marketing plan is consistent with that company's processes and values. Disagreements on decisions between functional pairs often are then elevated to a task team or operating committee level. Similarly, key disagreements at the operating committee level typically will be addressed by the steering committee.

When the strategic decision-making exercise is completed, the alliance team has tremendous clarity on what decisions need to be made, who will make the decisions, and what will happen if there is disagreement on a particular decision. Gary Stach, Lilly's executive director of OAM, summed up the strategic decision-making process as follows: "So you basically just map out the decisions each level needs to make, gain alignment to make those decisions, put the boundaries on them, and then let the team do its work. Of course, that's often a lot easier said than done."

Communication and Work Planning Documents

In addition to creating a decision-making template, Lilly's alliance team develops a communication and work planning document that (1) identifies each major task that the team needs to perform; (2) for each task, identifies who is responsible for doing the work, who is accountable for the end product, and who needs to be consulted or informed once the work is completed (Lilly refers to this as the "RACI process"); and (3) outlines the primary methods of communication, including the frequency of communication, among those who are responsible, accountable, or need to be consulted or informed.

One of the unique features of alliance teams is that they often tend to be large, principally because functional expertise is duplicated within the team. As a result, it is easy for tasks to fall through the cracks ("I thought you were responsible for that task") or for there to be a lack of communication among those who believe that they should be consulted or informed ("You should have consulted with me about those results; I could have told you a different way to interpret the data"). Lilly has found that the RACI work planning process is extremely effective at ensuring that work planning on alliance teams is done properly. States Lilly OAM alliance manager Michael Ransom:

> The bottom line is that the RACI process is basically a way to divide and assign responsibilities for the work, and develop effective work processes. Who's going to be responsible for doing the work? Who's accountable for the end product? Who do you need to consult with, and then who needs to be informed once you get the work done? We've found this to be a very effective work-planning approach. The RACI process keeps all of the right people involved.

After going through the RACI process for each task, the team discusses and agrees on how and what kind of information they are going to share with each other. This is a practical way of deciding when to use e-mail, voice mail, videoconference, electronic data interchange, and face-to-face meetings (see chapter 13 on how virtual teams use technology to communicate). Their goal is to make communication within the alliance team as open and transparent as possible. However, there is also the need for a common understanding of what kind of information or technology is proprietary to a particular partner organization and will not be shared. This helps identify the boundaries of what information can, and cannot, be shared within the alliance team.

Keeping the Alliance Team on Track: Annual Health Check

Lilly does regular team building on its alliance teams through a process it calls the "annual health check." It has developed a proprietary survey to check the health of its alliance teams on an annual basis. The annual health check survey provides an understanding of how the alliance team is performing in terms of fit:

- *Strategic fit* between partners, including commitment of the partners, alignment of the partners' objectives, and relationship qualities such as trust and fairness
- *Operational fit,* including attributes of effective organization and management, leadership, communication, and conflict management processes
- *Cultural fit,* including compatible values and ways of working together, especially ways appropriate to a knowledge industry

Lilly uses the health check survey to assess the relative health of its larger partnerships at a particular point in time. The survey captures the differences between the way that Lilly participants and partner participants on the alliance team view the partnership in terms of how well the team is working together to achieve common goals.

Conceptually, the health check survey evaluates the degree to which the alliance team is succeeding on the broad categories of strategic fit, operational fit, and cultural fit. It then defines fourteen categories that underlie those macrodimensions. For strategic fit, the Lilly survey uses three categories to define the dimension: commitment, strategy, and trust and fairness. For operational fit, the survey uses eight categories: communication, conflict management, decision making, leadership, performance measurement, roles, skills and competence, and team coordina-

Figure 14.1 Measuring Alliance Health

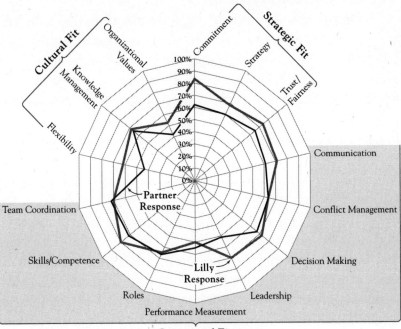

Note: Percentage of team members rating each dimension as favorable.
© 2001 Eli Lilly and Company.

tion. For cultural fit, the survey uses three categories: organizational values, knowledge management, and flexibility (see figure 14.1). To measure each dimension, the instrument asks respondents to rate their degree of agreement with specific statements or questions. For example, to measure commitment to the alliance team, the survey questions focus on such things as each partner's follow-through or understanding of the importance of the alliance for both companies. To measure knowledge management, the questions probe respondents' views on each partner's knowledge sharing and use of learning practices. Finally, the survey asks a set of broad "outcome" and "satisfaction" questions to assess the extent to which respondents believe the alliance is achieving its goals and objectives.

Although the survey and the specific questions that Lilly asks are proprietary, we offer a sample of the types of questions that Lilly might ask in each category based on our understanding of alliance teams and the challenges they face in succeeding (see figure 14.2). The survey respondent is asked to indicate the extent to which he or she agrees with each statement. Once the data are gathered and analyzed, they are reported back to the alliance team by the alliance manager from the OAM, who facilitates a discussion of the results. The most useful report for Lilly is the "spider web" chart that graphs the findings for both Lilly and the partner on a circular grid. Using this graphic, Lilly and its alliance partner can easily see the categories that Lilly and the partner agree are strong, the categories both view as areas needing improvement, and categories that they evaluate differently—the gaps in perception. For example, in figure 14.1, at least 70 percent of the survey respondents at both Lilly and the partner give a favorable rating on skills and competence (meaning 70 percent of the respondents agreed or strongly agreed with the survey items that assess the extent to which Lilly is bringing the necessary skills and competence to the alliance). Both also view "performance measurement" as a relatively weak area, giving it less than a 60 percent favorable rating. But they have clear differences on "commitment" and "flexibility," with Lilly participants indicating that they think Lilly is quite committed and flexible, whereas the partner does not feel that Lilly is as committed and flexible. In this case, the gap in perception on commitment and flexibility would point to areas that would be addressed in the health check review session. Of course, "performance measurement" would also be addressed since both Lilly and the partner felt this was a problem area.

The survey is used when there are at least ten direct participants on the alliance team from both Lilly and the partner. That size ensures that the quantitative results will be meaningful. In the case of alliances with fewer than ten team members from each partner in which a large-scale survey would not be statistically meaningful, Lilly has developed a focus group process that allows the alliance manager to probe into the same issues. The initial effort was to use the survey to evaluate only Lilly's capabilities and performance as a partner, since a major purpose of the health check is to make sure Lilly is being a good partner. But in many cases, the partner requested that its capabilities and performance in the alliance be included in the survey as well. More recently, the survey has been modified so that both companies answer questions about the alliance and about the partner. The end result is the same. The survey helps pinpoint areas in which the alliance team can take steps to improve both the relationship and team performance.

Does the health check help build healthy alliance teams? Absolutely. Alliance partner respondents say that Lilly has substantially improved its ability to recognize and resolve team difficulties in the partnership at an early stage, before they become stumbling blocks. In some cases, Lilly found that it needed to replace its alliance leader. Former OAM executive director Sims said, "Through these assessments we found that we had to occasionally make some leadership changes. They were not bad leaders, just not a good fit with the particular alliance." Alliance team failure, like a failed marriage, is often the culmination of a chain of events that eventually escalates toward the collapse of the relationship. The health check allows Lilly to send in a "marriage counselor"—in this case, the alliance manager—to help get the relationship back on track before it ends in a messy divorce. Sometimes the health check session does not reveal any major problems but instead results in a simple improvement in the day-to-day working relationship. In other instances, the health check process directly improves project results and outcomes.

The case of an alliance with a small biotechnology company on the west coast of the United States illustrates how the health

Figure 14.2 Examples of Potential Survey Items for a Health Check Survey

Instructions: Respond to the following statements on a scale of 1 to 5:
1 = Strongly Disagree; 2 = Disagree; 3 = Neither Agree nor Disagree; 4 = Agree;
5 = Strongly Agree.

Strategic Fit

Commitment

___1. Lilly is committing the resources necessary to make the alliance successful.
___2. Lilly team members demonstrate their commitment to the alliance by following through on promises and commitments.
___3. Lilly is highly committed to the alliance relationship.

Strategy

___1. The alliance has a well-defined strategy for achieving the desired outcomes for both partners.

Trust and Fairness

___1. Lilly team members are willing to make adjustments in ways perceived as "fair" by the alliance partner (Lilly is fair).
___2. Lilly team members are trustworthy and would not take advantage of our firm in this alliance relationship even if they had the chance (Lilly is trustworthy and shows goodwill).

Operational Fit

Communication

___1. We are extremely satisfied with the communication processes that Lilly has established to maintain effective communication with our firm.
___2. Lilly team members are open and transparent in their communications with our firm.

Conflict Management

___1. We are extremely satisfied with Lilly's ability to resolve disputes or disagreements that we have had during the alliance.
___2. We frequently have conflicts and we are not effective at resolving those disagreements.

Decision Making

___1. Lilly's decision-making processes are efficient and timely.
___2. Lilly's decision-making processes are effective.
___3. The right people are always involved in making key decisions.

Roles

___1. Lilly is effectively fulfilling all of the obligations and the roles it was assigned at the beginning of the alliance.

Performance Management

___1. The alliance team has clear and measurable performance metrics.

Leadership

___1. Lilly's alliance leader is providing effective leadership for the alliance.

Figure 14.2 (Continued)

Skills and Competence

___1. Lilly has shown that it is highly competent and has the skills necessary to perform the tasks that it is responsible for completing.

Team Coordination

___1. The alliance team is coordinating very effectively to achieve the alliance's goals.

Cultural Fit

Organizational Values

___1. Lilly team members behave in ways that reinforce Lilly's espoused organizational values.
___2. We find that our organizational values frequently clash with Lilly's organizational values.

Knowledge Management

___1. Lilly team members quickly share whatever information and knowledge they have to help the alliance achieve its objectives.
___2. We trust that confidential knowledge and data shared with Lilly will be kept confidential.

Flexibility

___1. Lilly is very flexible and able to make quick adjustments when necessary.

Overall Success and Satisfaction

___1. Overall, this alliance is on track to deliver significant value to our company.
___2. We are highly satisfied with the results of the alliance to date.
___3. We are highly satisfied with Lilly as a partner.

check survey uncovered a gap in communication and knowledge sharing within the alliance team. The members of the team found that the problems were created by the geographical distance between Lilly and the partner and by information bottlenecks. Key alliance members at Lilly and the partner sent electronic messages to each other but sometimes did not share those messages more broadly or in a timely way.

To solve the problem, the partnership added a new communication tool to the alliance, a discussion database software application (much like the virtual work space described in chapter 13). The discussion database eliminates the gatekeeper role in the alliance and permits data to be shared in real time by all participants. For example, one alliance member can post a research result, and many people can read and comment on the results as well as any responses to the results. It has also increased the active engagement in the project of the scientists on both sides because the software gives them greater opportunity to comment and provide suggestions for the project. Videoconferences between scientists are more productive because the scientists now immediately post their experimental results on the database, which gives alliance team members additional time to review the results before a discussion begins. The intervention, which began with the health check survey, eliminated an important communication bottleneck and has increased the speed with which the alliance is pursuing its original objectives.

In another instance, the health check survey led to a dramatic improvement in the success of a Lilly alliance with a leading medical school. The purpose of the alliance is to determine which cancer therapies work most effectively with which patients on the basis of their genetic type. The project uses fairly elaborate tracking of cancer patients, therapies, and tumors and is heavily dependent on collecting and analyzing tissue samples from cancer patients. The survey uncovered concerns about the operational processes the alliance used to gather and record the data.

After discussions among the alliance leadership team, the alliance members together reengineered the processes used to gather and report the data. The changes resulted in a 96 percent reduction in cycle time, from 4.5 hours per patient for data management to 10 minutes, and an 18,000 percent increase in productivity, from 4 specimens and no accompanying clinical data in year 1 to 720 specimens with complete clinical data in the first two months of the following year. The medical school met its entire year's goal in just two months, which enabled the alliance to radically improve productivity without increasing cost.

In Summary

Alliance teams are becoming an important part of the business landscape, and organizations that are able to manage them effectively will have a distinct advantage in the marketplace. We have described some of the unique challenges associated with managing alliance teams, including incompatible cultures, shared decision making, differing goals, and large teams. In addition to the challenges we have identified, alliance teams are even more difficult to manage because they tend to be temporary and virtual. Thus, we recommend that managers of alliance teams understand how to effectively manage both temporary teams (see chapter 11) and virtual teams (see chapter 13).

Despite these unique challenges, some organizations, including Eli Lilly, have had a successful track record of creating and managing alliance teams. We believe that the process of planning and executing an alliance team that Lilly has developed provides an excellent template for other organizations to follow, recognizing that some of the steps in the process may need to be modified to meet specific needs and situations. If an alliance team regularly gathers data and assesses its performance, it then can engage in various team-building activities to improve its functioning and performance. To the extent that an organization thoughtfully creates these teams, actively manages them, regularly monitors their progress, and takes corrective action as needed, such teams can spell the difference between success and failure.

Part Four

THE CHALLENGE OF
TEAM BUILDING
FOR THE FUTURE

15

CHALLENGES FOR BUILDING EFFECTIVE TEAMS

In the preceding chapters, we have described what can be done to make teams more effective. We have placed particular emphasis on the ability of teams to change (engage in team building), which we have described as a meta-competency that is crucial for changing team context, composition, or competencies when necessary to improve team performance.

In this final chapter, we summarize what we believe are the important issues for managers, team leaders, and consultants as they help teams they work with be more effective. We also discuss the challenges that all of us will likely face in the future as organizations and their environments become more complex, while the need for teamwork remains high.

Implementing the Four Cs: The Key to Success

We have found that the key to the development of effective teams is successfully managing the Four Cs that we discussed in part 1. Leaders of organizations must be willing to create team-friendly environments for teams to function effectively. This means that they must do the following:

1. Identify the kinds of work activities for which teamwork is likely to prove essential to accomplish the task. Tasks that require reciprocal interdependence between team members typically need strong, well-functioning teams.

2. Use the structure of the organization to reinforce team membership in accomplishing the organization's goals.

This means organizing tasks by teams when teamwork is necessary and assigning accountability to those teams.

3. Select team members on the basis of clear criteria for team membership. We recommend that potential team members be considered based on their technical expertise, interpersonal skills, and motivation to help a team function effectively to achieve its goals. Remember that teams need people to play both task roles and relationship roles for the team to function effectively over time.

4. Train managers and team members on the dynamics of effective teams and team leadership. Too many managers assume that if we just put people together on a team, they will know how to function effectively. The information on effective team dynamics in chapter 4 should be presented to team members and discussed as to how they might apply to their specific team needs and goals. Assigning a team a task to perform without providing sufficient training is much like putting an athletic team out on the field to play the game without ever practicing.

5. Reward team members for team performance. Much like Bain & Company, organizations need to highlight and reward successful teams to create a culture that encourages teamwork. Team progress should be monitored and feedback obtained from team members to track not only team performance but also their feelings about participation on the team. Part of an individual's compensation or performance review needs to be tied to his or her performance on the team.

6. Set aside time for teams to be involved in regular team-building activities. Like the credit union we discussed in chapter 3, organizations need to be willing to set aside time for team development and be willing to pay for it.

7. Help teams develop a competency at team building. Learn to diagnose problems in team functioning as they arise and engage in team-building activities as needed to solve those problems. A variety of problems afflict teams, including interpersonal conflict, the Abilene paradox, and role confusion. Consequently team members need to be able to diagnose such problems and have the ability to identify the appropriate team-building activities for solving those problems and improving team performance.

8. Use appropriate technologies, particularly in the case of virtual teams, to communicate, solve problems, and make decisions.

9. Periodically review team performance, even if there are no apparent problems. We suggest the regular use (generally once a year) of the surveys found in this book—the team context and composition scale (figure 3.1), the team competencies scale (figure 4.2), the team-building checklist (figure 5.1), and measuring alliance health (figure 14.1). If these instruments indicate problems, then the team can engage in some type of team-building activity to solve the problems and improve performance. We have found that role clarification is a particularly useful exercise as a periodic check to see how team members feel about their roles and what might be done in the team to help each other function more effectively.

10. Provide support to help managers and team leaders improve team performance. This means that providing access to internal or external consultants or other resources can help the manager guide the team through the team-building cycle discussed in chapter 5.

We believe that if organizations, team consultants, and team leaders take these ten suggestions seriously, we would see improved performance and higher satisfaction for those who work in a team environment.

Challenges Facing Organizations of the Future

A number of trends will challenge organizations as they try to make their teams more effective:

- The lack of teamwork skills in tomorrow's workforce
- The increasing need for teams to work together in cross-cultural teams, in virtual workplaces, and across organizational boundaries
- The increasing need for team leaders who can manage team diversity inherent in a global economy

We briefly discuss each of these in turn.

Finding and Developing Employees with Team Skills

One of the challenges facing leaders of organizations is to find employees with the ability to work effectively in a team environment. They typically rely on our educational institutions to provide their prospective recruits with the skills needed to carry out their work. However, in our experience, few educators train students to be effective team players. Moreover, there is increasing evidence that more recent generations—Gen X and Gen Y and millennials—are terrific with technology but are often very self-focused and do not develop the interpersonal skills or patience to work effectively with others in teams. They also typically expect and need lots of praise to stay motivated and are not adept at handling critical feedback.

Our experience in working in academia for several decades is that most education systems undermine the development of team skills in their students. Students are encouraged to work independently and not collaborate with one another. Grades (performance) are explicitly tied to individual performance. This creates an emphasis in self-interest—rather than an orientation to collaborate with others—that can work against the kinds of behaviors needed for successful teamwork. Jerry Harvey, in a rather controversial chapter titled "Encouraging Future Managers to Cheat," argues that the emphasis on "doing one's own work" has a negative impact on the cooperative spirit needed in organizations today.[1] Harvey argues that "cheating" is often defined as helping someone else with an assignment or doing their work for them. Thus, the only "good" student is one who works alone without collaboration or help. Moreover, grades typically are based on individual and not group performance, and thus group-oriented work is not rewarded. And even when an instructor makes group assignments, often he or she offers little or no training to students to help them function effectively as a group in carrying out the assignment. Thus, in our experience, due to the lack of thought, preparation, and training for group work, most student groups function rather poorly, and many students see group work as "dragging them down" and hurting their grade point average. Rather than a positive or even neutral view of teams, students graduate with a rather negative view about the role of teams in achieving goals.

Furthermore, the key interpersonal skills needed to function in groups, such as communication, problem solving, and conflict management, are not part of the curriculum. Students often are well prepared for the technical aspects of a team assignment but ill prepared to work through the difficult interpersonal issues that must be managed in any team. Uncooperative team members are avoided rather than confronted, social loafing is allowed to take place, and conflicts are swept under the rug or allowed to remain unresolved. Students know that the semester will soon end, so they can sweat it out until the end of the semester, the class will end, and then they no longer have to deal with those group members.

We believe that educators need to be more skilled in team learning and development and need to provide meaningful assignments that allow students to develop team skills and have positive team experiences. This may be particularly important in the future, because many students will not have had the experience of positive team experiences in their first learning environment, the home, given that about 50 percent of all marriages end in divorce and many still-intact families are rife with conflict. In such cases, students' "team of origin" will not have provided them with a positive view of being dependent on others, since those others (family members) may have let them down or even inflicted harm. Given that our first experience and view of what a team is comes from our experience in our families, one must wonder how effectively the families of the future will be preparing children to live in a world that requires teamwork. Such a condition makes it imperative that educators strive to help students develop a positive attitude toward group work and the development of skills that will allow them to function effectively in groups.

Unfortunately, not all families or educators will prepare future generations to work effectively in teams. Hence, it will likely be up to organizations themselves to develop training programs to orient employees to teamwork and provide them with the skills necessary for success in a team environment.

Teams Without Clear Boundaries

In chapters 13 and 14, we discussed the important role that virtual teams and alliance teams are playing now. We believe that there will be a continued trend for the use of these types of teams in the future. Organizations will find it increasingly important for individuals who are not in the same physical space to work together. Hence, they will have to learn to function effectively as virtual teams. Furthermore, joint ventures and strategic alliances will continue to be important features of the strategies of many firms. The creation of effective alliance teams to manage their shared interests will be critical for the success of such ventures.

As we have noted, building trust, developing effective means of communicating and problem solving, and creating common incentives for group members to work together are key aspects of developing successful virtual or alliance teams. Technology will likely continue to advance and will speed and improve communications, whether it's through handheld video communication, teleconferencing, or more effective e-mail systems, allowing people to effectively coordinate their work. The ability of organizations to use communication technologies to coordinate effectively will likely be a source of team success and may give a competitive advantage in the future. Moreover, when the boundaries of the team are more ambiguous, the need for monitoring team performance and engaging in team-building activities likely will become even more important.

Globalization and Teamwork

The globalization of industry will make teamwork more challenging in the future. Teams of the future will be composed more and more of members who speak dissimilar languages and have dissimilar cultures, values, and approaches to solving problems. In chapter 12, we noted the cultural differences in how people view relationships, power, uncertainty, and other factors that are important for individuals to communicate and coordinate their efforts effectively. To the extent that we find more multicultural teams in the future, team building will become more important. Creating a context that creates incentives for team members to work together will be critical for success, as will creating a common understanding among team members of what effective team dynamics are and of how they should function effectively as a team. Moreover, developing a common language whereby team members can understand one another and communicate effectively will be crucial. Thus, team-building exercises such as role clarification likely will prove to be important activities for such teams to succeed, given that different cultural values and language may foster misunderstandings among team members, making effective performance difficult.

The nature of work in the twenty-first century and increasing globalization will continue to make team-building activities a high priority for managers in the future. Without such an emphasis on teams, the likelihood of success on the part of global organizations will be reduced.

Conclusion

Throughout this book, we have described what can be done to improve the effectiveness of teams. In our experience, much of our own personal success, satisfaction, and also frustration has come from working on teams. Teams that work well give us energy, motivation, and a sense of accomplishment. Those that function poorly leave us feeling frustrated and unwilling to expend our best efforts to see the team succeed. To make a team successful requires not only the knowledge that we have presented in this book, but also a commitment on the part of individual team members to take the initiative to make their team function more effectively.

One of our father Bill Dyer's favorite, yet sad, lines in literature comes from *Walden*, when Thoreau writes, "The mass of men [and women] lead lives of quiet desperation."[2] To avoid such feelings of desperation, Bill's vision of a better world was to help family, church, and work teams function in such a way that members of those teams felt the rewards and satisfaction of collaborating with and supporting others to achieve meaningful goals.

For those of you who are working on an ineffective team, we encourage you to change your team for the better by speaking up to encourage the team to develop new ways of functioning that will help improve its performance. It takes courage to say, "I don't think our team is functioning as well as it could. What can we do to make it function more effectively so we can have a more positive team experience?" The ideas presented in this book have proven effective in improving team performance, and we believe they will prove helpful to you as you encourage your team to diagnose its problems and develop plans to improve its effectiveness. Our hope is that this book will provide you with both the motivation and the information you will need to improve your team's performance.

NOTES

Introduction

1. S. Milgram, *Obedience to Authority* (New York: HarperCollins, 1974); D. McGregor, *The Human Side of Enterprise* (New York: McGraw-Hill, 1960).
2. J. Campbell and M. Dunnette, "Effectiveness of T-Group Experiences in Managerial Training and Development," *Psychological Bulletin* 70 (1968): 73–103.
3. W. G. Dyer, *Team Building: Issues and Alternatives* (Reading, MA: Addison-Wesley, 1977), 23.
4. Jeff H. Dyer, Hal Gregersen, and Clayton Christensen, *The Innovator's DNA* (Boston: Harvard Business School Press, 2011).

Chapter One

1. J. Collins, *Good to Great* (New York: HarperCollins, 2001).
2. For an in-depth description of how Toyota shares knowledge across interorganizational boundaries to improve performance, see Jeffrey H. Dyer and Nile Hatch, "Using Supplier Networks to Learn Faster," *Sloan Management Review* (Spring 2004): 57–63.

Chapter Two

1. J. D. Thompson, *Organizations in Action* (New York: McGraw-Hill, 1967).
2. R. W. Scott, *Organizations: Rational, Natural, and Open Systems*, 2nd ed. (Englewood Cliffs, NJ: Prentice Hall, 1981), 212–13.

Chapter Three

1. L. C. McDermott, N. Brawley, and W. W. Waite, *World Class Teams: Working Across Borders* (New York: Wiley, 1998).
2. G. M. Parker, *Cross-Functional Teams: Working with Allies, Enemies, and Other Strangers* (San Francisco: Jossey-Bass, 2003).
3. J. R. Katzenbach and D. K. Smith, *The Wisdom of Teams* (New York: HarperCollins, 2003), 275.
4. Parker, *Cross-Functional Teams*, 166.
5. Mark Gottfredsen, partner at Bain & Company.
6. The MBA dream companies list is available at Jonathan Thaw, "Google Is Top Dream Company' for MBA Students, Survey Finds," May 4, 2007, http://www.bloomberg.com/apps/news?pid=newsarchive&sid=a18GLUPScNzs.
7. N. J. Perry, "A Consulting Firm Too Hot to Handle," *Fortune*, April 27, 1987, 91.

Chapter Four

1. D. McGregor, *The Human Side of Enterprise* (New York: McGraw-Hill, 1960). Also see J. Lipman-Blumen and H. J. Leavitt, *Hot Groups* (New York: Oxford University Press, 1999).
2. *Meetings, Bloody Meetings* (Chicago: Video Arts, 1994), videotape.
3. For examples of such exercises, see D. L. Anderson, *Organization Development: The Process of Leading Organizational Change*, 2nd ed. (Thousand Oaks, CA: Sage, 2012).
4. J. Hilburt-Davis and W. Gibb Dyer, *Consulting to Family Businesses* (San Francisco: Jossey-Bass, 2003).

Chapter Five

1. E. H. Schein, *Process Consultation: Its Role in Organization Development* (Reading, MA: Addison-Wesley, 1988).

Chapter Six

1. For a description of a variety of team-building activities, see www.pfeiffer.com and review the books and exercises developed by Lorraine L. Ukens or Steve Sugar and George Takac; the latter are the authors of *Games That Teach Teams: 21 Activities to Super-Charge Your Group!* (San Francisco: Jossey-Bass/Pfeiffer, 1999), or see B. C. Miller's *Quick Teambuilding Activities for Busy Managers: 50 Exercises That Get Results in Just 15 Minutes* (New York: Amacom, 2004).

2. Kurt Lewin, "Group Discussion and Social Change," in T. M. Newcomb and E. L. Hartley (eds.), *Readings in Social Psychology* (New York: Holt, 1947); W. G. Dyer, *Strategies for Managing Change* (Reading, MA: Addison-Wesley, 1984).

3. J. K. Cherney, "Appreciative Teambuilding: Creating a Climate for Great Collaboration," 2005, www.teambuildinginc.com/article_ai.htm.

4. Ibid.

5. Ibid.

6. R. Beckhard, "The Confrontation Meeting," *Harvard Business Review* 45 (1967): 149–55. M. Weisbord and S. Janoff, *Future Search: Getting the Whole System in the Room for Vision, Commitment, and Action* (San Francisco: Berrett-Koehler, 2010).

7. R. Harrison, "Role Negotiations: A Tough-Minded Approach to Team Development," in W. Burke and H. Hornstein (eds.), *The Social Technology of Organization Development* (Washington, DC: NTL Learning Resources, 1971).

8. R. W. Boss, *Organization Development in Health Care, Part II* (Reading, MA: Addison-Wesley, 1989).

9. R. W. Boss, "Team Building and the Problem of Regression: The Personal Management Interview as an Intervention," *Journal of Applied Behavioral Science* 19 (1983): 75. See also a more extended discussion in ibid.

10. R. W. Boss, personal communication to the editors, May 31, 2006.

11. R. Likert, *The Human Organization* (New York: McGraw-Hill, 1967), chap. 4.

Chapter Seven

1. The problem is just as acute with children, especially teenage children. Parents have expectations about how children ought to behave, study, treat their elders, handle their money, do work around the house, wear their clothes, and so on. Children often do not understand these expectations until the expectations are violated—and then conflict arises because their parents clearly aren't happy when the children don't dress "appropriately" or don't spend enough time doing homework. In the same way, children have expectations of parents that parents may not understand. Children may like parents to be seen but not heard when their friends are around, not make a scene when the restaurant bill is added incorrectly, not to get uptight if one of their children flunks an exam once, and try to understand rather than jump to conclusions. It is not uncommon for children to feel frustrated and powerless when parents violate their expectations (in much the same way that a subordinate feels powerless when his boss violates his expectations) because they feel their parents are too powerful to confront.

2. For more on the nature of conflict and how to manage it, see K. A. Jenn and E. A. Mannix, "The Dynamic Nature of Conflict: A Longitudinal Study of Intragroup Conflict and Group Performance," *Academy of Management Journal* 44 (2001): 238–51; and R. E. Walton, *Managing Conflict: Interpersonal Dialogue and Third-Party Roles*, 2nd ed. (Reading, MA: Addison-Wesley, 1987).

3. For a discussion of diversity and innovation in organizations, see L. Thompson, *Making the Team: A Guide for Managers* (Upper Saddle River, NJ: Pearson, 2011); T. Kelly, *The Art of Innovation: Lessons in Creativity from IDEO, America's Leading Design Firm* (New York: Doubleday, 2001); and D. Tjosvold,

Team Organization (New York: Wiley, 1991), especially chap. 10. See also Tjosvold's book *The Conflict-Positive Organization: Stimulate Diversity and Create Unity* (Reading, MA: Addison-Wesley, 1991).

4. R. A. Lutz, *Guts* (Hoboken, NJ: Wiley, 2003), chap. 9.

Chapter Eight

1. Much of the material in the "The Abilene Paradox" was contained in J. Harvey, "Managing Agreement in Organizations: The Abilene Paradox." Reprinted by permission of the publisher from *Organizational Dynamics*, Summer 1974, copyright © 1974 by AMACOM, a division of the American Management Association. It is also found in Harvey's book *The Abilene Paradox and Other Meditations on Management* (Lexington, MA: Lexington Books, 1988).

2. Ibid., 63–80.

3. The term *own up* has a precise meaning. Essentially, owning up is (1) a first-person statement beginning with the word *I* ("I think," "I believe," "I want") in which the individual (2) clearly communicates his or her own ideas and feelings about an issue (3) in a descriptive way (4) without attributing an idea, a feeling, a belief, or a motivation to another.

4. See C. Argyris, *Intervention Theory and Method: A Behavioralz-Science Approach* (Reading, MA: Addison-Wesley, 1970); and C. Argyris and D. Schön, *Theory in Practice* (San Francisco: Jossey-Bass, 1974).

5. R. Beckhard, "The Confrontation Meeting," *Harvard Business Review* 45 (1967): 149–55. W. W. Burke, *Organization Development: A Process of Learning and Changing*, 2nd ed. (Reading, MA: Addison-Wesley, 1994), esp. chap. 4; and E. H. Schein, *Process Consultation*, 2nd ed. (Reading, MA: Addison-Wesley, 1988).

6. *The Abilene Paradox* (Carlsbad, CA: CRM Learning, 2002), videotape. This humorous yet effective video illustrates the perils of the Abilene paradox.

Chapter Nine

1. The early research on interdepartmental conflicts can be found in P. R. Lawrence and J. W. Lorsch, *Organization and Environment: Managing Differentiation and Integration* (Boston: Division of Research, Harvard Business School, 1967).

2. The basic theory and method for intergroup processes are found in R. Blake, H. Shepard, and J. Mouton, *Managing Intergroup Conflict in Industry* (Houston: Gulf, 1954). For other discussions on intergroup team-building strategies, see J. K. Fordyce and R. Weil, *Managing with People* (Reading, MA: Addison- Wesley, 1971), pp. 123–30; R. Beckhard, *Organization Development: Strategies and Models* (Reading, MA: Addison-Wesley, 1969); and E. H. Schein, *Organizational Psychology*, 3rd ed. (Upper Saddle River, NJ: Prentice Hall, 1980), chap. 5. A more recent review of intergroup conflict is L. L. Thompson, *Making the Team: A Guide for Managers* (Upper Saddle River, NJ: Pearson, 2011).

Chapter Ten

1. This research was done by J. Dyer, H. Gregersen, and C. Christensen as part of The Innovator's DNA research project, some of it published in *The Innovator's DNA* (Boston: Harvard Business School Press, 2011). Quotations in this chapter from Gil Cloyd, A. G. Lafley, David Neeleman, Herb Kelleher, John Gardner, Michael Dell, Kevin Rollins, Pierre Omidyar, David Kelley, Matt Adams, John Foster, and other executives are taken from this original research.

2. You can gain an idea of your propensity to engage and use these five skills through a self-assessment or 360-degree assessment found at www.InnovatorsDNA.com.

3. A. Edmondson, "Psychological Safety and Learning Behavior in Work Teams," *Administrative Science Quarterly* 44 (1999): 350–83.

4. D. Ariely, *The Upside of Irrationality* (New York: HarperCollins, 2010).

5. J. H. Dyer, H. B. Gregersen, and C. Christensen, "Entrepreneur Behaviors, Opportunity Recognition, and the Origins of Innovative Ventures," *Strategic Entrepreneurship Journal* 2 (2008): 317–38.

6. Nightline, *Deep Dive video*, February 9, 1999, videotape.

7. Ibid.

8. For more details on QuestionStorming, see chapter 3 in Dyer, Gregersen, and Christensen, *The Innovator's DNA*.

9. Nightline, *Deep Dive*.

10. Interview with David Kelley at Stanford University's business and design school, August 21, 2006, http://sites.google.com/site/wyndowe/iinnovateepisode3:davidkelley,founder ofideo.

11. Nightline, *Deep Dive*.

Chapter Twelve

1. E. B. Magnus, "The Conceptualization of Social Complexity in Global Teams," *Nordic Psychology* 63 (2011): 35.

2. D. C. Hambrick, S. C. Davidson, S. A. Snell, and C. C. Snow, "When Groups Consist of Multiple Nationalities: Towards a New Understanding of the Implications," *Organization Studies* 19 (1998): 182.

3. E. H. Schein, *Organizational Culture and Leadership*, 4th ed. (San Francisco: Jossey-Bass, 2010).

4. G. Hofstede, *Culture's Consequences: International Differences in Work-Related Values* (Thousand Oaks, CA: Sage, 1980).

5. K. Lagerstrom and M. Andersson, "Creating and Sharing Knowledge Within a Transitional Team: The Development of a Global Business System," *Journal of World Business* 38 (2003): 84–95. See also T. M. Paulus, B. Bichelmeyer, L. Malopinsky, M. Pereira, and P. Rastogi, "Power Distance and Group Dynamics of an International Project Team: A Case Study," *Teaching in Higher Education* 10 (2005): 43–55.

6. N. Goodman, "Cultivating Cultural Intelligence," *Training* 48 (March-April 2011): 38.

7. D. J. Pauleen, "Leadership in a Global Virtual Team: An Action Learning Approach." *Leadership and Organization Development Journal* 24 (2003): 157.

Chapter Thirteen

1. Reported in C. M. Solomon, "Managing Virtual Teams," *Workforce* 80, no. 6 (2001): 60.
2. This example of a virtual work space is taken from A. Majchrzak, A. Malhotra, J. Stamps, and J. Lipnack, "Can Absence Make a Team Grow Stronger?" *Harvard Business Review* 82, no. 5 (May 2004): 134–35.
3. Ibid.

Chapter Fourteen

1. P. Drucker, "Nonprofit Profit," *Alliance Analyst*, November 11, 1996, http://allianceanalyst.com.
2. Columbia University, European Trade Commission, Studies by Booz Allen & Hamilton, 1999 as reported in a presentation by William Lundberg, President of the Association of Alliance Professionals at its Fall Summit, November 6, 2001.
3. P. Kale, J. H. Dyer, and H. Singh, "Alliance Capability, Stock Market Response, and Long-Term Alliance Success: The Role of the Alliance Function," *Strategic Management Journal* 23 (2002): 747–67.
4. PricewaterhouseCoopers study reported in exhibit 2 of N. Sims, R. Harrison, and A. Gueth, "Managing Alliances at Lilly," *In Vivo: The Business and Medicine Report*, June 2001.
5. We thank numerous members of the Office of Alliance Management (OAM) at Eli Lilly and Company for providing insights into how Lilly manages its alliances teams. This chapter draws heavily on interviews with Gary Stach and Nelson Sims, current and past executive directors of OAM, and Michael Ransom and Dave Haase, current and past managers of OAM, as well as the following publications by individuals from OAM:

Nelson Sims, Roger Harrison, and Anton Gueth, "Managing Alliances at Lilly," *In Vivo: The Business and Medicine Report*, June 2001; and David Futrell, Marlene Slugay, and Carol H. Stephens, "Becoming a Premier Partner: Measuring, Managing and Changing Partnering Capabilities at Eli Lilly and Company," *Journal of Commercial Biotechnology* 8 (Summer 2001): 5–13.

6. Interview with OAM executive director Nelson Sims, October 2000.

Chapter Fifteen

1. Jerry Harvey, *The Abilene Paradox and Other Meditations on Management* (Lexington, MA: Lexington Books, 1988).
2. D. Thoreau, *Walden* (New York: Harper and Row, 1961), 8.

THE AUTHORS

W. Gibb Dyer Jr. is the O. Leslie Stone Professor of Entrepreneurship and the academic director of the Center for Economic Self-Reliance in the Marriott School of Management at Brigham Young University (BYU). He received his BS and MBA degrees from BYU and his PhD degree in management philosophy from the Massachusetts Institute of Technology. He has also served as a visiting professor at IESE (Instituto de Estudios Superiores de la Empresa) in Barcelona, Spain, and in 2005 was a visiting scholar at the University of Bath in England. He publishes widely on the topics of family business, entrepreneurship, organizational culture, and managing change in organizations, and his articles have appeared in many of the top journals in his field, including *Academy of Management Review, Sloan Management Review, Entrepreneurship: Theory and Practice,* and *Family Business Review.*

Because of his innovative approach to teaching, Dyer was awarded the 1990 Leavy Award for Excellence in Private Enterprise Education by the Freedoms Foundation at Valley Forge. He has consulted with numerous organizations such as General Growth Properties and NuSkin Enterprises and is a recognized authority on organizational change, family business, and entrepreneurship. He has been quoted in publications such as *Fortune,* the *Wall Street Journal,* the *New York Times,* and *Nation's Business.* At BYU, he has previously served as chair of the Department of Organizational Behavior, as director of the Master's Program in Organizational Behavior, and on the University Council on Faculty Rank and Status. In 2008 he was given the Outstanding Faculty Award from the Marriott School. He and his wife, Theresa, are the parents of seven children—six daughters and one son.

Jeffrey H. Dyer (PhD, UCLA) is the Horace Beesley Professor of Strategy at the Marriott School, Brigham Young University, as well as professor of strategy at the University of Pennsylvania's Wharton School. He was formerly a manager at Bain & Company, a management consultancy. Dyer regularly delivers speeches and workshops on innovation and strategy and consults with leaders at companies like General Electric, General Mills, Gilead Sciences, Harley Davidson, Hewlett Packard, Intel, Sony, Johnson & Johnson, and Medtronic.

Dyer is the only strategy scholar in the world to have published five times in the *Strategic Management Journal* (the top academic journal in strategy) and *Harvard Business Review* (the top practitioner journal). He was ranked the fourth most cited management scholar in the world from 1996 to 2006. His research has been featured in the *Economist, Forbes, BusinessWeek, Fortune,* CNN, *Fast Company*, and the *Wall Street Journal*. His research has won awards from McKinsey & Company, the Strategic Management Society, the Institute of Management Science, and the Academy of Management. His Oxford University Press book, *Collaborative Advantage*, won the Shingo Prize Research Award. His most recent book, *The Innovator's DNA*, coauthored with Hal Gregersen and Clayton Christensen, is a business best-seller published by Harvard Business Review Press.

William G. Dyer was the past dean of the Marriott School of Management and founder of the Department of Organizational Behavior at Brigham Young University (BYU). He served as a private consultant to many companies, including Exxon, General Foods, AT&T, and Honeywell. He was the author of numerous books and articles on the topics of organizational change and team dynamics. During the last years of his life, he devoted much of his time to the plight of Native Americans and others who were in need or disadvantaged. He received his BA and MA degrees from BYU and his Ph.D. degree from the University of Wisconsin. He passed away in 1997.

Index

f represents figure; *t* represents table.

A

Abilene paradox, 155–160, 166
Absenteeism, 163
Academic programs, 22; lack of collaboration in, 272–274; modular interdependence in, 26–27
Accountability, 67
Accounting departments, 27
Action planning: description of, 99, 119; goals of, 119; options for, 119–120
Action summaries, 216–217
Ad hoc teams. *See* Temporary teams
Adams, M., 197, 202
Agenda, meeting: for personal management interviews, 121, 122; purpose of, 67–68
Agreeableness, 155
Agreement, unhealthy, 155–166
Aircraft design, 29
Alliance teams: annual checks of, 257–265; challenges of, 274–275; communication and work planning documents in, 256–257; communication solutions in, 263–264; cultural assessment in, 251–253; definition of, 13; example of, 250–265; failure rate of, 248, 251; growth in, 247; versus internal teams, 248–250; need for, 12–13; strategic decision making for, 254–256; strategic futures exercise for, 253–254
Amazon.com, 40–42, 186
Amnesty, 69
Anger, 161, 162
Annual health checks, 258–264
Anonymous sources, 97
Anthony, C., 28–29
Appreciative inquiry approach: benefits of, 115–116; for cross-cultural teams, 228; description of, 114–115; for interteam conflict management, 174
Argyris, C., 2

Ariely, D., 191
Artifacts, 220–221
Asian people, 228, 232
Assessments: online, vii; of organization's culture, structure, and systems, 55; of team competencies, 76, 77–81*f*; of team context and composition, 52–53*f*; of team leaders, 49–50; of team members' skills, 40; of team satisfaction, 49–50
Assignment summaries, 120, 216–217
Association of Strategic Alliance Professionals, 250
Associational thinking, 186
Assumptions, shared, 223–226
Atomic Energy Committee, 208–209
Audioconferences, 241, 242*t*, 243
Authoritarian leaders, 87
Automobile companies, 209
Autonomous teams. *See* Self-directed teams
Avoiding conflicts, 86–87

B

Bain & Company, 37, 270; team building in, 91; team composition in, 42–51
Banting, F., 250
Baseball teams, 27, 28
Basketball teams, 28–29
Beckhard, D., 2–3, 6, 118, 165
Benioff, M., 186, 240
Best, C. H., 250
Bezos, J., 186
Bias, 191
Biotech companies, 250, 251
Blame, 135, 161, 162
Blank slide presentation, 46
Board of directors, 82–84
Bonuses, 54
Boss, W., 120–122
Boss-team relationships, subordinate, 58, 59*t*, 87
Boston Consulting Group, 50
Boundaries, 274–275

Boy Scouts, 222
Brainstorming, 187, 199–201
Buddies, team, 48
Burke, W., 165
Bushe, G., 115
Business expertise, 195–196

C

Campbell, J., 5
Car manufacturers, 34–35
Case analysis, 111
Cell phone assembly plants, 35–36
Challenges, innovation, 187
Change, attitudes about, 106, 107f
Change management skills of teams: in
     cross-cultural teams, 230; definition of,
     14f; description of, 17–18; of temporary
     teams, 217–218. *See also* Team building
Change, resistance to: versus innovation,
     72; team leaders versus team members
     and, 87
Chatter, 240
Cheating, 273
Cheese graters, 197–202
Children: subordinate role of, 282–283;
     swapping of, among families, 3–4
Christensen, C., 7, 183, 186, 190, 197
Chrysler, 34–35, 236–237
Classroom culture, 223, 226
Closed-ended surveys, 95
Cloyd, G., 188
Coaches: description of, 74; mistakes of, 75;
     team leaders as, 74–75
Collaboration: barriers to, 110; developing,
     71–72; importance of, 61; lack of, in
     schools, 272–274; of virtual teams,
     239–240
Commitment, 259
Communications: in agreement management,
     165; in alliance teams, 256–257,
     263–264; brainstorming problems with,
     200–201; conflict management and,
     135–136; of cross-cultural teams,
     228–229, 231; cultural norms and, 221;
     diversity and, 149; importance of, 61;
     opening channels of, 70–71; problems
     with, 110; of staff versus teams, 59t; with
     stakeholders, 218; temporary teams and,
     218; of virtual teams, 236–243
Competencies of teams: in cross-cultural
     teams, 229–230; definition of, 14f;
     description of, 17, 57; developing
     guidelines and metrics for, 64–65;
     development of, 58–76; example of, 76,
     82–84; identifying, 64; levels of, 73;
     measurement of, 76, 77–81f; most
     important of, 60–61; team leaders as
     educators and, 60–64

Complementary skills, 192–196
Composition of teams: assessment of, 50;
     characteristics of team leaders and
     members in, 37–39; in cross-cultural
     teams, 228–229; culture of organization
     and, 44–45, 55; definition of, 14f;
     description of, 15–17; example of, 42–51;
     finding team members and, 39–41;
     importance of, 50; measurement of team
     satisfaction and, 49–50; motivation of
     members and, 39–40; organizational
     rewards and, 51, 54; personal
     development and, 48–49; team
     assignments and, 56; team chemistry and,
     47–48; team development and, 51, 54–55;
     team dynamics and, 47; team leadership
     skills and, 45–46; team process in, 46–47;
     team size and, 41–42
Compromise, 143
Confirmation-disconfirmation process, 118
Conflict management: clarification exercise
     in, 135–142; of cross-cultural teams,
     230–233; importance of, 61, 71; for
     interteam conflicts, 170–181; negotiating
     agreement in, 134–135; start-stop-
     continue exercise in, 142–144; of
     temporary teams, 215–216
Conflicts: in alliance teams, 252; among team
     members, 88–91; avoidance of, 86–87;
     cause of, 170; description of, 129;
     diversity as source of, 147–149;
     expectation theory of, 129–134; feedback
     and, 71; managers as center of, 144–147;
     one team member as source of, 149–153;
     signs of, 88; of staff versus teams, 59t; in
     temporary teams, 214
Conformity, 86–87
Confrontations, 150–151, 232
Congruent person, 3
Consensus, 66, 214–215
Consequence symptoms, 85–86
Consultants: in action planning, 99; for
     agreement management, 164–165; in
     appreciative inquiry approach, 114–115;
     in data analysis phase, 110; for data
     gathering, 94–96, 109; to elicit
     information about team leaders, 145; in
     evaluation efforts, 100; in preparation
     phase of team building, 105; recruitment
     of, 44–45; role of, 93; seeking help from,
     90f, 92
Consulting magazine, 50
Consulting to Family Businesses (Dyer &
     Hilburt-Davis), 82
Context of teams: assessment of, 50; in cross-
     cultural teams, 226–228; culture of
     organization and, 33–34; definition of,
     14f; description of, 14–15; importance of,
     25, 50, 169; interteam problems and, 172;

lack of teamwork and, 21–25, 169; nature of task and, 25–30; structure of organization and, 34–35; systems of organization and, 35–36; types of teams and, 30–33; of virtual teams, 244
Continuous improvement, 18, 91
Contract negotiations, 119
Controversies, constructive, 148
Coons, T., 239
Creativity, 189, 199
Crisis, 136
Critiquing, 149
Cross-cultural teams: benefits and drawbacks of, 219; cultural variables influencing, 224–225t; description of, 234; Four Cs in, 226–230; increasing number of, 219; need for, 12–13; violated expectations in, 230–233
Cultural assessments, 251–253
Cultural fit, 258, 259
Culture, ethnic: of alliance teams, 251–253; artifacts of, 220–221; definition of, 220; future challenges involving, 275–276; norms of, 221–222; shared assumptions in, 223–226; types of, 220; values of, 222–223; of virtual teams, 236, 244
Culture, of organization: assessment of, 55; assumptions underlying, 34; description of, 33–34; example of, 42–43; importance of, 33, 34
Curriculum committee, 208–210

D

Daimler-Benz, 236–237
Data analysis: alternatives to, 111–112; goals of, 110–111; process of, 98–99
Data gathering: for agreement management, 164–166; alternatives to, 106–109; for evaluation of team building, 100; for follow-up, 125; in team-building process, 93–98, 106–109
Data sharing, 59t, 97–98
Dateline (TV show), 196–197
Decision making: in alliance teams, 252, 254–256; of cross-cultural teams, 232; process for, 66–67; of temporary teams, 209–210, 214–215; unhealthy agreement and, 155–166
Decision teams, 30
Deep dives, 199
Dell Computer, 193
Dell, M., 193
Descriptive feedback, 117
Diabetes care, 250–251
Direct feedback, 146
Discovery: description of, 184; developing skills of, 185–188; execution balanced

with, 193–194; innovation and, 185; time engaged in, 185t
Discussion databases, 264
Disruptive people, 149–150, 186
Diversity: brainstorming and, 201; of opinions, 87; source of, 147; as source of conflict, 147–149; in temporary teams, 215–216; of virtual teams, 236
Documentation: of meetings, 68; of virtual communication, 241
Drucker, P., 247
Due diligence, 251–253
Duncan, T., 28
Dunnette, M., 5
Dyer, B., 1, 4, 276
Dyer, G., 82
Dyer, J., 4, 42, 183, 186, 190, 197
Dyer, M., 4
Dyer Student Team Assessment, vii
Dyer Team Assessment, v
Dyer, W. G., 1, 2–7

E

eBay, 193
Education systems, 272–274
Educators, team leaders as, 60–74
Eli Lilly and Company, 250–265
E-mail, 238, 240–241, 242t
Employee satisfaction, 45–46
Envelope exchange, 118
Ergonomics, 198
Ethnic groups, 147
Evaluations, 100
Execution: complementary types of, 192–193; description of, 184; discovery balanced with, 193–194; innovation and, 185; time engaged in, 185t
Executive committees, 27–28
Expectation theory, 129–134
Expectations, 148–149; in cross-cultural teams, 230–233; of temporary teams, 212–213
Experimenting process, 201–202
Experimenting skills, 186
Expertise, complementary, 192–196
Extraordinary teams, 44–45, 47
Extrinsic motivation, 39

F

Facebook, 240
Facilitators: for interteam conflict management, 174–175; seeking help from, 90f, 92; team leaders as, 75–76
Failure, 46–47; of alliance teams, 248, 251; psychological safety and, 190; risk taking and, 72
Failure-to-listen problem, 200

Family dynamics, 3–4
Fault, 135, 161, 162
Feedback: conflict and, 71; description of, 70; to disruptive people, 150–151; form for, 70–71; goals of, 117; guidelines for, 117; leaders asking for, 145; problems of, 116; in role clarification exercise, 140; for staff versus teams, 59t; types of, 117–119
FIBA (International Basketball Federation) World Championship, 28–29
Financial departments, 27
First-idea-in-line problem, 200
Focal person, 139–140
Focus groups, 261
Follow-up: importance of, 120; for interteam conflict management, 176–177; personal management interviews for, 120–123; team sessions for, 123–126
Force-field analysis, 113
Forcing, 144
Foster, J., 202
Four Cs of Team Performance: description of, 13–18; implementation of, 269–272. *See also specific factors*
Free-rider problem, 201
Friendships, 134
Frustration, 161, 162
Functional pairs, 255–256

G

Gandhi, M., 203
Gardner, J., 192
Gen X and Gen Y, 272
Genentech Inc., 251
Gibb, J., 1, 2, 6, 7
Global economy, 12–13
Globalization, 275–276
Goal setting: description of, 65; importance of, 65; problem-solving method for, 46; of staff versus teams, 59t; team assignments and, 56; team selection and, 40
Goals: of action planning, 119; of alliance teams, 253–254; of data analysis phase, 110–111; of data gathering phase, 106; diversity and, 148; of feedback, 117; in follow-up sessions, 124; importance of, 61; of problem solving, 114; in role clarification exercise, 137, 138; of team-building preparation phase, 104–105; of team-building programs, 103, 171; of temporary teams, 213–214
Golf team, 26
Goodman, N., 229
Greetings, 221
Gregersen, H., 7, 183, 186, 190, 197
Ground rules, 138–139, 171
Group dynamics, 2

H

Haase, D., 253
Harvey, J., 155–156, 160, 273
Health check surveys, 258–264
Hilburt-Davis, J., 82
Hofstede, G., 223
Honda, 35
Honest broker, 251
Honesty, 3
Howorth, M., 44
Human factors, 195
Human resources, 137
Human Side of Enterprise (McGregor), 2
Humanistic psychology movement, 2

I

IDEO, 192, 194–202, 222–223
Ignoring, 143
Implementing plans, 99–100
Individual assignments, 151–152, 200
Individual performance, 272–273
Informal communication, 135–136
Innovation, encouraging, 72
Innovative teams: characteristics of, 183–184; leaders of, 183–196; processes that encourage, 196–202
The Innovator's DNA (Gibb, Gregerssen, & Christensen), 7, 183, 197
Insulin, 250–251
Intellectual leadership, 45
Interdependency, 46–47
International Basketball Federation (FIBA) World Championship, 28–29
Interns, 44
Interorganizational alliance teams. *See* Alliance teams
Interpersonal skills, 272–274
Interpreters, 228
Interteam development programs, 170–181
Interventions, 151
Interviews: for data gathering, 95–97; for follow-up, 120–122, 125; to recruit employees, 43
Intimidating people, 201
Intranet, 239
Intrinsic motivation, 39
Isolating people, 151, 152
Iverson, A., 28

J

Japanese culture, 220–221, 234
Job descriptions, 135
Jobs, S., 186

K

Kaizen, 18, 91
Katzenbach, J. R., 41
Kelleher, H., 189–190
Kelley, D., 196, 198, 201
Knowledge management, 259

L

Laboratory training, 146
Lafley, A. G., 188
Language differences, 228–229, 237
Large teams, 41
Layoffs, 32–33
Leaders. *See* Team leaders
Leadership, shared, 63–64
Leadership skills, 45–46
Likert, R., 123
Lilienthal, D., 208
Limited participation, 151
Listening, 200
Lutz, B., 150

M

Majority voting, 216
Management profiles, 118
Managers, ineffective: relationships of, with
    team members, 57, 58; scenario about,
    11–12, 18–19; support of team
    development by, 51; team-building time
    and, 24–25; transition of, to effective
    managers, 59–60
Managers, role of: in action planning, 99;
    clarification of, 140–141; in conflict,
    144–147; in evaluation of team building,
    100; in preparation phase of team
    building, 105; in rewards systems, 51, 54;
    in staff versus team, 58, 59t; in success of
    team, 4; in team building, 51, 93
Marketing, 255–256
Married people, 130–132, 274
Maslow, A., 2, 3
Maslow, B., 3
McGregor, D., 2, 60
McLean, H., 4
Meetings: conflicts regarding, 135, 136; of
    cross-cultural teams, 226–227; data
    analysis during, 112; effective running
    of, 61, 67–68; for follow-up, 120–122,
    123–126; paying employees for, 55;
    presenting data in, 96, 97; for problem
    solving, 55; for role clarification,
    138–139; of temporary teams, 215; of
    virtual teams, 237–238
Meetings, Bloody Meetings (video), 68
Metrics, development of, 64–65
Milgram, S., 2

Millennials, 272
Minority groups, 147
Mission statement: importance of, 51;
    organization culture in, 44–45; temporary
    teams and, 213–214
Mixed teams, 172–173, 175
Modular interdependence: description of,
    26–27; frustrations associated with, 29
Motivation, of team: definition of, 37;
    employee satisfaction and, 46; goal setting
    and, 40, 46; need for, 37, 39; skills and,
    40; tools for, 39–40; training and, 39f
Multicultural planning, 147
Multidisciplinary teams, 195
Myers-Briggs Type Indicator, 227

N

National Training Laboratories, 1
NBA basketball, 28, 29
Neeleman, D., 189
Negative people, 150
Negotiating agreements, 134–135
Networking process, 198–199
Networking skills, 186
Newsletters, company, 45
Nonverbal communication, 161
Norms, 221–222, 237

O

Observing process, 198
Observing skills, 186
Office of Alliance Management, 251, 260
Olympics, 28, 29
Omidyar, P., 193
Open feedback sessions, 119
Open-ended surveys, 95
Operating committees, 255
Operating guidelines, 214–218
Operational fit, 258
Organization development, 2–3
Organization men, 2
Organizational analysis, 118
Ouchi, B., 6
Outsourcing, 247
Overbearing people, 152
Overt resistance, 87

P

Parker, G., 41–42
Participation, of disruptive people, 151
Passionate team members, 40–41
Passive resistance, 87, 144
Patience, 272
Pay raises, 54
Pay system: ineffective types of, 35–36; to
    support problem-solving meetings, 55

Performance reviews: lack of team-building efforts in, 24; promotions and, 45; tips for success involving, 271

Personal development, 48–49

Personal improvement plans, 119

Personal management interviews (PMIs), 120–123

Personalities, conflicting, 129–130

Personality assessment, 227

Pessimistic people, 150

Peter principle, 45

Pharmaceutical industry, 248, 250–251

Phone conversations, 243

Pizza teams, 42

Pooled interdependence. *See* Modular interdependence

Power, shared, 40; effective teams and, 58–60; importance of, 63; methods for, 63

Prescription writing, 119

Priorities: in data analysis, 98; questioning process and, 197; of temporary teams, 211–212

Private interviews, 96

Problem solving: barriers to, 110–111; holding meetings for, 55; to promote team production and interdependence, 46; in team-building process, 113–114; unhealthy approach to, 155

Problems, categories of, 113

Process consulting, 99

Product development teams, 29, 31

Production, manager's role in, 4

Productivity: problems with, 86; promotion of, 46–47

Professional development: importance of, 48–49; managers' support of, 51

Promotions, 45

Prototyping, 201–202

Psychological safety, 68, 189–192, 201

Q

Questioning process, 197–198

Questioning skills, 186, 187

Questionnaires, 125

QuestionStorming method, 197

R

RACI process, 256, 257

Ransom, M., 257

Reciprocal interdependence, 28–30

Reciprocity, 72

Regression effect, 120

Relationships, of successful teams, 73

Resource personnel, 137, 145, 147

Respect: creating, 71–72; importance of, 61

Responsibility, 151

Retreat, for team building, 92

Reward systems: in alliance teams, 252; as barriers to effective teamwork, 15; example of, 45; lack of, for team-building efforts, 24; managers' role in, 51, 54; for risk taking, 72; tips for success involving, 270

Ridgeway, K., 50

Risk taking: encouraging, 72; importance of, 61; for innovation, 188–192; rewards for, 72; unhealthy agreement and, 163

Role clarification exercise, 146; description of, 135–142; in virtual teams, 245

Role models, 188

Role negotiation, 113

Rollins, K., 193

Root cause analysis, 111

S

Safe environment, 188–192

Sales managers, 123, 124

Sales teams, 123, 124

Salesforce.com, 186, 240

Schedule reviews, 120

Schein, E., 2–3, 6, 99, 165

Self-directed teams: description of, 31–33; difficult issues of, 32–33; leader's role in, 31–32

Self-images, 108–109

Self-interest, 273

Semiautonomous work teams. *See* Self-directed teams

Sequential interdependence, 27–28

Shell Chemicals, 239–240

Sims, N., 252–253, 261

Skills, of team leaders, 186, 192–196

Skills, of teams: composition of team and, 15–17; importance of, 39; lack of, 40; in leadership, 45–46; motivation and, 39*f*, 40; planning professional development to enhance, 48–49; team assignments and, 56, 66

Skoll, J., 193

Small teams, 41, 47

Smart failures, 190

Smith, D. K., 41

Smoothing, 143

Social media, 240

Socratic method, 75

Southwest Airlines, 189–190

Spider web chart, 259*f*, 260

Stach, G., 256

Staff, versus teams, 58, 59*t*

Stakeholders, 218

Standards, importance of, 61

Start-stop-continue activities, 118, 142–144

Steering committees, 255

Stereotypes, 219

Strategic fit, 258

Strategic futures exercise, 253–254

Structure, of organization: alliance teams and, 252; assessment of, 55; description of, 34–35

Student behavior, 221–222, 223

Subordinate relationships, 58, 59t, 87

Subunits: action plans for, 120; analysis of, 118; role of, 113

Success, manager's role in, 4

Suggestions, example of, 117

Summary presentations, 96, 97

Summer interns, 44

Surveys: for annual health checks, 258–264; description of, 94–95; to elicit feedback about team leaders, 145–146; as follow-up tool, 125

Systems, of organizations: assessment of, 55; description of, 35–36

T

Task force, 175

Task teams: in alliance teams, 255; description of, 31; role of, 113

Team assignments: accountability for, 67; for difficult people, 151–152; follow-up on, 120; importance of, 61; members' refusal of, 48; process of making, 47–48, 65–66; for staff versus teams, 59t

Team building: appreciative inquiry approach to, 114–116; challenges for, 269–277; checklist for, 89–90f; consultant's role in, 93; versus continuous improvement, 91; cycle of, 93–100; data gathering in, 93–98; definition of, 12, 85; description of, 91; engaging in, 73–74; format of, 103–104; frequency of, 91; importance of, 61–62; initiation of, 88; instruction in, lack of, 22–23; lack of, 12, 21–25; major tasks in, 101; making time for, 54–55; manager's role in, 93; mangers' follow-through with, 51; negative effects of, 23; obstacles to, 22–25; outside consultant for, 92; primary obstacle of, 22; process of, 91–92, 103; rationale for, 85–86; to solve interteam problems, 170–181; versus T-groups, 5; time needed for, 91–92; unhealthy agreement and, 163–166; in virtual teams, 244–245. *See also* Change management skills of teams

Team chemistry, 47–48

Team development, 54–55

Team dynamics, 47

Team leaders: in action planning, 99; assessment of, 49–50; as center of conflict, 144–147; challenge of innovation for, 191; characteristics of, 37–38, 39, 203; as coaches, 74–75; creation of vision and, 51; decisions made by, 66; dilemmas of, 31; discovery skills of, 185–188; as educators, 60–74; employee satisfaction and, 45–46; expectations violated by, 133; as facilitators, 75–76; in follow-up team sessions, 123; of innovative teams, 183–196; most valued type of, 183; power sharing of, 40; in role clarification exercise, 142; role of, 31–32, 58, 59t; in self-directed teams, 31; as skill builders, 40; tasks of, 184; versus team members, 86–88; training of, 38; of virtual teams, 238, 243

Team members: differences among, 88–91; expectations violated by, 133–134; measuring satisfaction of, 49–50; problems of, 110; recruitment of, 272–274; selection of, 270; versus team leaders, 86–88

Team performance: Four Cs in, 14f; scenario about, involving inadequate performance, 11–13, 18–19; serious problems of, 11–13, 18–19, 85–86

Team production: emphasis on, 46–47; manager's role in, 4; T-group research on, 5

Team size: benefits of, 47; determining, 41; example of, 47; for follow-up sessions, 124; ideal, 41–42; importance of, 16; small versus large, 41; team assignments and, 56

Team-building program: action planning in, 119–120; appreciative inquiry approach to, 114–116; data analysis and problem solving in, 109–114; data gathering climate in, 106–109; feedback in, 116–119; follow-up sessions in, 123–126; goal of, 103, 171; implementation and evaluation phases in, 120–123; preparation phase of, 104–106

Teams, high-performing: assessing competencies of, 76, 77–81f; challenges confronting, 272; characteristics of, 13, 38; determinants of, 13–18; developing competencies of, 58–76; finding members of, 40–41, 43–44; generic types of, 30–33; goal of, 30; identification of, 33; interdependence of, 26–30; member selection for, 40–41; self-assessment of, 54; shared power among, 40, 58–60; versus staff, 58, 59t; transition to, 59–60

Teamwork: assessing structure for, 55; barriers to, 15; benefits of, 4; challenges to, 272; continuum of, 26f; in cross-cultural teams, 227–228; culture of organization and, 33–34; improving, 170–177; increased need for, 12–13; lack of, 169, 170; nature of task and, 25–30; structure of organization and, 34–35; systems of organization and, 35–36

Tech boxes, 199

Technical expertise, 195

Technology: advances in, 235; growth in alliances and, 247; increased use of, 275; problems of virtual teams involving, 239–243; virtual team communications and, 237, 241, 243; for virtual work spaces, 239–240

Temporary teams: description of, 207; design of, 211–218; preliminary conditions for, 207–211; tasks of, 210

T-groups: central ideas of, 4; description of, 1–2; history of, 2–3; versus team building, 5

Theory X and Theory Y assumptions, 2

Theory Z management, 6

Thoreau, H. D., 276

Thoughtful failures, 72

Time: for leadership tasks, 184–185, 243; for team building, 91–92, 136

Time zones, 237

Total unit analysis, 118

Toyota, 18, 35

Training: to elicit feedback about team leaders, 146; keys to success of, 270; motivation and, 39f; of team leaders, 38; of virtual teams, 239–243

Trust: building of, 68–70; in cross-cultural teams, 227; importance of, 61, 68–69; lack of, 87–88; personal management interviews and, 121; team leaders versus team members and, 87–88; team size and, 41

Turnover, reducing, 48–49

Twitter, 240

U

Unhealthy agreements: alternatives to, 163–166; cause of, 163; description of, 155–160; symptoms of, 160–163.

The Upside of Irrationality (Ariely), 191

V

Values, 148, 222–223, 252

Video conferencing, 241, 242t, 243

Virtual teams: challenges of, 274–275; common problems in, 238–243; communication of, 236–243; demands of team leaders of, 238; frustrations of, 29; need for, 12–13; popularity of, 235; team-building tips for, 244–246; versus traditional teams, 236–238

Virtues, 59t

Vision: diversity and, 148; leaders' role in, 51

Voting processes, 216

W

Wade, D., 28–29

Walden (Thoreau), 276

Web pages, 238, 239, 242t

WebEx conferencing, 243

Weisbord, M., 118

The Wisdom of Teams (Katzenbach & Smith), 41

Work planning documents, 256–257

Z

Zyliss, 197, 198